Israel's Prophets and the Prophetic Effect of Pope Francis

Israel's Prophets and the Prophetic Effect of Pope Francis

A Pastoral Companion

Michael Ufok Udoekpo

Forewords by Patrick J. Russell and Javier I. Bustos

Preface by Christophe Pierre

WIPF & STOCK · Eugene, Oregon

ISRAEL'S PROPHETS AND THE PROPHETIC EFFECT OF POPE FRANCIS
A Pastoral Companion

Copyright © 2018 Michael Ufok Udoekpo. All rights reserved. Except for brief quotations in critical publications or reviews, no part of this book may be reproduced in any manner without prior written permission from the publisher. Write: Permissions, Wipf and Stock Publishers, 199 W. 8th Ave., Suite 3, Eugene, OR 97401.

Wipf & Stock
An Imprint of Wipf and Stock Publishers
199 W. 8th Ave., Suite 3
Eugene, OR 97401

www.wipfandstock.com

PAPERBACK ISBN: 978-1-5326-4717-8
HARDCOVER ISBN: 978-1-5326-4718-5
EBOOK ISBN: 978-1-5326-4719-2

Manufactured in the U.S.A.   JUNE 27, 2018

Contents

Foreword I by Patrick J. Russell, Ph.D. | ix

Foreword II by Fr. Javier I. Bustos, S.T.D. | xiii

Preface by Archbishop Christophe Pierre. | xvii

Acknowledgements. | xix

Introduction. | xxi

Part I: Israel's Prophets in Light of Pope Francis | 1

- Israel's Prophets: Meaning, Function, and Nature | 1
- Classification of Prophets | 6
- Effect of Israel's Pre-Classical Prophets | 8
    - i. Effect of Abraham, Moses, and Miriam | 8
    - ii. Effect of Balaam | 9
    - iii. Effect of Former Prophets | 10
    - iv. Effect of Deborah, the Prophetess | 11
    - v. Effect of Samuel, the Prophet | 12
    - vi. Effect of Nathan, the Prophet | 15
    - vii. Effect of Ahijah, the Prophet | 16
    - viii. Effect of Shemaiah, the "Man of God," and an Unnamed Prophet | 18
    - ix. Effect of Other Pre-Classical Prophets | 21
    - x. Effect of Elijah, the Prophet | 22
    - xi. Effect of Elisha, the Prophet | 25

- xii. Effect of Micaiah Ben Imlah, the Prophet (1 Kgs 22) | 26
- xiii. Effect of Huldah, the Prophetess (2 Kgs 22:14–20) | 27
- Effect of Israel's Classical Prophets | 28
  - i. Effect of Amos, the Prophet | 28
  - ii. Effect of Hosea, the Prophet | 32
  - iii. Effect of First Isaiah (Isa 1–39) | 34
  - iv. Effect of Micah, the Prophet | 35
  - v. Effect of Zephaniah, the Prophet | 37
  - vi. Effect of Nahum, the Prophet | 38
  - vii. Habakkuk, the Prophet | 39
  - viii. Effect of Jeremiah, the Prophet | 57
  - ix. Effect of Obadiah, the Prophet | 61
  - x. Effect of Ezekiel, the Prophet | 62
  - xi. Effect of Second Isaiah (Isa 40–55) | 65
- Effect of Post-Exilic Prophets | 66
  - i. Effect of Haggai, the Prophet | 66
  - ii. Effect of Zechariah, the Prophet | 67
  - iii. Effect of Malachi, the Prophet | 68
  - iv. Effect of Third Isaiah (Isa 55–66) | 69
  - v. Effect of Joel, the Prophet | 71
  - vi. Effect of Jonah, the Prophet | 72
- Summary of Part I | 73

Part II: The Life, Writings, and Ministry of Pope Francis & His Prophetic Effect | 75

- Life of Pope Francis (Jorge Mario Bergoglio) | 75
- Effect of *Lumen Fidei* ("On the Light of Faith") | 77
- Effect of *Evangelii Gaudium* ("The Joy of the Gospel") | 81
- Effect of Laudato Si' ("On Care for Our Common Home") | 87
- Effect of *Amoris Laetitia* ("The Joy of Love") | 99

- Effect of *Gaudete et Exsultate* (Rejoice and Be Glad) | 108
- Effect of Other Letters, Messages, and Visits | 112
    - i. "Fraternity, the Foundation and Pathway to Peace" | 112
    - ii. "Apostolic Letter to the Consecrated People" | 114
    - iii. "No Longer Slaves, but Brothers and Sisters" | 116
    - iv. "Overcome Indifference and Win Peace" | 117
    - v. *Misericordia et Misera* ("Mercy with Misery") | 118
    - vi. Francis's "Letter to the Bishops of Nigeria" | 121
    - vii. "Nonviolence as a Style of Politics for Peace" | 123
    - viii. "Migrants and Refugees: Men and Women in Search of Peace" | 124
- Summary of Part II | 125

Part III: Prophetic Effect of Francis and Challenges to Contemporary Society | 127

- Francis's Prophetic Effect on the U.S.A. | 127
    - i. The Prophetic Effect of Francis's Visits | 128
    - ii. Pew Research Center Report & Francis's Effect | 130
    - iii. Publication of John Gehring & Francis's Effect | 131
    - iv. Center for Climate Change & Francis's Effect | 136
    - v. Michael Wright & Francis's Prophetic Effect | 139
    - vi. John Allen Jr. & Francis's Prophetic Effect | 140
    - vii. McElwee Joshua & Francis's Effect | 142
- Echoes of Francis's Prophetic Effect in Asia | 142
- Echoes of Francis's Prophetic Effect in Africa | 144
- Summary of Part III | 152

Summary and Conclusion | 154

Bibliography | 161

Author Index | 169

Subject Index | 171

Scripture Index | 179

Foreword I

Pope Francis within the Prophetic Landscape

Recently I arrived at my neighborhood donut shop with a biography of Pope Francis and a newspaper tucked under my arm, looking forward to some quiet reading as I enjoyed a cup of hot coffee and calorie-heavy pastry. As I was paying for my order, the barista spied my book's cover and jovially exclaimed, "Dude, Francis is the man! I'm not Catholic and more spiritual than religious, but I love that guy. He walks the talk." As I sat down and opened up the newspaper, a headline blared, "The War Against Pope Francis," with the article delineating certain bishops' backlash reaction to the papacy's direction in allowing the divorced and remarried without an annulment to receive communion.

How do we come to understand and explain this dichotomy of opinions about Pope Francis? Is it because he exercises his magisterial teaching office in a manner consistent with the famous injunction of St. Francis of Assisi – to "preach the gospel always and, if necessary, use words," – that he simultaneously comforts but challenges, clarifies and confuses, consoles yet confounds? If so, then is there some sort of background – a landscape, if you will – upon which we can place Pope Francis' pastoral practices and everyday expressions which might give us a clearer picture of the purpose and meaning of the gospel of mercy which he preaches so emphatically?

In *Israel's Prophets and the Prophetic Effect of Pope Francis: A Pastoral Companion*, Rev. Michael Ufok Udoekpo offers just such a framework. He masterfully traces for a broad audience – from questioning scholars to questing souls – the congruent lines between those by-gone bold biblical voices and the present provocative

Foreword I

papal teaching. In Part I, Fr. Udoekpo's trained hand as a biblical exegete draws for the reader the particular contours of each prophetic book's message by depicting the ways that the prophet's theological framework is applied to the pressing social needs of his day. In Part II, Fr. Udoekpo as a Catholic theologian paints upon this biblical landscape the shape of Pope Francis' down-to-earth teachings and jaw-dropping acts of mercy by unpacking his encyclicals and other significant writings in relation to their "prophetic effect." Then, in Part III, he taps the "Pope Francis Effect" assessment of various commentators and other resources, including Pew Research. Through Fr. Udoekpo's scholarly artistry in weaving together these three parts, the Pope's theological outlook and ministerial objectives take form. In this manner, new hues of color in Pope Francis' prophetic effect emerge.

As a consequence of this examination of the biblical prophets side-by-side with Pope Francis' ministerial activity, Fr. Udoekpo's work moves the discussion from a facile comparison to a robust analysis. This is, in the true sense of the phrase, an innovative work of biblical theology, as it examines Pope Francis' words and deeds through an interpretative matrix constructed from an exegetical evaluation of the nature and scope of the actions, oracles, and purposes of the biblical prophets. No previous systematic and sustained evaluation of this type has been undertaken, so this is certainly a constructive and needed contribution to the ongoing understanding and assessment of the Francis papacy. However, another value of this work is not to be overlooked, as Fr. Udoekpo's summaries of the prophetic books serve as helpful and succinct overviews of each of the biblical prophets.

Few scholars could reduplicate Fr. Udoekpo's effort here, as his own unique story provides him with an indispensible lens for perceiving the flow and function of the messages of the biblical prophets and Pope Francis. Educated on three continents (Africa, Europe, and North America), he has a worldview that enables his work to avoid being detrimentally parochial. As a first-generation citizen of the United States, he has direct experience with the issues of migration and immigration. Not only are these major prophetic emphases of Pope Francis, but the forced migration of the people of Judah after the Babylonian conquest fundamentally shaped the theological expression of the exilic and post-exilic prophets. Further, Fr. Udoekpo has personally experienced the complications and struggles of entering an American culture in which the color of one's skin fundamentally effects a person's engagement with the broader culture. Hence, he is particularly situated to explore the impact of oppression and injustice, which are leitmotifs for the biblical prophets and Pope Francis. In this book, as he has done in his previous publications, Fr. Udoekpo nimbly navigates these issues in productive ways. He heuristically draws upon the cultural contexts of the United States and Nigeria to unpack the modern-day application of the biblical prophets' messages, as well as employs these viewpoints as means for examining Pope Francis' thought from different global perspectives. His background thus provides a canvas which few others are capable of employing when painting a portrait of the modern-day significance and real-life consequences of the oracles of biblical prophets and the vision of Pope Francis.

However, my appreciation of Fr. Udoekpo extends beyond his scholarship. Since we serve together as Scripture professors at Sacred Heart Seminary and School of Theology, I am also blessed to know him as a colleague. As the academic dean, I have been deeply impressed by Fr. Udoekpo's unflagging commitment to developing a prophetic vision within his students. The prophetic vision involves perceiving the connections between God's revelatory actions in the past and the pressing needs of society today. Such vision is essential for effective pastoral ministry and enlightened ministerial leadership. As the reader will discover through this book, the seminarians – and the laity we train for lay ecclesial ministry – are indeed fortunate to have the gift of Fr. Udoekpo's insight and wisdom on developing a prophetic vision for ministerial service.

The timeliness of this book is indeed a great gift as we are certainly in one of those "turning times." As Pope Francis often says, we are living in change of eras, not just an era of change. Broadly speaking, it is in such pivotal moments in history that the prophetic vocation in ancient Israel and Judah flourished. Fr. Udoekpo's book is thus a propitious resource, as it provides us with the perspective of time by producing a richly textured landscape of the various shapes and forms of the prophetic message from ages past upon which the current "prophet of the times" can be understood, gauged, and even appraised. Enjoy this penetrating gaze into the prophetic effect of those distant, daunting figures found in pages of sacred books written many millennia ago and of the joy-filled, indomitable elder who appears on the pages of bestselling books, current periodicals, and popular websites in our current days.

Patrick J. Russell, Ph.D.
Chief Academic Officer
Vice President for Intellectual Formation
Professor of Scripture Studies
Sacred Heart Seminary and School of Theology

Foreword II

ON DECEMBER 16, 2013, Pope Francis reminded those present in the Chapel of the *Domus Sanctae Marthae* that all baptized are called to be prophets (*L'Osservatore Romano*, Weekly ed. in English, n. 51, 20 December 2013). Michael Udoekpo masterfully explains the meaning of these words coming out of the mouth, work and life of the Latin American Pope.

By embarking on a demanding revision on the effects of the prophets of Israel, Fr. Udoekpo outlines the different categories of prophets, their historical contexts, their mission, and their accomplishments. A prophet is a true mediator between God and his people through time: past, present, and future. It is worth noting that the ministry of the prophet is as unique as his or her own person: enigmatic, strong, persistent, playful, persecuted, direct, just judges of what they see or hear, wholeheartedly committed to a cause, loyal to truth, and eager to embrace suffering for the sake of truth.

Fr. Udoekpo's review of the prophets of the past leads us to reflect on the prophets of our times; especially on the prophetic ministry of Pope Francis. According to Udoekpo, the effects of the prophets of Israel on Francis are present in the contents of his ministry and in his own person: "Ethical conduct, justice, judgement, the sovereignty of God, the people of God, Israel, Zion or Jerusalem, repentance and hope for restoration, and God's mercy dominates the minds of Israel's Prophets. Similar themes and gestures, we argued, would directly or indirectly influence Pope Francis' pastoral achievements."

For the Argentine Pope, "the prophet is a man of three times: the promise of the past, the contemplation of the present, the courage to point out the path toward the future" (*L'Osservatore Romano*,

Weekly ed. in English, n. 51, 20 December 2013). Udoekpo helps us to connect the valuable ministry of the prophets of the Old Testament with Pope Francis by articulating his prophetic ministry in the tension of past-present-future.

For Francis, "the prophet is aware of the promise and he holds God's promise in his heart, he keeps it alive, he remembers it, he repeats it." Fr. Udoekpo clearly emphasizes Pope Francis' genuine love for the Tradition and God's promise by highlighting his call to understand and proclaim the *kerigma* in *Evangelii Gaudium*: "Nothing is more solid, profound, secure, meaningful and wisdom-filled than that initial proclamation. All Christian formation consists of entering more deeply into the kerygma, which is reflected in and constantly illumines, the work of catechesis, thereby enabling us to understand more fully the significance of every subject which the latter treats" (165).

A prophet, according to the Pope, is the one who "looks into the present, he looks at his people and he experiences the power of the spirit to speak a word to them that will lift them up, to continue their journey toward the future." By providing a number of parallels with the prophets of the past, Udoekpo delineates Pope Francis' commitment to the present time and his invitation to a "journey toward the future."

Francis' call for the place and meaning of authentic missionary disciples reminds us of Ezekiel's instructions to priests (Ez. 42-44): "Missionary discipleship is a vocation: a call and an invitation. It is given in the 'today,' but also in tension. There is no such thing as static missionary discipleship. A missionary disciple cannot be his own master, his immanence is in tension towards the transcendence of discipleship and towards the transcendence of mission. It does not allow for self-absorption: either it points to Jesus Christ or it points to the people to whom he must be proclaimed. The missionary disciple is a self-transcending subject, a subject projected towards encounter: an encounter with the Master (who anoints us as his disciples) and an encounter with men and women who await the message. That is why I like the saying that the position of missionary disciples is not in the center but at the periphery: they live poised towards the peripheries . . . including the peripheries of eternity, in the encounter with Jesus Christ. In the preaching of the Gospel, to speak of existential peripheries decentralizes things; as a rule, we are afraid to leave the center. The missionary disciple is someone 'off center': the center is Jesus Christ, who calls us and sends us forth. The disciple is sent to the existential peripheries" (Pope Francis, Address to the Leadership of the Episcopal Conferences of Latin America during the General Coordination Meeting, Rio de Janeiro, 28 July 2013).

Along with a strong call to serve the poor and the immigrant (those in the peripheries), the prophetic ministry of Pope Francis reads the sign of the times and helps us to turn our eyes to the future: the environment and the family. Fr. Michael Udoekpo also opens the eyes of the reader by bringing hope to those who await a time of justice and peace; at the end of this book, you will realize that God has not forgotten his people and He is still sending prophets among us.

Very Rev. Javier I. Bustos, S.T.D.
Sacred Heart Seminary and School of Theology
Archdiocese of Milwaukee, USA

Preface

I WAS PLEASED TO receive Father Michael Ufok Udoekpo's latest work, entitled "Israel's Prophets and the Prophetic Effect of Pope Francis: A Pastoral Companion," in which he examines the prophets of Israel in their historical, cultural and literary contexts to show how their charism, nature and function foreshadows, in many ways, the prophetic charism demonstrated by the Holy Father. Udoekpo's work also presents a succinct overview of the prophetic nature of Pope Francis' writings, including *Lumen Fidei, Evangelii Gaudium, Amoris Laetitia, Laudato Si'* and *Gaudete et Exsultate*. Finally, Udoekpo's work proposes the prophets and His Holiness' embodiment of the prophetic message as a paradigm for the Church today in the context of the New Evangelization.

A prophet, as the author's work explains, can be one who calls or one who is called. Certainly, Pope Francis is one who calls the Church today to be a Church that goes forth from its comfort zone to the spiritual and existential peripheries to proclaim the Good News of Salvation, encouraging and challenging the whole Church to deeper pastoral conversion for the sake of evangelization and mission.

However, the Holy Father is also one who is called. He was called by God, through the Cardinal-electors, to guide and lead the Church, strengthening her in faith and unity through concrete, pastoral activity. Five years removed from his election, one can more deeply appreciate how the Spirit of God moves and works in the Church, calling the Archbishop of Buenos Aires to shepherd the universal Church, bringing with him the cultural, religious, and pastoral richness of the holy and faithful People of God. Called by God, he has exercised his prophetic charism as a mediator of the Mercy and Tenderness of God, seen especially in the face of Christ the Redeemer.

PREFACE

It is my hope that Father Udoekpo's original work will reach the hands of theologians, pastors, and the lay faithful, stimulating them not only to think more deeply about the prophets and the ongoing call to conversion to the Lord, but also to encourage them to receive and live the Magisterium of Pope Francis in their words and actions, so that the joy of the Gospel may fill the whole world.

Grateful for this service which Father Udoekpo has rendered to the Church, I am

Sincerely yours in Christ,

Archbishop Christophe Pierre
Apostolic Nuncio
United States of America
March 20, 2018

Acknowledgements

THE PAPACY OF POPE Francis, like those of his predecessors, has uniquely captured global attention. Commentators, theologians, scientists, philosophers, Christians and non-Christians, Catholics and non-Catholics, the poor, and the rich have all been drawn to offer their perspectives on this Pope of Mercy's ongoing prophetic ministry and unique contributions. The volume in your hand, *Israel's Prophets and the Prophetic Effect of Pope Francis: A Pastoral Companion*, offers one of those perspectives. My hope is that this book will be accessible to everyone.

I am thankful to God for his grace. I am also thankful to my Bishop, Most Rev. Camillus R. Umoh, and his predecessor, Most. Rev. Camillus Etokudoh, of Port Harcourt Diocese, for their encouragement. This project commenced as I developed, taught, and shared the theology and relevance of the biblical prophets in light of the timely and universal faith context, shepherded by Pope Francis, with my graduate students at Sacred Heart Seminary and School of Theology (Wisconsin).

Its draft-versions were proposed at two scholarly conferences: the Eightieth International Meeting of the Catholic Biblical Association of America (CBA) on August 5-8, 2017, at the Catholic University of America, Washington D.C.; and the Academic Faculty Colloquium on October 4, 2017, at Sacred Heart Seminary and School of Theology (SHSST). I was very surprised and gratefully encouraged by the volume of positive and constructive feedback I received from my colleagues at both conferences.

I am very grateful to the Apostolic Nuncio to the United States, His Excellency Archbishop Christophe Pierre, who was not only

ACKNOWLEDGEMENTS

pastorally and fatherly present to the faculty, staff, and students during his visit to SHSST on November 8, 2017, but who also read and wrote an inspiring, inviting, and theologically engaging letter of preface to this work. His words are very encouraging to me.

To my friends and colleagues Dr. Patrick J. Russell (my dean) and Very Rev. Fr. Javier Bustos, I cannot thank you enough for finding time to read and evaluate this work and for writing such affirming and thoughtful forewords that reflect the theology, spirituality, and pastoral essence of this book.

On hearing that I was working on a book concerning Pope Francis, Sister Professor Teresa Okure, SHCJ (the Catholic Institute of West Africa), and Sister Leonie-Martha O'karaga, HHCJ (Superior General of the Handmaids of the Holy Child Jesus), generously offered me resources that were very useful for this work. I am grateful to them as well as to Very Rev. Fr. Anselm C. Etokakpan, Rev. Dr. Gerald Emem Umoren, Rev. Dr. Jean Pierre-Ruiz, Fr. Donald M. Baeir, Fr. James Akpan, Dr. James Stroud, Mr. Bill Bowden, Mr. and Mrs. Werner, and Doris Debis, my colleagues and library staff at Sacred Heart for their encouragement, endorsements, prayer, and support.

The editors at Wipf and Stock Publishers have been outstanding, as have Ms. Susanna Pathak and Ms. Elizabeth Vince in editing various stages of this publication. A special "thank you" to the President-Rector and board of administration of SHSST for granting me a sabbatical for the 2018-19 academic year, part of which was used in completing this work.

All this would not have been easy without the support of my family (brothers, sisters, nieces, and nephews), friends, brother-priests, religious students, and parishioners, with whom we share the Lord's Vineyard during this time of Pope Francis, a mediator a of God's tender mercies and boundless riches of Christ.

Fr. Michael Ufok Udoekpo
September 12, 2018

Introduction

> "In time past God spoke in partial and various ways to our ancestors through the prophets, but in these last days he has spoken to us by a Son, whom he appointed heir of all things, through whom he also created the worlds." (Heb 1:1–2)

THIS TEXT FROM HEBREWS 1:1–2 endorses various ways through which Israel's God addresses us through the prophets from one generation of the covenant to another. Commonly speaking, prophets are God's spokespersons. They interpret the will of God. They act as a society's conscience—as defenders of the poor and voiceless. They prefer to lean on the side of the marginalized and thus love to champion social justice and reject every form of injustice. They are also familiar with their communities, whom they strive to influence, change, and morally impact.

Prophets are risk takers for the sake of truth. Some forecast the immediate future with eyes on the present. They mediate between the human and the divine. Prophets are servants of God. They are guided by divine providence to plead and intercede for all. Prophets are commonly seen as evangelizers and challengers of social sins. They are good leaders and lead with humility. They teach and freely preach God's word. Prophets also serve as conduits of divine judgment and mercy. They transmit God's love and divine promises. Through them, religious people—whether Jews or Christians—engage with God. Prophets act as agents of change, promoting positive alternatives and newness of life.

We know of many people today who, by their actions, courageous behavior, leadership styles, writings, and pastoral outreach, would fit our simple definition of a prophet. Mother Theresa of Calcutta, Pope

INTRODUCTION

St. John Paul II, Benedict XVI, Rev. Dr. Martin Luther King Jr., and Blessed Oscar Romero are some of them. People like Mahatma Gandhi, the Dalai Lama, Nelson Mandela, Desmond Tutu, Fannie Lou Hamer, Dom Helder Camara, Dorathy Kazel, Ita Ford, Maura Clark, Jeanne Donovan, Ella Baker, and Jorge Mario Bergoglio (Pope Francis) are also good examples of prophetic figures.

Since time is greater than space, this work focuses on Pope Francis, the first Latin American to be elected to the Chair of Peter.[1] A native of Buenos Aires, Argentina, Jorge Mario Bergoglio was ordained as a priest in 1969 and served as head of the Society of Jesus in the Argentina province from 1973 to 1979. He became the archbishop of Buenos Aires in 1998 and was made a cardinal in 2001 by Pope John Paul II. Jorge Mario Bergoglio was elected as pope on March 13, 2013. He has been outstanding since then.[2]

Given that Pope Francis is such a popular global religious leader, a theologian, and a spiritual father who loves the poor, families, the planet, and the environment with striking prophetic courage, this work undertakes three tasks. First, it historically and theologically examines Israel's prophets in their contexts—including their meaning, nature, and function. This is done to show how their prophetic charism, courage, and ministries foreshadow the ministry of Pope Francis.

Second, it examines how the pastoral achievements of Pope Francis—specifically, his teachings, sayings, preaching, major writings (*Lumen Fidei, Evangelii Gaudium, Amoris Laetitia, Laudato Si' and Gaudete et Exsultate*), letters, visits, and other messages—may have influenced contemporary society. Part II examines basic questions such as:

- Who is a prophet?
- Could Francis be seen as a prophet?
- How does the pastoral Francis fit among Israel's prophets?
- How does Francis's pastoral imitation of the biblical prophets impact the church and modern society?

1. In this work, Pope Francis will be addressed as the Holy Father, Jorge Mario Bergoglio, and Francis to reflect the simplicity of his lifestyle and pastoral approach.

2. Additional comments on Francis's biographical data will be made in Part II of this work.

INTRODUCTION

We will also examine what changes Francis's papacy have brought to bear on the church and society. We will discuss what impact Francis has had on how people view the church or whether they have responded verbally or in writing to his ministry. We will examine whether his prophetic courage has encouraged more people to celebrate the sacraments (especially penance and mercy, love, and forgiveness), attend papal events, or become more concerned about global warming, the planet, ecology, integral spirituality, family, and poverty. We will discuss how his writings and messages have helped increase not only dialogue with all people, but have increased public engagement on a variety of issues that are challenging to our society today.

Third, this text explores the prophetic effect of Francis and proposes that the entire volume be seen as a pastoral companion to introductory books and commentaries on the biblical prophets and spirituality.[3]

This tripartite theological survey on Israel's prophets and their impact on Pope Francis's "prophetic effect" challenges us to actively be prophetic in our daily lives. It serves as a prophetic paradigm for contemporary evangelizers, leaders, exegetes, pastors, theologians, preachers, teachers, and members of all faith communities.[4]

---

3. Introductory books referred to here include: Lindblom (*Prophecy in Ancient Israel)*; Westermann (*Basic Forms of Prophetic Speech*); Wilson (*Prophecy and Society in Ancient Israel*); Heschel (*Prophets*); Brueggemann (*The Prophetic Imagination*); Leclerc (*Introduction to the Prophets*); Wifall (*Israel's Prophets*); Cook (*Hear, O Heavens, and Listen, O Earth*); Hays (*Message of the Prophets*); Udoekpo (*Day of YHWH*) and Branick (*Understanding the Prophets*). Others are: Vawter, "Prophetic Literature," 186–200; Huffmon, "Prophecy," 477–82.

4. See Reese ("Francis Effect"); Maibach ("Francis Effect," 1–92); Orobator ("Francis Effect and the Church in Africa," 3–76), and Irwin (*Laudato Si'*, 254–55) for insight into the "Francis effect." To a certain extent, in this study, what many writers have already described as "the Francis effect" qualifies as the "prophetic effect" or "impact" of Pope Francis and the challenges his ministry poses to contemporary society and religious communities. Note also that in *The Merriam Webster Dictionary*, the singular noun "effect" means three things: (1) "intent," (2) "result," and (3) "influence." The plural noun "effects" means "moveable property, goods." For example, "personal effects. As a verb, as also used in this study, it goes beyond influence, result, and intent. It also refers to actual achievements and results of Francis's ministry. Therefore, the "prophetic effect" of Francis, which we are examining—whether this Vicar of Christ's contributions, achievements, or effects—can be interpreted or appreciated through the prism or activities of the biblical prophets.

Part I

Israel's Prophets in Light of Pope Francis

Israel's Prophets: Meaning, Function, and Nature

DEFINING ISRAEL'S PROPHETS, THEIR function, and their nature in light of Pope Francis requires two things. First, we must appreciate the fact that the Israelites lived within the larger context of the ancient Near East; their neighboring countries had a sense of the phenomenon of prophecy that was parallel to the Israelites'. These neighbors include the Assyrians, Egyptians, Babylonians, and Mesopotamians. Israel shared with these countries some basic practices and beliefs about "gods and heavenly rule, kings and earthly rule, as well as priests and temple."[1] Affirming this point, Gerhard von Rad writes:

> We may take it for granted that men possessed by the spirit only appeared in Israel after the conquest of Canaan. In the eleventh-century Syria and Palestine there are signs of the rise of an ecstatic and mantic movement whose origins are apparently outside that area and perhaps lie in the mantic of Thrace and Asia Minor. Canaanite religion must, then, have been the medium by which the movement came to Israel.[2]

Vawter agrees with von Rad that, from the beginning, a common pattern of seers and diviners existed throughout the ancient

---

1. See Leclerc (*Prophets*, 18–36) for a full explanation of these shared beliefs and assumptions.
2. Von Rad, *Old Testament Theology*, 7–8.

Near East.³ These seers and diviners were employed in discerning the will of their protective deity.⁴ Huffmon also ascertains belief in the existence of such deities. He points out that, during the Old Testament period, seers and diviners who acted as prophets and intermediaries were common in royal palaces throughout the ancient Near East (Syria-Palestine, Anatolia, Mesopotamia, and Egypt). He argues that evidence abounds in stories told in Egypt and in the eighteen-century BC texts from Uruk (Southern Babylonia) and Mari (Middle Euphrates), and particularly in the Assyrian texts from the reigns of Esarhaddon (680–669 BC) and Ashurbanipal (668–627 BC).⁵

In studying these texts, we discover a variety of titles worn by those persons who sought to mediate the will of the gods to their kings and communities. These titles include: *Āpilu/āpiltu* ("answerer"), *Assinnu* ("cult functionary"), *Muḫḫûtu* ("ecstatic"), *Nabû//nābî* ("diviners"), and *Qam(m)ātum* (probably meaning "speaker").⁶ Evidence in Babylonian temples points to the existence of *bārū* priests, who delivered a *tērtu* ("a message"; probably a cognate to Hebrew *Torah*) to their client using liver divination. There was no distinction between prophets and priests in the ancient Near East—except in Israel. (It is worth noting that priesthood in Israel was hierarchical and hereditary, while prophecy was charismatic. Prophets like Jeremiah and Ezekiel probably were also priests, though the prophet Amos was not.⁷)

However, the recognition of this common pattern in the ancient Near East, especially as presented in the Mari Texts, does not detract from the uniqueness of true prophecy in the Old Testament. Rather, as noted by Leclerc, both the form and content of prophecy in the ancient Near East and in royal courts was very different from what we have in biblical Israel.

The Mari archive contains letters sent by an official who may have been instructed by the prophet to write to a king. The prophecies

---

3 See Leclerc (*Prophets*, 27–30), where he discusses the two kinds of divinations: "inductive or instrumental" and "intuitive or mediated divination." Plato calls the former "artificial divination" (by casting lots) and the later "natural divination" (verbally and through dreams and visions). See also Vawter's opinions on the common phenomenon of prophecy in the ancient Near East.

4. Vawter, "Prophetic Literature," 187.

5. Huffmon, *Prophecy*, 477–78. See also Leclerc (*Prophets*, 29–36) for detailed examples of these stories.

6. Ibid., 478–82.

7. Vawter, "Prophetic Literature," 187.

in these letters differ from those in the Bible in several ways. For instance, unlike biblical prophecies, the Mari letters were contaminated with other businesses and administrative issues. Additionally, the Old Testament prophecies were directly delivered to the addressee. Furthermore, while the Mari letters are privately limited to the kings, Israel's prophecies had a broader audience (kings, the elite, priests, the poor, the rich, and all nations and kingdoms). The contents of the Mari texts concern mostly politics, the cult, and the military. In contrast, the major concerns of authentic Old Testament prophecies, even when read in light of the New Testament, are ethics, spirituality, society, and the common good.[8]

Besides the shared concept of prophecy between Israel and their ancient Near Eastern neighbors, when dealing with the meaning, nature, and function of Israel's prophets and how these prophets have served as treasures to Francis's prophetic effect, we must also consider that the words, semantics, and language used in defining prophets and prophecy could be misleading unless measured in proper perspective and used in the right context. To this second point of proper contextualization, the English words "prophets" or "prophetess" semantically and linguistically come to us from the Greek word *prophētēs*, which literally means "the one who speaks for another, especially for a deity."[9] In Hebrew we have the corresponding term *nābî'* in singular and *nəbî'îm* in plural, which is very close to the Akkadian verb *nabû*, meaning "to call, to announce, to name."[10] In Anderson's view:

> There is some uncertainty, however, as to whether the Hebrew form has an active meaning ("one who calls, an announcer") or a passive meaning ("one who is called"). In the former case, the emphasis would be on the role of a prophet to proclaim a message; in the latter, the stress would be on the prophet's vocation to be a messenger in the service of the deity. Both views are relevant for understanding Israelite prophecy, but one would have to turn to particular biblical texts to see how prophets actually function in different situations. In any case, the term refers to one who communicates the divine will. The

---

8. This study will later focus on this argument in light of Pope Francis. Leclerc, *Prophets*, 34.

9. Anderson, *Understanding the Old Testament*, 248.

10. Ibid., 248.

prophet is an intermediary, a spokesperson—one who acts and speaks on behalf of another.[11]

Hays and many other scholars affirm Anderson's definition of biblical prophets or prophecy. They do this with certain nuances and explication beyond the spontaneous or basic definitions noted in the introductory section of this study. First, Hays identifies three biblical terms used in the Old Testament to represent "those special people who speak and transmit the word of Yahweh." These terms are *nābî* ("prophet"), "seer," and "man of God." Samuel (a prophet, judge, and priest) is an embodiment of these three terms, which indicates their similarity in meaning (1 Sam 9:8–10). The term "seer" also occurs in multiple places in the Hebrew Bible (1–2 Sam; 1–2 Chr).[12] In some of the occurrences (1 Sam 8–10), one of these three terms would sometimes describe an individual. In 2 Samuel 24:11, for instance, Gad is called *hannābî' hozēh Dāwid* ("the prophet, David's seer"). When King Jeroboam's palace priest, Amaziah, attacks and calls Amos a "seer" (Amos 7:12), Amos of Tekoa replies sarcastically, *lō'-nābî' ā'nōkî wᵉlō' ben- nābî' ā'nōkî* ("I am not a prophet, nor a prophet's son," Amos 7:14), thereby distancing himself from professional prophets who prophesied for profit and personal glory (1 Kgs 20:35; 2 Kgs 2:3, 5, 7, 15; 4:1, 38; 5:22; 6:1; 9:1).[13] In 1 Samuel 9:9 we read, "formally in Israel, anyone who went to inquire of God would say, 'Come, let us go to the seer'; for the one who is now called a prophet was formally called a seer." This implies that "seer" (*hozēh*) was perhaps an older word for "prophet" (*nābî'*). The term "man of God" also appears in connection with the one who delivers the word of God. Good examples include Moses (1 Chr 23:14; Ezra 3:2) and David (Neh 12:24, 36).[14]

Wifall argues that the term "prophet" has at least three distinct meanings, which are useful in shedding light on the meaning of prophecy in Israel. First, a prophet is one who foretells or predicts future events—in the sense of the Old Testament foreshadowing the events of the New Testament. Second, a prophet is one who "proclaims" or "forth-tells"—in the sense of the preaching of pastors in Christian churches. Third, a prophet can also be one who

11. Ibid., 248.
12. Hays, *Message of the Prophets*, 25.
13. Ibid, 26.
14. Ibid., 26.

"speaks for" or "on behalf of" someone as a mediator or messenger between two parties.[15] Wifall nevertheless warns that the role and meaning of "prophet" in Israel cannot be restricted to any one of these definitions; further, it cannot be restricted to any segment of time—past, present, or future. Instead, Israel's prophets were divinely called to preach and reinterpret the covenant theology for their time and culture. Such a message would include God's acts in Israel's past, his dealings with them in the present, and how God will continue to relate with them in the immediate future.[16] The purpose of God "speaking through a prophet was not to communicate information about a timetable of events for the distant future."[17] Rather, their words were "intended for their own time, and represented God's continued involvement in history."[18]

According to Abraham J. Heschel, while engaging in such divine representation, a prophet remains sensitive to evil (Amos 8:4–8; Jer 2:12–13).[19] A prophet recognizes the importance of trivialities, luminous and explosive, and pursues the highest good. He or she is one whose octave is too high, an iconoclast, who practices austerity and compassion and makes sweeping allegations (Jer 5:1, 5; 6:13; 8:10; Hos 4:1–2). In their engagements, prophets make sure that few are guilty while all are responsible. A prophet is like a blast from heaven who faces a coalition of callousness and authority and embraces loneliness and misery. He is an assayer—a messenger and a witness and one who is merely tolerated by the people. A prophet, above all, is God's partner and associate.[20] As a divine associate, a prophet is a person of agony, whose "life and soul are at stake in what he says," yet who is able to perceive "the sigh of human anguish."[21] A prophet makes God audible, reveals God's will and inner life, and is in fellowship with God's feelings—his perspective and divine consciousness in history.[22]

15. Wifall, *Israel's Prophets*, 12.
16. Ibid,. 12–13.
17. Anderson, *Understanding the OT*, 249.
18. Daniel L Smith-Christopher, "Returning to Sources: The Hebrew Bible," 25.
19. See Heschel, *Prophets*, 1–31.
20. Heschel, *Prophets*, 3–31.
21. See Heschel (*Prophets*, xiii), where Susannah Heschel comments on her father's thoughts.
22. Ibid., xiii.

Whether Pope Francis shares in these prophetic qualities will come to light when we examine his ministry. We will keep in mind Walter Brueggemann's understanding of the task of prophetic ministry, which "is to nurture, nourish, and evoke a consciousness and perception alternative to the consciousness and perception of the dominant culture around us."[23] Pope Francis would identify Brueggemann's "dominant culture" with current acts of injustice, capitalism, consumerism, the exclusion of the poor from the sociopolitical and economic livelihood, the globalization of indifference, and human hostility to nature and the environment. Therefore, a prophet's mission is to offer alternative exhortation to this current "dominant culture" by "letting people see their own history in the light of God's freedom and his will for justice."[24]

Brueggemann suggests the prophetic ministry includes three tasks in addition to offering alternatives in light of God's freedom. Some of these additional tasks are evident in Francis's ministry. First, he argues that "the practice of prophetic ministry is not some special thing done two days a week. Rather, it is done in, with, and under all the acts of ministry—as much in counselling as in preaching, as much in liturgy as in education. It concerns a stance and posture or a hermeneutic about the world of death and the world of life that can be brought to light in every context." Second, he argues that "Prophetic ministry seeks to penetrate the numbness in order to face the body of death in which we are caught." And third, he argues that "Prophetic ministry seeks to penetrate despair so that new futures can be believed in and embraced by us."[25]

Classification of Prophets

Prophets are grouped under the titles "Former Prophets" and "Latter Prophets" in the Hebrew Bible (*Tanak*).[26] The Former Prophets are early or pre-classical prophets such as Samuel and Elijah who are mentioned in the Historical Books (Joshua–2 Kings 25).

---

23. Brueggemann, *Prophetic Imagination*, 3.
24. Brueggemann, *Prophetic Imagination*, 116.
25. Brueggemann, *Prophetic Imagination*, 117.
26. *Tanak* is an acronym for *Torah* (the Pentateuch), *Nəbîʾîm* (the Prophets), and *Kətubîm* (the Writings).

The Latter Prophets are the classical prophets (Isaiah, Jeremiah, Ezekiel [Major Prophets], and the Book of the Twelve [the Minor Prophets]). In the Jewish canon, the books of Daniel and Lamentations are classified among the Writings. So also are the books of Psalms, Job, Proverbs, Ruth, Ecclesiastes (*Qoholot*), Esther, Ezra-Nehemiah, and 1 and 2 Chronicles.[27]

The Greek Old Testament groups its books into four units: the Pentateuch, the Historical Books, the Wisdom literature, and the Prophets. The Prophetic Books begin with the four Major Prophets (Isaiah, Jeremiah, Ezekiel, and Daniel); the book of Lamentations is placed in between Jeremiah and Ezekiel (rather than among the Writings, as is the case in the Hebrew Bible). Unlike the Hebrew Bible, the Greek Old Testament grouping ends with the Minor Prophets (Hosea, Joel, Amos, Obadiah, Jonah, Micah, Nahum, Habakkuk, Zephaniah, Haggai, Zechariah, and Malachi).[28] A majority of scholars classify the book of Daniel as "apocalyptic" literature rather than a prophetic book because, apart from its genre and literary style, its message differs from the Prophetic Books.[29]

What follows is a chronological discussion of the prophetic effect of these different classes of prophets (pre-classical, classical, and post-exilic). Considering the above definition of prophetic functions, our goal is to highlight how their prophetic roles or tasks form a bedrock or foundation for Francis's ministry.

---

27. See Binz (*Introduction*, 68–75) and Dawes (*Introduction*, 11–26) for a simplified study on the canon of the Bible.

28. See Udoekpo (*Day of YHWH*, 25–26), which contains an extensive study of several titles for the Book of the Twelve and the order of the Twelve in the MT (Hosea, Joel, Amos, Obadiah, Jonah, Micah, Nahum, Habakkuk, Zephaniah, Haggai, Zechariah, and Malachi) and in the LXX (Hosea, Amos, Micah, Joel, Obadiah, Jonah, Nahum, Habakkuk, Zephaniah, Haggai, Zechariah, and Malachi).

29. See Leclerc (*Prophets*, 388–89), Branick (*Understanding the Prophets*, 267–92) for additional comments on the book of Daniel.

Effect of Israel's Pre-Classical Prophets

i. Effect of Abraham, Moses and Miriam

Because of his intercessory role, faith, and obedience, Abraham is named as a prophet in Genesis 20:7. His radical response to God's call to leave his hometown and travel to a strange land, to which the Lord directed him, in faith is deemed prophetic (Gen 12).

Moses is also a prophet and a leader who intercedes for his people and delivers God's words to them (Exod 3; 32). Moses, we are told, will be "like God to Pharaoh, and Aaron . . . shall be your prophet," communicating the divine will to Pharaoh (Exod 7:1 NRSV). In Brueggemann's *Prophetic Imagination*, "Moses represents a radical break with the social reality of Pharaoh's Egypt."[30] Likewise, today, Francis challenges the "Pharaohs" of his time.

Continuing to examine the pre-monarchical biblical tradition, after the Lord had defeated the Egyptian army at the Red Sea (Exod 15:1–18), Moses and Aaron's sister, Miriam, is mentioned as a prophet or prophetess—not only in a scene of holy war, but as a leader.[31] Miriam recognizes the victories of the Lord and leads the people in a hymn of praise to the Lord:[32]

> Then the prophet Miriam, Aaron's sister, took a tambourine in her hand; and all the women went out after her with a tambourine and with dancing. And Miriam sang to them: "Sing to the Lord, for he has triumphed gloriously; horse and rider he has thrown into the sea." (Exod 15:20–21 NRSV)[33]

Does not Miriam's joyful recognition of God's role foreshadow the *Joy of the Gospel* of Francis, a leader of 1.2 billion global Catholics?

---

30. Brueggemann, *Prophetic Imagination*, 5–7.

31. Miriam's significance cannot be overstated. Women were prophetesses in ancient Israel. Miriam poses a paradigmatic challenge to all women today in the church and in the society to be prophetic in their various positions.

32. Affirming this, Leclerc (*Prophets*, 46) states that, "the prophet is one who recognizes the victory won in battle as a deed of the Lord. This, too, is a job of the prophet: to see in the unfolding of events—war, famine, oppression, deliverance—the hand of God at work. The prophet interprets the meaning of history in light of God's larger plan for the people and the world."

33. Unless stated otherwise, biblical quotations will be drawn from *The New Oxford Annotated Bible: NRSV with the Apocrypha*.

Recognition of Miriam's leadership and vocation will be heard again in the mouth of Israel's prophet as follows: "For I brought you up from the house of slavery; and I sent before you Moses, Aaron and Miriam" (Micah 6:4). Miriam's story "reminds us that women served as prophets, even though no prophetic books attributed to women are known.[34] Her story also reinforces the tradition that prophecy is an ancient institution in Israel, known and esteemed in the time before kingship was established."[35] In other word, God has always used his human instruments to bring about positive changes.

ii. Effect of Balaam

What about the effects of the Mesopotamian Balaam, son of Boer, who appears—ironically—as a prophet? In his role, Balaam is a mouthpiece of the God of Israel and not of the Moabite King Balak (Num 22–24). Balaam is hired by a foreigner to curse Israel, but Balaam offers an alternative notion of prophetic ministry. In this story, rather than cursing, Balaam extends God's blessings to Israel. Coming to King Balak, he says, "I have come to you now, but do I have power to say anything? The word God puts in my mouth, that is what I must say" (Num 22:38).

The stories of Abraham, Moses, Aaron, Miriam, and Balaam present a broad historical view of biblical prophecy that would come to foreground the ministry of Pope Francis. From them, we learn that prophets are leaders, intercessors sent to the people as God's viceroys and spokespersons, and they perform great deeds and act as intermediaries between God and the community. They also endure hardship and criticism.

In biblical tradition, Moses remains the greatest embodiment of all these functions and attributes.[36] In the books of Exodus and Deuteronomy, Moses is the prophet *par excellence* and the one sent to deliver the word of God to his contemporaries, even in the face of criticism, suffering, and, occasionally, rejection.[37]

---

34. See Paul ("Review of *Prophets Male and Female*," 584–86) for an interesting analysis of female prophets in ancient times in comparison to male prophets.
35. Leclerc, *Prophets*, 47.
36. Ibid., 49.
37. Hays, *Message of the Prophets*, 23.

In his study on Moses's prophetic role, "'Face to Face': Moses as Prophet in Exodus 11:1–12:28," Bernon Lee presents the interplay of Moses's communication with God concerning the rite of Passover (Exod 11:1—12:28). In this study, Moses is an exemplary and inspiring prophet who not only listens to God, but also sees God "face to face," receives his blessings, and converses with God. He speaks with God, and God speaks through him.[38] He meets the criteria of the authentic prophet as defined in Deuteronomy: authentic prophecy conforms to the law (Deut 12:32—13:4) and sees fulfillment (Deut 18:15–22).[39] In each of these pre-classical prophets, one can see hidden treasures of Francis's prophetic qualities.

iii. Effect of Former Prophets

In the historical books—particularly the Deuteronomistic History (the DH, Josh–2 Kings 25) or the Former Prophets—when Israel monarchy and the priesthood were not keeping to the covenant promises, several prophets played a role in the history of biblical prophecy that would come to inform Pope Francis.

One of those Former Prophets is Joshua (Josh 1–24). Gorden Oeste comes to categorize Joshua as a prophet by employing a synchronic, theological reading of the DH. He convincingly argues that, although the DH never explicitly calls Joshua a prophet (*nābî'*), Joshua fulfills the popular roles of Israel's prophets (leader, intercessor, and successor of Moses).

The qualities that characterize Joshua as a prophet are reflected in the pastoral activities of Pope Francis today. For instance, Joshua works several signs. Before the Israelites cross the Jordan, Joshua reminds them of God's presence (Josh 3:8). He points to the Ark of the Covenant and the movement of the Jordan as a sign of God's presence (Josh 3:10–13).[40] Oeste also notes that a close examination of Joshua 24 together with other passages reveals the following five criteria (some of which are evident in the ministry of Francis):

---

38. Lee, "Moses As Prophet," 3–21.
39 See Leclerc (*Prophets*, 54–55) for further details.
40. Oeste, "Joshua in Deuteronomistic History," 23–36.

1. Joshua, like Moses, is raised up by Yahweh (Josh 1:1-9; Deut 18:15, 18).
2. Joshua is not only placed among his brothers as a leader (Deut 18:15, 18) but is buried in his own *naḥălāh* ("inheritance"), symbolizing covenant membership with others (Josh 19:49-50; 24:30-32).
3. Joshua is faithful in passing on the commands of Yahweh and Moses (Josh 11:12, 15, 23; 15:13; 17:4; 22:9; 24:2-13; see 14:2, 5; 21:2, 8; Deut 18:18).
4. Joshua insists on complete fidelity to Yahweh (Josh 22:5; 23:7-8; 24:2-28; Deut 13:1-5; 18:20).
5. Joshua fulfils the traits required of a prophet like Moses because of his accurate predictions and courage (Josh 3:5, 13-16; 6:26; 1 Kgs 16:34; 24:19-20; Judg 2:1-5, 10-11; 3:6-8; 10:13-14; Deut 18:21-22).[41] No one doubts the missionary and courageous qualities of Pope Francis.

iv. Effect of Deborah, the Prophetess

In the book of Judges, the two main sections—the cyclical divine words (Judg 2:6-16:31) and the concluding narrative (Judg 17-21)—evidence the people of Israel receiving or requesting words from heaven. These units, which recycle heaven's words, are bound together by the introductory section (Judg 1:1-2:5), which is also filled with intermediary or prophetic figures such as Deborah.[42]

Remarkably, the book of Judges introduces Deborah as a judge and a prophetess (Judg 4-5). Besides this introduction, the book of Judges further indicates that, as a leader over military, political, and judicial matters, Deborah summons Barak against the Canaanites, who are oppressing the Israelites. As a prophetess, she effectively delivers divine messages from Yahweh to Barak using the first-person formula (Judg 4:6-7); additionally, she predicts the outcome of the war (Judg 4:9, 17-22; 5:24-27).[43] In Deborah's leadership, we see a

---

41. Ibid., 37-41.
42. Boda, "Recycling Heaven's Words," 43-67.
43. Leclerc, *Prophets*, 63.

prefiguring of the leadership found in Pope Francis. We will see the same in the prophetic qualities of Samuel.

v. Effect of Samuel, the Prophet

Israel's prophets appointed and rejected kings. Samuel acted as a prophet by appointing and rejecting kings (1 Sam 9:1—10:16; 10:17-27; 11:1-15) in moments of unfaithfulness and disobedience.[44] In the case of Saul, Samuel said:

> You have done foolishly; you have not kept the commandment of the Lord your God, which he commanded you. The Lord would have established your kingdom over Israel forever, but now your kingdom will not continue; the Lord has sought out a man after his own heart; and the Lord has appointed him to be ruler over his people, because you have not kept what the Lord commanded you. (1 Sam 13:13-14)

Samuel is also prophetic in calling out Saul for his failure to carry out the "ban" (that is, the *ḥerem*) regarding the Amelekites, as instructed by the Lord (1 Sam 15:15-19; Josh 6:17-19). He says to Saul:

> Has the Lord as great delight in burnt offerings and sacrifices, as in obedience to the voice of the Lord? Surely, to obey is better than sacrifice, and to heed than the fat of rams. For rebellion is no less a sin than divination, and stubbornness is like iniquity and idolatry. Because you have rejected the word of the Lord, he has also rejected you from being king. (1 Sam 15:22-23)[45]

Besides making or breaking kings,[46] Samuel is customarily prophetic in the eyes of DH historians in his acts of authorizing and prohibiting holy wars.[47] For example, Samuel informed Saul, "Thus

---

44. Ibid., 63.

45. Middleton ("A Conflicted Prophet's Resistance," 69-91) unfortunately, and unsatisfactorily, sees the role of Samuel in this text in a negative light—from a mere historiographical point of view rather than a theological and providential point of view. He thinks Samuel's refusal to intercede for Saul sets Samuel "apart from Moses in his paradigmatic prophetic intercession on behalf of Israel's sin."

46. This expression is borrowed from Leclerc, *Prophets*, 68.

47. See Von Rad, *Der Heilige Krieg* (cited in Cross, *Canaanite Myth*, 88); Von Rad

says the Lord of hosts, 'I will punish the Amalekites for what they did in opposing the Israelites when they came up out of Egypt. Now go and attack Amelek and utterly destroy all that they have; do not spare them, but kill both man and woman, child and infant, ox and sheep, camel and donkey (1 Sam 15:2–3).

Finally, Samuel's prophetic role is heightened in his interpretation of the Mosaic tradition for his contemporary society. In the context of ancient Israel, Samuel makes an adjustment for Israel's time of transition. He addresses Saul and the people of his time, place, and culture on the new role of the king as one who obeys rather than makes laws. Samuel says;

> See, here is the king whom you have chosen, for whom you have asked; see, the Lord has set a king over you. If you will fear the Lord and serve him and heed his voice and not rebel against commandments of the Lord, and if both you and the king who reigns over you will follow the Lord your God, it will be well; but if you will not heed the voice of the Lord, but rebel against the commandment of the Lord, then the hand of the Lord will be against you and your king. (1 Sam 12:13–15)[48]

In 1 Samuel 12:13–15, Samuel, without abrogating the law, adapts prophetically to the new social situation, which gave rise to the reign of David (2 Sam 3–6; 7, 11–12; 1 Kgs 1). Echoes of this adaptation will be seen in Christ, who came to renew, update, and fulfill the law rather than abolish it (Matt 5:17). Christ's mission of renewal resounds in the Acts of the Apostles and in various church teachings and ecclesiastical documents today.[49] An example of such a document is the eighth encyclical letter of Saint John Paul II, entitled *Mission of the Redeemer* (*Redemptoris Missio*), dated to December 7, 1990, which was written in celebration of the twenty-fifth

---

(*Holy War*, 44–51); Craigie (*Problem of War*, 22–26) and Udoekpo (*Day of YHWH*, 59–60) for additional comments on holy war in ancient Israel.

48. Leclerc (*Prophets*, 69–70) has detailed comments on this.

49. See, for instance, Flannery, *Vatican Council II*, especially those basic sixteen documents (*Lumen Gentium, Dei Verbum, Scrosanctum Concillium, Gaudium et Spes, Christus Dominus, Presbyterorum Ordinis, Optatam Totius, Pefectae Caritatis, Apostolicam Actuositatem, Ad Gente Divinitus, Unitatis Rdintegratio, Orientalium Ecclesiarum, Inter Merifica, Dignitatis Humanae, Nostra Aetate the Gravissimum Educationis*).

anniversary of the Second Vatican Council's Decree on the Church's Missionary Activity, *Ad Gentes*.

As a foundational document for reflection on the Church's missionary activity, *Ad Gentes* prophetically declares:[50]

> Having been sent by God to the nations to be "the universal sacrament of salvation," the church, in obedience to the command of her founder (Matt 16:15) and because it is demanded by her own essential universality, strives to preach the gospel to all. The apostles, on whom the church was founded, following the footsteps of Christ "preached the word of truth brought churches to birth." It is the duty of their successors to carry on this work "so that the word of God may speed on and triumph" (2 Thess 3:1), the kingdom of God be proclaimed and renewed throughout the world.[51]

In his Apostolic Exhortation *Evangelii Nuntiandi*, Pope Paul expresses the same zeal for prophetic renewal when he speaks of evangelization as the grace and vocation of the church. Prophetic renewal is her deepest identity. The church exists to evangelize, preach, teach, and reconcile sinners to God, as did Samuel and Israel's other prophets.[52]

Built on this prophetic teaching, which flows from *Ad Gentes* and *Evangelii Nuntiandi*, John Paul II develops his teachings on the church's missionary mission in his *Redemptoris Missio*. Here, John Paul II's discussions include:

- Christ as the savior (chapter I)
- The kingdom of God (chapter II)
- The Holy Spirit as the primary agent of the mission (chapter III)
- The vast horizon of the mission of *Ad Gentes* (chapter IV)
- The paths of mission (chapter V)
- Leaders and workers in the missionary apostolate (chapter VI)
- Cooperation in missionary activity (chapter VII)
- Missionary spirituality (chapter VIII)

---

50. Wuerl, *Gift of John Paul II*, 143.
51. *Ad Gentes*, no. 1.
52. Paul VI, *Evangelii Nuntiandi*, no. 14.

In all this, it is the Holy Spirit who "makes them witnesses and prophets."[53]

An appropriation of this new way of interpreting the faith tradition of the church is seen in Pope Francis. Though not in the sense of secular kings, one can recall how many times Pope Francis has appointed and demoted church leaders for one reason or another.

vi. Effect of Nathan, the Prophet

Nathan is another important ancient prophet. He plays a significant prophetic role in the life of David and in what we may call the "royal theology" (2 Sam 7, 11-12; 1 Kings 1) that would directly or indirectly inspire contemporary prophets and forms the foreground for the papacy of Francis. Nathan appears in 2 Samuel 7 without any indication of his background. In this episode, David addresses his concerns to Nathan, who—without consulting God—instructs David to build a house for the Lord (2 Sam 7:1–17).[54] Through Nathan's vision (*ḥāzôn*), God instructs David not to build a house (*bāyît*; "temple," "dwelling place," "physical structure").[55] In this vision, the Lord instructs Nathan: "Go and tell my servant David: Thus says the Lord: Are you the one to build me a house to live in? . . . Why have you not build me a house of cedar?" (2 Sam 7:4–7). Surprisingly, through Nathan, the Lord announces to David that he should not build him a house—a physical dwelling place. Rather, the Lord promises to build for David and his offspring ("descendants" or "seed") an everlasting dynasty, royal dignity, or kingdom:

> From the time that I appointed judges over my people Israel; and I will give you rest from all your enemies. Moreover the

---

53. John Paul II, *Redemtoris Missio*, no. 24. See also John Paul II's teachings in the *Redemptor Hominis*, nos., 1–22 and *Dominum et Vivifcantem*, nos. 1–67 on the Holy Spirit.

54. Leclerc, *Prophets*, 72–73.

55. *bāyît*, "temple," "a dwelling place," also has different connotations in different contexts in the Bible: household, physical building, family, caretaker, steward, etc. In my native African languages, "*Efik*" "*Ibibio*," "*Annang*," it is translated as "*Ufok*," or "*Ubon*." I want to believe the author's parent knew of this passage when they named him Ufok Udoekpo (Udoekpo's household, "caretaker," of my dynasty, dignity, or family).

Lord declares to you that the Lord will make you a house. When your days are fulfilled and you lie down with your ancestors, I will raise up your offspring after you, who shall come forth from your body, and I will establish his kingdom. He shall build a house for my name, and I will establish the throne of his kingdom forever. I will be a father to him, and he shall be a son to me. When he commits iniquity, I will punish him with a rod such as morals use, with blows inflicted by human beings. But I will not take my steadfast love from him, as I took it from Saul, whom I put away from before you. Your house and your kingdom shall be make sure forever before me; your throne shall be established forever. (2 Sam 7:11–16)

What is also significant in this passage (2 Sam 7:1–17) is the Deuteronomic criterion of an authentic prophet (Deut 18:18). A true prophet is one who speaks God's words and has "fellowship with the feelings of God."[56] In this text, Nathan is considered a true prophet who receives and speaks God's words to King David.[57] Generally, the appearance of the prophets in the history of Israel's kingship reminds us of God's presence among his people, despite their history. God is in our midst no matter what! Of course, Nathan would also dominate the royal maneuvering that would eventually lead David to select Solomon, whom Nathan would anoint as king (1 Kgs 1).[58] Francis, who appoints many church leaders—especially bishops and cardinals—can relate to the prophetic duties of biblical Nathan.

vii. Effect of Ahijah, the Prophet

The prophet Ahijah is responsible for the designation of the northern kings. He presides over the division of the kingdom soon after the death of Solomon.[59] Historically, Solomon began his kingship well; he reigned with wisdom. Later, however, he strayed from the Lord when he, through the influence of his foreign wives and concubines,

---

56. Heschel, *Prophets*, xiii.

57. See Leclerc (*Prophets*, 73–78) for additional insight on Nathan and elements of royal theology (kingship forever, unconditional promise, the king is the "son of God," and Jerusalem is God's dwelling).

58. Branick, *Understanding the Historical Books*, 79.

59. See Beal ("Prophetic Word for Two Kingdoms," 105–124), which, though short of theological details, has extensive comments on the different sets of prophetic words spoken to both of the divided kingdoms, north and south (1 Kgs 11–14).

chose to worship foreign gods. According to Scripture, "among his wives were seven hundred princesses and three hundred concubines, and his wives turned away his heart" (1 Kgs 11:3). This behavior was sinful and in violation of God's covenant relationship with Israel. First Kings 11:4–8 details the remainder of Solomon's sins, which led to a socio-religious crisis and the division of the kingdom:

> For when Solomon was old, his wives turned away his heart after other gods; and his heart was not true to the Lord his God, as was the heart of his father David. For Solomon followed Astarte the goddess of the Sidonians, and Milcom the abominations of the Ammonites. So Solomon did what was evil in the sight of the Lord, and did not completely follow the Lord, as his father David had done. Then Solomon built a high place for Chemosh the abomination of the Ammonites, on the mountain east of Jerusalem. He did the same for all his foreign wives, who offered incense and sacrificed to their gods.

Because of Solomon's sins and his unpopular extravagance, the Lord rejected Solomon's ways, tore the kingdom from him, and gave it to his servants (1 Kgs 11:9–13), as Samuel had predicted (1 Sam 8:10–18). Solomon's behavior not only breached the covenant but led to social and religious unrest. Ahijah was sent to manage this unrest. In 1 Kings 11:29–41, the Prophet Ahijah from the northern town of Shiloh symbolically announces God's rejection of the sitting king and designation of a new king, Jeroboam:

> Take for yourself ten pieces; for thus says the Lord, the God of Israel, "See, I am about to tear the kingdom from the hand of Solomon, and will give you ten tribes. One tribe will remain his, for the sake of my servant David and for the sake of Jerusalem, the city that I have chosen out of all the tribes of Israel. This is because he has forsaken me, worshiped Astarte the goddess of the Sidonians, Chemosh the god of Moab, and Milcom the god of the Ammonites, and has not walked on my ways, doing what is right in my sight . . . I will take you, and you shall reign over all that your soul desires; you shall be king over Israel." (1 Kgs 11:29–37)

Besides this symbolic action, the Prophet Ahijah also made it clear to Jeroboam, the new king of the northern kingdom, that if he walked in God's ways and kept his commands and statutes, as David did, God would build an everlasting house and dynasty for Israel (1 Kgs 11:38). Ahijah's prophetic role is comparable to that of Samuel (1 Sam 15:26; 16:13; 2 Sam 7:12–16). Israel's prophets were instrumental in anointing, intervening in, indicting, bringing changes and reforms to, and rejecting Israel's kings and political sphere for a variety of reasons.

Another good example is found in the case of Rehoboam and Jeroboam. Rehoboam succeeded his father, Solomon, as the king of Israel.[60] It was only when Jeroboam and the assembly of Israel felt the burden of taxation, neglect, and labor imposed on them by Rehoboam that the north decided to secede and rebel against Rehoboam, thereby fulling the prophecy of Ahijah: "so the king did not listen to the people, because it was a turn of affairs brought about by the Lord that he might fulfill his words" (1 Kgs 12:15). Ahijah's actions here—indicting corrupt kings and leaders, initiating changes and reforms, and intervening in the face of poor leadership and injustice—would require courage even in our day. This is also true in the contemporary sense of the papacy of Francis, who has done things differently or broken away from traditions in many ways. Francis, in light of the Prophet Ahijah, "is a challenge. He shakes us up to make us better. He disturbs us from our complacency and status quo attitude. He humbles us with his humility. He has slowly moved the Church from being dogmatic, self-engrossed and authoritative institution to being gentle, outreaching—compassionate and persuasive Church through the power of love and mercy."[61]

viii. Effect of Shamaiah, the "Man of God," and an Unnamed Prophet

Shemaiah, a "man of God," intervenes in the prophetic wars among the communities of Israel. He unequivocally warns the kings, "Thus says the Lord, you shall not go up or fight against your kindred the people of Israel. Let everyone go home, for this thing is from me" (1 Kgs 12:24). Shemaiah is worthy of imitation as a champion of peace, dialogue, and reconciliation. In both Ahijah and Shemaiah's roles, as well as Francis's and other contemporary prophets' roles, "God's effective word is at work guiding the events of history."[62]

60. Branick, *Understanding the Historical Books*, 94.
61. See Tan, "Foreword," 7–8.
62. Leclerc, *Prophets*, 82.

Further stories of God guiding historical events through prophets, his divine agents, appear in relation to Jeroboam king of Israel (922–901 BC). In his attempt to consolidate power, Jeroboam ignored the central place of worship in Jerusalem. To rival the central place of worship in Jerusalem, preferred by the Deuteronomistic Historians (Deut 12:5–7), he established shrines in the far north of Dan (Judg 18:30) and on the southern border in Bethel (Gen 28:18–22). He also fashioned golden calves, in violation of God's commandments (Deut 5:8–9), supported a non-Levitical priesthood (Deut 18:1–8), and even altered the religious calendar. Additionally, he offered sacrifices that were meant for a priest to offer. As a result, an unnamed prophet ("man of God") from Judah denounces the king and his foreign altars (1 Kgs 13:1–10):

> O altar, altar, thus says the Lord, "A son shall be born to the house of David, Josiah by name; and he shall sacrifice on you the priests of the high places who offer incense on you, and human bones shall be burned on you. . . . The altar shall be torn down, and the ashes that are on it shall be poured out."
> (1 Kgs 13:2–3)

Upon hearing this rebuke from the man of God, Jeroboam stretched out his hand and ordered the prophet to be seized—only to have his hand wither (1 Kgs 13:4). The king then asked for help from the prophet, and with the prophet's effective intercession, the king's hands were restored. Here, we may ask: Is Pope Francis a contemporary "man of God," whose prophetic papacy is guided by prayer and intercession for the church and the world?

First Kings relates further details about this unnamed "man of God" (1 Kgs 13:1–10). It records that "an old prophet" lured the "man of God" from Judah to disobey God by eating, dining, and drinking with the false prophet against God's will. Consequently, "the man of God" is devoured by a lion on his way back (1 Kgs 13:11–25). This confirms that an "uncompromising obedience to God's command is required of kings, prophets, and people alike."[63] It also confirms that prophets were mouthpieces of God. They spoke the truth, condemned, and interceded on behalf of the people. They were fully commissioned to communicate judgment on behalf of God, as was typical of Ahijah against the sinful Jeroboam:

63. Ibid., 83.

> Thus says the Lord, the God of Israel: because I exalted you from the people, made you leader over my people Israel, and tore the kingdom away from the house of David to give it to you; yet you have not been like my servant David, who kept my commandments and followed me with all his all his heart, doing only that which was right in my sight, but you have done evil above all those who were before you and have gone and made for yourself other gods, and cast images, provoking me to anger, and have thrust me behind your back; therefore, I will bring evil upon the house of Jeroboam. (1 Kgs 14:7–10)

The evils visited upon the house of Jeroboam include (1 Kgs 14:12–18):

1. Cutting off every male in Israel, both bond and free
2. Consuming the house of Jeroboam as one would burn up dung with fire
3. Allowing dogs to eat up every deceased person from the house of Jeroboam
4. Feeding anyone from his house who dies in the open field to the birds of the air
5. Raising a king who will take Israel into exile[64]

Noticeably, the themes of the prophecies of Ahijah, Shemaiah, and the man of God are not different from the themes we hear often from the Deuteronomistic Historians: that the exiles Israel experienced were a result of the Israelites' sins of disobedience, idolatry, and infidelity. In fact, according to Anderson, "the Deuteronomistic historians were horrified at Jeroboam's innovations, especially the setting up of golden bulls in high places other than Jerusalem."[65]

---

64. Anderson (*Understanding the OT*, 258–59) points to the brief report in 1 Kings 14:25–28 about King Shishak of Egypt (935–914 BC). After Solomon's death, Shishak was "no fonder of Jeroboam than he was Rehoboam." He used Jeroboam as an instrument to destabilize the united kingdom of Israel. Under the same Shishak, Egypt invaded the united kingdom as well as Edom, Philistia, Judah, and Israel in the fifth year of King Rehoboam.

65. Anderson, *Understanding the OT*, 259.

ix. Effects of Other Pre-Classical Prophets

Other pre-classical prophets who were active during the divided monarchy include Elijah, Elisha, Micaiah Ben Imlah, and Huldah. During this period of the divided monarchy, the southern kingdom of Israel was somewhat steady under the kingship of Asa and Abijam (1 Kgs 15); the northern kingdom was less stable under Jeroboam's numerous successors (922–901 BC). For instance, Jeroboam's son, Nadab, reigned for just two years (1 Kgs 15:25; 901–900 BC) before he was assassinated by Baasha (900–877 BC). Baasha was in turn eliminated by his son Elah (877–876 BC) after ruling for twenty-two years. Elah ruled for two years before he was assassinated by Zimri (876 BC). Zimri ruled for only one week and was succeeded by Omri (876–869 BC).[66] It was against this unstable political background that another prophet, Jehu, son of Hanani, did what prophets were known for: Jehu challenged the status quo (as we see in Francis) and reminded people about God. Jehu's prophetic words against King Baasha were as follows:

> Since I exalted you out of the dust and made you leader over my people Israel, and you have walked in the way of Jeroboam, and have caused my people Israel to sin, provoking me to anger with their sins, therefore, I will consume Baasha and his house, and I will make your house like the house of Jeroboam son of Nebat. Anyone belonging to Baasha who dies in the city dogs shall eat; and anyone of his who dies in the field the birds of the air shall eat. (1 Kgs 16:1–4)

Following Jehu are the prophetic episodes of Elijah, Elisha, and Micaiah—all Ephraimite prophets who were active during the period of the Omride Dynasty.[67] Omri was an astute politician and successful military leader who came to the throne by a coup d'état.[68] He fought and conquered the Moabites in the Transjordan. Evidence of this is found on the Moabite Stone, which records the boasts of the last king of the Omride dynasty, Mesha:

> I (am) Mesha, son of Chemosh. [...], King of Moab, the Dibonite- my father (had) reigned over Moab thirty years ... As for

---

66. See Leclerc (*Prophets*, 85) for additional information.
67. Anderson, *Understanding the OT*, 268–69.
68. Anderson, *Understanding the OT*, 264.

> Omri, king Israel, he humbled Moab many years (lit., days), for Chemosh was angry at his land. And his son followed him and he also said, "I will humble Moab." In my time he spoke (thus), but I have triumphed over him and over his house, while Israel hath perished forever![69]

Omri eventually purchased Samaria and turned it into the capital of Israel, which it remained until 722 BC. He tried to check Syria by engaging in diplomatic alliances and political marriages with international partners such as Judah and Phoenicia. For example, his son, Ahab, was married to Jezebel, daughter of the Phoenician king Ethabaal (1 Kgs 16:31). His daughter, Attaliah, was given in marriage to King Jehoram of Judah. These actions indicate that Omri was more interested in political success than worship of Yahweh. Like father, like son. The religious behavior of Ahab (869–850 BC) "was entirely wrongheaded: he built a temple to the Canaanite god Baal in the capital city of Samaria (I Kgs 16:30–32). With the influence if his wife Jezebel, this put Baal-Melkart, a protective deity of Tyre, at the center of the kingdom's religious and cultic life."[70] First Kings 16:30–33 pointedly criticizes Ahab for his sins:

> Ahab son of Omri did evil in the sight of the Lord more than all who were before him. And as if it had been a light thing for him to walk in the sins of Jeroboam son of Nebat, he took as his wife Jezebel daughter of King Ethbaal of the Sidonians, and went and serve Baal, and worshiped him. He erected an altar for Baal in the house of Baal, which he built in Samaria. Ahab also made a sacred pole. Ahab did more to provoke the anger of the Lord, the God of Israel, than had all the kings of Israel who were before him. (1 Kgs 16:30–33)

Every time, place, and culture has its own challenges that call for prophetic intervention. The time of Ahab was no exception.

x. Effect of Elijah, the prophet

Elijah was commissioned to challenge the idolatry and tyrannical culture of his time (1 Kgs 17–19; 21). Elijah's exemplary prophetic ministry would come to impact the ministry of Pope Francis in

---

69. Pritchard, *Ancient Near East*, 320.
70. Leclerc, *Prophets*, 87; see also Anderson, *Understanding the Prophets*, 272.

many ways, directly or indirectly—particularly his prophetic promotion of the sovereignty of Yahweh and in his promotion of God as the source of fertility. Like Elijah and Elisha, Pope Francis continues to challenge modern idolatry, such of the "globalization of indifference," especially in his 2016 New Year Message.[71] Elijah's emphasis on the exclusive worship of God as the father of the poor and needy also foregrounds Francis's contemporary passion for the plight of the poor today.

Just as the election of Pope Francis was a surprise to some, Elijah of Tishbete appeared on the scene seemingly from nowhere and announced drought in the name of the God of Israel in other to challenge Ahab and his gods (1 Kgs 17). He was like Moses, the prophet who stood toe to toe, shoulder to shoulder, with Pharaoh. In 1 Kings 17, Elijah effectively drives home the truth that the God of Israel has authority over all lands, nations, water, and fertility. For Elijah, people's lives—even those outside Palestine—are in God's hand. Elijah finds joy in reaching out to the widow of Zeraphat in the Phoenician town of Jezebel, particularly during the famine (1 Kgs 17:8–24), even though it was not politically and socially conducive. This same pastoral approach to the poor and the marginalized would come to mark the ministry of Pope Francis.

In 1 Kings 18, Elijah dramatically contests, defeats, and massacres 450 prophets of Baal and 400 prophets of Asherah on Mount Carmel. Without fear, he points out to Israel the danger of "limping with two different opinions" (1 Kgs 18:21)—that is, worshiping many gods instead of the true God of Israel. Echoing Joshua 24, Elijah foregrounds the functions of Francis and of today's prophets, who are called to discourage syncretism in all its disguises, to challenge the Jezebels of all times, and to bring people to acknowledge the presence of God in their midst.

Usually this comes with the price of persecution and harsh criticism. Every prophet must be willing to pay such a price. In the case of Elijah, his life was threatened by the status quo. In 1 Kings 19, Elijah flees from such threats to the wilderness and toward the south of Beer-sheba, away from Jezebel's persecution. Fatigued after a day's dusty journey into the wilderness, Elijah is frustrated and wishes for death (1 Kgs 19:1–4). But the grace of God is sufficient for God's

---

71. This will be elaborated further in Part II and Part III.

prophet (1 Kgs 19:5–8). God provides for Elijah as he had provided for the Israelites in the wilderness (Exod 16). After traveling for forty days and forty nights in the wilderness, Elijah finally arrives at Mount Horeb (Sinai), the sacred mountain of the covenant, where Moses once received the Ten Commandments (Exod 19–24; 32–34). Elijah also encounters God on this mountain—not necessarily in thunder, wind, fire, and earthquakes, but in a gentle sound of divine silence (1 Kgs 19:11–13). In all this, Elijah is God's mouthpiece—a kingmaker and a king breaker.[72] God instructs him to anoint Hazael as king over Aram (1 Kgs 19:15), Jehu as king in Israel (in place of Ahab), and Elisha as his prophetic successor (1 Kgs 19:15–21).[73]

Several significant facts emerge from Elijah's prophetic stories and journey to Sinai, where Moses received the revelation from God after the exodus. First, we see that prophets—even modern prophets—must reinterpret or build on Israel's faith covenant tradition. Second, we see that prophets are reformers who cherish the importance of Sinai. Third, we see that prophets like Elijah must keep the Mosaic tradition alive, in new forms and ways and with a renewed spirit, especially in a world where the poor are neglected.[74]

Richard Sklba's comment also underscores the importance of Elijah's prophetic ministry of Elijah for us today:

> Among the most influential of the spirited prophets of Israel towers the figure of Elijah the Tisbite from the land of Gilead just east of the Jordan River (1 K 17:1). He is presented as an individual woven into the theological legends and reminiscences of the Deuteronomistic history (1 K17–2 K2) . . . In the age of syncretistic distractions and dangerous flirtation with the religious foundations of the political power in neighboring nations, Elijah stood tall and strong, firmly recalling the people of Israel to the life-giving core of their ancestral faith.[75]

Also significant for us in light of Francis's ministry is that the Prophet Elijah was not indifferent to the plight of the poor. This is made clear in the story of Naboth's vineyard (1 Kgs 21). In this story, Naboth refuses to sell his family land to Ahab and Jezebel.

---

72. Leclerc, *Prophets*, 90.
73. See Branick, *Understanding the Historical Books*, 100.
74. Anderson, *Understanding the OT*, 277.
75. Sklba, *Pre-Exilic Prophecy*, 28.

Of course, this ancestral estate belongs to God (1 Kgs 21:3). Ahab cannot have it, and Jezebel is not happy. Naboth is falsely accused and unjustly executed (1 Kgs 21:14). Elijah is sent to address this social injustice. In fulfilling his mission, Elijah effectively reminds everyone—especially modern prophets and followers of Pope Francis—that prophets are not confined to critiquing worship; their ministry also extends to the area of social justice. Elijah confirms that Israelite prophets were champions of ethical conduct, bearers of the word (1 Kgs 17:24), confronters of kings (1 Kgs 21:20), and advocates for the poor and the voiceless.[76]

xi. Effect of Elisha, the Prophet

Elisha succeeded Elijah in his prophetic ministry (2 Kgs 2–9; 13:14–21). He effectively picked up "the mantle of Elijah that had fallen from him" (2 Kgs 2:13–15). Elsewhere Scripture records that "Elijah passed by him and threw his mantle over him" (1 Kgs 19:19–21). In both accounts, Elijah transfers his prophetic authority to Elisha with implicit divine guidance and blessing. From then on, like Moses and Elijah, Elisha remains an agent of the mighty deeds of God in various capacities and contexts. For instance:

- He parted the Jordan River (2 Kgs 2:8, 13–14).
- He supplied the needy widow (1 Kgs 17:14–16; 2 Kgs 4:1–7).
- He raised the widow's son from the dead (1Kgs 17:17–24; 2 Kgs 4:32–37).[77]
- He miraculously fed the hungry and had leftovers (2 Kgs 4:42–44).

Additionally, Elisha brought God's healing mercy to the ailing Naaman (2 Kgs 5:1–19)—an act that foreshadows Francis's message of divine mercy. Elisha also announces an end to starvation and famine in Samaria (2 Kgs 6:24–7:20). In that context, he "restored land to a poor widow, again demonstrating the Mosaic roots of his faith and power."[78] Elisha also prophesied effectively in God's name (2 Kgs 2:21;

---

76. See Sklba (*Pre-Exilic Prophecy*, 29–42) for additional analysis on the spirituality of Elijah.

77. Leclerc, *Prophets*, 97.

78. Sklba, *Pre-Exilic Prophecy*, 43.

3:16; 4:43). He interceded for the dead (2 Kgs 4:33) and designated Hazael as the king of Aram. He sent a prophet to anoint Jehu as the king of Israel (2 Kgs 9:1–13).[79] Scripture further reveals Elisha's human side—especially when he commanded the angry bears to devour the little boys who made fun of his baldness (2 Kgs 2:23–25).

In his prophetic role, Elisha proves to be an inspiring agent of the God of Moses, who protects the poor and the immigrant, and whose prophecy would come to a fulfillment and beyond (Deut 18:21–22). Elisha reminds us that, wherever we are, we are called to protect the immigrant, the poor, and the widow—a theme that has dominated the papacy of Pope Francis in a unique way.

Elijah and Elisha were not only authentic and zealous; they were also effective prophetic agents of the God of Moses. Many of Israel's classical prophets were also effective prophetic agents, including Amos, Hosea, and others. But before we discuss these classical prophets, we should mention the story surrounding the Prophet Micaiah Ben Imlah, who is another good example of one who delivers a true prophecy in Israel that came to fulfillment (1 Kgs 22).

xii. Effect of Micaiah Ben Imlah, the Prophet (1 Kgs 22)

At the heart of Micaiah Ben Imlah's prophetic story is whether King Jehoshaphat of Judah and King Ahab of Israel should fight together against Aram (Syria) over the territory of Ramoth-gilead. The story highlights a surprising moment of cooperation between Judah and Israel and emphasizes the role of prophecy in Israel.[80] Prophets had the role of anointing kings and counseling them on military matters—including whether to go to war. They were also responsible for reinterpreting traditions. Even though Ahab's palace prophets recommended that the king go to war, Jehoshaphat of Judah preferred a second opinion from Micaiah, a prophet outside of the king's palace (1 Kgs 22:5–28). Ahab and Jehoshaphat received conflicting prophetic advice. Ahab's palace prophets predicted victory, while Micaiah provided alternative advice. Despite political pressure from the king's messengers and chief of staff (1 Kgs 22:14), Micaiah

---

79. Anderson, *Understanding the OT*, 279; Leclerc, *Prophets*, 97.
80. Branick, *Understanding the Historical Books*, 101.

denounced the palace prophets' prophecies of victory as the words of "a lying spirit" (1 Kgs 22:22).[81]

It turned out that the prophet of God, Micaiah, was right, while the lying palace prophets were wrong (Jer 23:9–32). Micaiah suffered punishment and humiliation for standing up against falsehood (2 Kgs 22:24–28). Like Jeremiah and Jesus, Micaiah "suffers the indignity of a slap on the face and imprisonment (Matt 26:67 and John 18:22). He defends his world by appealing to his prophetic experience of the great council of God, giving in effect the foundation of authentic prophecy."[82] Micaiah effectively appeals to modern prophets, preachers, and pastors to be aware of falsely rubber-stamping the king's opinion for a paycheck. He also reminds us that suffering and endurance are part and parcel of prophetic ministries. Above all, Micaiah shows us that that which the Lord has promised us through the mouth of his prophets will always come to fulfillment (Deut 18:21–22).

xiii. Effect of Huldah, the Prophetess (2 Kgs 22:14–20)

Huldah was a late pre-exilic and pre-classical female prophet who lived during the time of King Josiah's reforms (640–609 BC). In the Bible, she stands among strong female figures like Sarah (Gen 11:29–23:20), Miriam (Exod 15:20; Num 12:1–12; 20:1), Deborah (Judg 4:4–5:31), Hannah (1 Sam 1–2), Abigail (1 Sam 25:28–31), Esther, Noadiah (Neh 6:14), and Isaiah's wife (Isa 8:3). What an inspiration to all—especially women in the church and contemporary worship communities.

Huldah's effectiveness came to light when King Josiah embarked on religious reforms in 622 BC (2 Kgs 22–23; 2 Chr 34–35). In the eighteenth year of his reign, as narrated in 2 Kings, he commissioned the repair of the temple in Jerusalem. Hilkiah, the high priest, found the Book of the Law (2 Kgs 22:8), which he handed over to Josiah's secretary, Shaphan, who in turn read it to the king. Moved by the words of the Lord, which Josiah believed had been neglected, the king tore his garment and mourned. He sought prophetic confirmation, which he received from the prophetess Huldah (2 Kgs 22:15–20).

---

81. Leclerc, *Prophets*, 92.
82. Branick, *Understanding the Historical Books*, 102.

Huldah's readiness to respond to the situation could be considered as analogous to Francis's readiness for spreading the gospel.

It is fair to say that, among Israel's early and pre-classical prophets of God, including Abraham, Moses, Deborah, Samuel, Elijah, Elisha, Nathan, Ahijah, Shamaiah, Micaiah, and the unnamed "man of God," Huldah proves to be a notable divine agent. In their time and culture, these prophets were effective in their respective missions. These missions, some of which we have discussed, could be seen as foreshadowing the prophetic ministry of Pope Francis (discussed further in Part II of this work).

Effect of Israel's Classical Prophets

Classical prophets include Hosea, Amos, Joel, Isaiah, Micah, Obadiah, Jeremiah, Ezekiel, Jonah, Nahum, Habakkuk, Zephaniah, Haggai, Zechariah, Malachi, and Daniel. These individuals prophesied in the beginning of the mid-eighth century BC, through the time of Ezra and the beginning of Judaism (400 BC). Each of these prophets has a collection of sayings and writings attributed to his name. These prophets (Amos–Malachi) are also considered classical in the sense that, among all the Old Testament books, their prophetic writings or sayings "make a 'classical' presentation of Israel's unique monotheistic faith."[83] Each of these prophets (Amos –Malachi) effectively challenge us to be prophetic and pose unique questions for us today in matters of ethical conduct, justice, peace, dialogue, unity, judgment, fairness, worship of God alone, mercy, forgiveness, courage to lead with example and preach with righteousness, truth, and hope for salvation. Pope Francis would come to emphasize each of these matters in his ministry.

i. Effect of Amos, the Prophet

Amos is one of the foundational classical prophets in Israel. He foregrounded the papacy of Francis and has bequeathed for our times tremendous prophetic effects and challenges. Prior to his calling to prophesy to the people—especially the establishments of the northern kingdom of Israel—Amos grew up as a farmer and businessman

---

83. Wifall, *Israel's Prophets*, 10.

in his humble village of Tekoa, located in southern Jerusalem (Amos 1:1; 7:14–17).[84] From his personal business setting, he received a calling to the "prophetic mission" to serve many nations and people. This took place during the mid-eighth century BC, when Jeroboam II reigned as king in the northern kingdom (786–746 BC) and Uzziah governed in the southern kingdom (783–742 BC). It was a time of relative peace and prosperity.

During this time, the advancing Assyrian Empire had expanded as far as Damascus in Syria. Israel and Judah enjoyed a time of prosperity, as their enemy Aram concentrated on defending itself against the threat of the rising Assyrian political might. Because of the political deficits suffered by Aram, "Israel was able to concentrate for a few decades on building its commercial activities and gain greater influence over its smaller neighbors."[85] Adding to Israel's political and economic progress was expanded territorial gains and political equilibrium comparable to the times of King David and King Solomon (2 Kgs 14:23–29; 2 Chr 26:6–8).[86] However, the rise of business opportunities and the expansion of trade, farming, and transportation stifled small farm and business owners; this growth, combined with the lack of military threat, made the elite people of Israel indifferent to the plight of the poor.

Israel's success was short-lived and marked by abuse of wealth by the rich.[87] The rich appropriated food, grain, chariots, horses, linen, winter and summer homes, jewelry, perfume, spices, and ivory for themselves and their friends and families (Amos 3:15). They also dined and drank sumptuously while the poor were starving. According to Scripture, the elite classes traded the voiceless and the poor for a pair of sandals (Amos 2:6–7; 8:6) and were indifferent to the ruins of the house of Joseph (Amos 6:4–6).

In Amos's time, corruption became the norm in Judah and Israel. Owners of big farms and businesses used false weights of measurement in business transactions (Amos 8:5–6). The political class and the officials at the gate and law courts became accustomed to bribery (Amos 5:12). During worship and religious activities, the

84. See Udoekpo, *Worship in Amos 5*, 1–8.
85. Matthews, *Prophets of Israel*, 46.
86. Paul, *Amos*, 1.
87. Premnath, "Amos and Hosea," 127.

same rich and elite class led idle songs at shrines in Bethel, Gilgal, and Dan (Amos 4:1–13). They engaged in various hypocritical worship gestures for their own benefit (Amos 5:21–27).[88]

Amos could not stand by in the face of these acts of injustice and abuses of the poor and religion. As Francis does today, Amos—an inhabitant of a rural village of Tekoa—responded to a divine calling. In responding, Amos does not "rejoice with the rich over their good fortune, nor does he take comfort in the lavish rituals and sacrifices at the royal shrines in Bethel."[89] He challenged sinners, acts of sin, and injustice. He boldly called out the corrupt elite for what they were. With great sarcasm, he mocked their wives (i.e., collaborators) as the fat "cows of Bashan" (Amos 4:1). Scholars have interpreted these "fat cows" variously as: (a) the elite women of Samaria who pressured their ruling husbands to subjugate and violate the poor; (b) all the elite (both male and female) citizens of Samaria who did not care for the poor; or (c) all the inhabitants of the city of Samaria, as well as their deities.[90]

Like Pope Francis, Amos uses a very simple and down-to-earth pastoral language while criticizing these elite citizens and their wives. Amos is convinced that Israel's God is not just the sovereign of all creation, but he judges every nation as well as Israel for their crimes (Amos 1–2). He urges them to listen to, worship, and seek God alone, practicing justice and righteousness both in private and in the public marketplaces and plazas (Amos 3–6). Even though God punishes unfaithfulness and those who refuse to listen, Amos's views and visions (Amos 7–9:10) still offer a prophetic hope for salvation for the repentant remnant of the house Judah (Amos 9:11–15). It is this interaction of doom and hope in Amos's message that prompts some to argue that Amos's literature betrays signs of updates and redaction to meet the tastes and challenges of different times, people, and culture.

In the initial verses (Amos 1:1), the prophecy of Amos is addressed to the northern tribe of Israel after their split from Judah (1 Kgs 12; Amos 2:6–16; 7:15). After this, Amos addresses several other

---

88. Udoekpo, *Worship in Amos* 5, 12.
89. Matthews, *Prophets of Israel*, 46.
90. See Irwin ("Cows of Bashan," 231–46) and Udoekpo (*Worship in Amos* 5, 11) for various interpretation of "cows of Bashan."

nations, including Aram (Amos 1:2–5), Philistia (Amos 1:6–8), Tyre (Amos 1:9–10), Edom (Amos 1:11–12), Ammon (Amos 1:13–15), Moab (Amos 2:1–3), and Judah (Amos 2:4–5). The concluding chapter offers a more hopeful and less dooming message of optimism, hope, and salvation for the remnant of Joseph (Amos 9:11–15). This demonstrates that Amos's message is not a mere historical record or time-bound prophecy whose message is relevant for solely his original eighth-century BC audience. Rather, Amos's "message has the power to address more than one audience in one place at one time,"[91] including our society today.

Sometimes—as was the case with Amos—being a prophet demands courage and endurance in the face of challenges, criticism, and rejection. Therefore, Amos challenges us to boldly and positively reassess the unethical status quo and courageously withstand the prophetic opposition of our time (Amos 7:10–12). Even though we, as humans, like to manufacture our own prophetic criteria for missionary work, social justice, judgment, righteousness, and worship, the daily situation in our nations, towns, cities, inner cities, villages, parishes, and dioceses are analogous to those of the prophet Amos. In our contemporary communities, the gap between the "haves" and the "have-nots" is still obvious. Few people in our communities can afford quality education, medical care, food, grain, housing, and employment. Various factors contribute to these problems, including corruption in our nation's capital and insensitivity among our nation's leaders—especially among the elite.

Amos foregrounds the message of Pope Francis. He employs major themes, such as social criticism and empty worship, to challenge us to defend and the poor (Amos 2:6–7; 4:1; 5:7–13; 8:4–7) and to reinterpret with orthodoxy the traditions of Israel's theology of judgment (Amos 3–4), election, the exodus (Amos 2:9–10; 5:25), and the Day of the Lord (Amos 5:18–20). Amos summons us to speak against all forms injustice and idolatry (Amos 5:1–17). Amos calls us to combat the unrighteous, to seek the Lord (Amos 4:6–11), to offer hope to the hopeless (Amos 9:11–15), and to expose the worthlessness of hypocritical religion. Amos invites us to unequivocally promote ethical worship of God alone (Amos 4:4–5; 5:4–6, 21–27). These themes are inherent in the writings and preaching of Francis.

91. Leclerc, *Prophets*, 129.

ii. Effect of Hosea, the Prophet

Hosea foregrounds the ministry of Pope Francis and many other contemporary prophets. He is a prophet of the covenant. Hosea's prophecy is like a love story about God, who constantly loves his chosen people. It is a story of the relationship between Israel and God. Despite Israel's unfaithfulness, God is always faithful and will never walk away from his covenant promises.

Hosea pleads with Israel "to return to strict compliance with the covenant, to renounce all other gods, and to recognize their obligation to 'know God' by trusting in his command."[92]

Other prophetic themes resounding throughout Hosea include justice and worship (Hos 4–8), judgment (Hos 9–11), divine compassion (Hos 11–14), and fertility and infertility. The most remarkable theme in Hosea is the relationship between the Lord and Israel. This theme is presented as a marriage metaphor in which Hosea is instructed to marry Gomer, a woman who will be unfaithful to Hosea. Hosea's marriage to Gomer represents God's covenant with the nation of Israel, which the people have violated by engaging in idolatry (Hos 1–3).[93]

Hosea's marriage metaphor sets the tone for all twelve of the Minor Prophets; it further sets the tone for part of Pope Francis's *Amoris Laetitia* ("The Joy of Love"). For instance, in the first chapter of this Post-Synodal Apostolic Exhortation (which will be fully reviewed in Part II), Francis appeals to Hosea's prophecy, saying, "we can think of the touching words that prophet Hosea puts on God's lips: When Israel was a child, I loved him . . . I took them up in my arms . . . I led them with cords of compassion, with the bands of love, and I became to them as one who eases the yoke on their jaws, and I bent down to them and fed them" (Hos 11:1, 3–4).[94]

Hosea conveys this prophecy through his three children, who are given symbolic names. He also conveys his message through words of love, sadness, judgment, and hope. Hosea does not spare either kings or priests in Israel. He points to the "calf of Samaria" (Hos 8:6; 13:2) and to the political class of people, who "build palaces"

---

92. Matthew, *Prophets of Israel*, 52.
93. Ibid., 52–53.
94. Francis, *Amoris Laetitia*, no. 28.

(Hos 8:14) and promote "multiple altars" (Hos 8:11). Hosea further sets the tone for Francis's ministry by condemning the idolatrous actions of his time, which "reflect the leadership's desire for political and personal power and have precipitated the coming crisis (5:1-2; 7:1-10; 8:4-6)."[95]

Hosea emphasizes the importance of salvation history and dwells on the themes of faithfulness and unfaithfulness, fertility and infertility.[96] For him, Israel (symbolized by his wife, Gomer) can return to the Lord provided she renounce her foreign attire, strange lovers, and idolatry.

Branick sums up Hosea's theological perspective with the following points:

- God's love for Israel as his wife (Hos 2:21–22)
- God's love for Israel as his beloved son or little child (Hos 2:1; 11:1–4)
- Israel's sin as adultery with Israel's illegitimate lover, Baal (Hos 2:7, 12; 4:12–15; 13:1)
- God's suffering because of Israel's sin (Hos 11:8)
- The consequences of sin as the degradation of the land (Hos 2:11–14; 4:3) and the destruction of society (Hos 4:1–2)
- The error of thinking of religion as a substitute for morality (Hos 6:6)
- A future recovery and salvation (Hos 2:1–3, 16–24; 11:8–11; 14:5–9)
- The importance of "returning to God" (Hos 2:9; 3:5; 5:4; 6:1; 12:7; 14:2–3)
- The place of intimacy with God (Hos 2:16) and a place of new espousal (Hos 2:21–22)[97]

In other words, God, out of his mercy, loves people regardless of their own brokenness and level of faithfulness—themes dear to Francis's heart.

---

95. Matthews, *Prophets of Israel*, 53.
96. Cook, *Hear, O Heavens, and Listen, O Earth*, 77–85.
97. See Branick, *Understanding the Prophets*, 66.

iii. Effect of First Isaiah (Isa 1–39)

Significant themes in the prophecies of Isaiah include:

- The relationship between God and Israel (Isa 1)
- The house of David
- Jerusalem and the threats it faces (Isa 9; 11; 32:1–8)
- The city of Jerusalem (Isa 2; 4; 28–30)
- Social justice (Isa 3; 5; 10:1–4)
- God's sovereignty over all creation (Isa 10:5–34)
- The need to trust in Yahweh (Isa 12; 33)
- The Day of the Lord, eschatology (Isa 13–27)
- Hope for salvation of the remnant of Israel

Some of these themes also carry over into Second Isaiah (Isa 40–55) and Third Isaiah (Isa 56–66). These themes, and many others, provide the tone for Isaiah's contemporaries, including Hosea, Micah, and Zephaniah. Isaiah's prophecies laid the foundation for some of the prophets that came after him, and they also influenced the writings and preaching of Pope Francis and many other contemporary prophets and leaders.

In his first Apostolic Exhortation, *Evangelii Gaudium* ("The Joy of the Gospel"), Francis appeals to one of Isaiah's joyful and hopeful prophecies foreshadowing the expected Messiah: "you have multiplied the nation, you have increased its joy (9:3)."[98] Isaiah, whom Francis loves, is noted for exhorting the inhabitants of Zion to go forth to meet the Savior with songs. Francis again quotes Isaiah thus: "shout aloud and sing for joy!" (Isa 12:16).[99]

Like the Prophet Nathan, whom we discussed earlier, Isaiah stands as an authoritative prophetic figure worthy of consultation in moments of crisis, as when the enemy Assyrian armies approached. Isaiah preached that Israel's kings—including Ahaz—should trust in the Lord, who would one day send them the Messiah, who would be born of a virgin and come from the line of David (Isa 7:10–17; 9:6–7;

---

98. Francis, *Evangelii Gaudium*, no. 4.
99. Ibid., no. 4.

11:1–5; 32:1–8).[100] Even though Isaiah would attribute Israel's fall to their alliance with foreign power instead of trusting in the Lord, Isaiah never ceased to stress the importance of hope and the future restoration of the remnant.

Other theological points in Isaiah that are relevant to Francis's prophetic papacy include:

- Isaiah sees God as the Holy One of Israel (Isa 1:4; 12:6; 30:15)
- For Isaiah, politics and peace go hand in hand (Isa 7)
- For Isaiah, it is important to have faith and remain calm (Isa 7:9; 28:16–17)
- Isaiah teaches that God is with us and with Israel (in Immanuel; Isa 7:14–16)
- Isaiah portrays sin as resulting from lack of knowledge of God (Isa 1:2–3)
- Isaiah stresses the need for judgment and justice (Isa 1:27; 5:7)
- Isaiah speaks of restoration and salvation of the just (Isa 1:18–31)

iv. Effect of Micah, the Prophet

Micah of Moresheth is an eighth-century prophet and thus a contemporary of Isaiah, Amos, and Hosea. By implication, Micah shares in the same historical events that led to the fall of the northern kingdom of Israel to Assyria in 721/22 BC.[101] He also shares many theological themes with these prophets, such as the sweep of history, that God is the God of all nations, and that God is the Holy One of Israel (compare Isa 1–39). For this reason, Joan E. Cook suggests that the two prophets "might well have been familiar with common tradition. Canonically, the effect of the similarity is that the two books offer a commentary on each other, enriching the message of the both books."[102] For example, Micah 4:1–3 appears verbatim in Isaiah 2:2–4:

---

100. Matthews, *Prophets of Israel*, 62.
101. Matthews, *Prophets of Israel*, 77.
102. Cook, *Hear, O Heavens, and Listen, O Earth*, 94.

> In the days to come the mountain of the Lord's house shall be established as the highest of the mountains, and shall be raised above the hills; all the nations shall stream to it. Many peoples shall come and say, "Come, let us go up to the mountain of the Lord, to the house of God of Jacob; that he may teach us his ways and that we may walk in his paths." For out of Zion shall go forth instruction, and the word of the Lord from Jerusalem. He shall judge between the nations, and shall arbitrate for many peoples; they shall beat their swords into plowshares, and their spears into pruning hooks, nation shall not lift up sword against nation, neither shall they learn war any more.

However, in contrast to Isaiah, Micah approaches his prophecies from a very simple and rural perspective. His simplicity is analogous to that of Pope Francis, who shares in the prophetic passion of Micah. Besides his simple approach, Micah anticipates Francis, as well as the goals and principles of the New York headquarters of the United Nations (at least ideally) in his passion for justice. Micah is uncomfortable with injustice and neglect of the poor, especially in matters of real estate, exploitation, and organized corruption among the leadership class, rulers, priests, and professional prophets.[103]

Additional major themes in Micah include:

- God's readiness to destroy Samaria and Jerusalem (Mic 1:6–7; 3:12)
- The evil of oppressing the poor in the quest for wealth (Mic 2:1–2)
- Resistance to the prophetic word (Mic 2:6), particularly on the part of the leaders (Mic 3:1–12)
- The strength of the prophet through the spirit of God to denounce sin (Mic 3:8)
- The restoration of Jerusalem (Mic 4:4–8)
- The remnant (Mic 4:6–7; 5:6–7)
- The preference for ethical conduct over cultic sacrifices (Mic 6:6–8)[104]
- The mercy of God (Mic 7:18–20)

---

103. Leclerc, *Prophets*, 191.
104. Branick, *Understanding the Prophets*, 102–103.

Micah's prophecies prompt contemporary readers and institutions (whether civil, political, social, economic, or ecclesiastical) to pay attention to the true nature of God—his kindness, justice, judgment, and mercy toward all, especially the poor and the oppressed. Micah calls us to listen to Pope Francis, who emphasizes the gospel of mercy in his ministry.

v. Effect of Zephaniah, the Prophet

Zephaniah is one of Israel's late pre-exilic prophets, prophesying during the reign of King Josiah of Judah (640–609 BC). I have discussed him extensively in a few other places.[105] He stressed judgment against all nations, particularly through the Day of the Lord (Zeph 1–2) and restoration of the remnant (Zeph 2–3). On that day, "the remnant of nation will have been purified, the proud will have been removed from their midst (3:1), and the people shall 'lie down, no one shall make them afraid' (3:12– 13)."[106]

Popular themes in Zephaniah are:

- The day of the Lord (Zeph 1:2–18)
- The importance of seeking justice and righteousness (Zeph 2:3)
- Promises for the Gentile nations (Zeph 3:9–10)
- Salvation for the repentant "remnant of Israel" (Zeph 3:12–13)
- The Lord, the mighty savior in your midst, and the joy of restoration (Zeph 3:15–17)[107]

Zephaniah foregrounds the prophets after him and foreshadows the ministry of Pope Francis. Just as Zephaniah proposes changes and ends his prophecies with hymns of joy and hope for Zion's liberation, Francis proposes changes as well as alternatives to bring about joy in place of sadness. This is evidenced in Francis's first prophetic Apostolic Exhortation, *Evangelii Gaudium*, where he appeals to Zephaniah's joyful message. Francis, the successor of Peter and Vicar of Christ, writes: "Perhaps the most exciting invitation is that of the prophet Zephaniah, who presents God with his people in the midst

---

105. Especially in Udoekpo (*Day of YHWH*); Udoekpo ("Seek the Lord," 77–91).
106. Matthews, *Prophets of Israel*, 85.
107. See Branick, *Understanding the Prophets*, 118; Leclerc, *Prophets*, 213–218.

of a celebration overflowing with the joy of salvation."[108] Francis continues, "I find it thrilling to reread the text: 'The Lord, your God, is in your midst, a warrior who gives you the victory; he will rejoice over you with gladness, he will renew you in his love; he will exult over you with loud singing, as on a day of festival'(3:17)."[109]

vi. Effect of Nahum, the Prophet

Nahum is another classical prophet who influenced the ministry of Pope Francis. Nahum sees God as a divine warrior and as the sovereign of all creation and nations. Although he is a Judean prophet, Nahum makes it clear to the inhabitants of Nineveh that their great city will fall due to God's judgement for their sinfulness and heartless subjugation of kingdoms throughout the ancient Near East, particularly Judah (Nah 1:2).[110]

Like Zephaniah, Nahum prophesies using ancient motifs portraying God's fury as a consuming fire: "Who can endure the heat of his anger? His wrath is poured out like fire" (Nah 1:6; Zeph 1:18). Nahum portrays God's blazing wrath as drying up the seas and rivers and making the lush, fertile lands of Carmel and Lebanon wither and fade (Nah 1:4; Amos 1:2).[111] By utilizing ancient motifs of power, Nahum supersedes any possibility of others ascribing the coming events to Baal, the false Canaanite storm god.[112]

This motif of power must have frightened Nahum's contemporaries. They must have been scared by the severe military language he uses in referring to shields, spears, swords, chariots, ramparts, fortresses, forts, officers, troops, guards, plunder, booty, enemies, foes, wounds, corpses, charging, besieging, and mustering.[113] In addition to this military language, Nahum courageously offers a graphic presentation of the neutralization of Nineveh by an irresistible army "whose chariots will careen through the streets while no one can stop the savage plundering of the city (Nah 2:3–12)."[114]

108. Francis, *Evangelii Gaudium*, no. 4.
109. Ibid., no. 4.
110. Leclerc, *Prophets*, 220.
111. Ibid., 220.
112. Matthews, *Prophets of Israel*, 84.
113. Leclerc, *Prophets*, 221.
114. Matthews, *Prophets of Israel*, 84.

In addition, Nahum's courageously advances his understanding of God as a divine warrior combating the dominant Assyrian Empire (Nah 3:1–10). God, for Nahum, is a God of justice. He is the ruler of the universe and creation. Both themes are familiar in the teachings of Pope Francis.

In his *Laudato Si'*, Francis utilizes themes reminiscent of those used by the Prophet Nahum. He acknowledges that "the writings of the prophets [including Nahum] invite us to find renewed strength in times of trial by contemplating the all-powerful God who created the universe."[115] For Francis, "God's infinite power does not lead us to flee his fatherly tenderness, because in him affection and strength are joined. Indeed, all sound spirituality entails both welcoming divine love and adoration, confident in the Lord because of his infinite power. . . . the God who liberates and saves is the same God who created the universe, and these two divine ways are intimately and inseparably connected."[116] These "divine ways" continue in the prophecies of Habakkuk.

vii. Effect of Habakkuk, the Prophet

Habakkuk's effect on contemporary prophets—particularly Pope Francis—is tremendous, especially in areas of faith, human suffering, justice, and righteousness. Therefore, although I have commented on Habakkuk's themes elsewhere in my writings, I will dwell a bit on Habakkuk here.[117]

Issues of theodicy and the sovereignty of God dominate Habakkuk's theology. Injustice within the prophet's Judean society and the threat of the inevitable invasion of the Babylonian troops make Habakkuk wonder why the wicked prosper over the righteous. Habakkuk laments, prays, and confronts the holy, mysterious, and majestic God (Hab 1:2–2:5). God convinces Habakkuk that, in times of hardship, the just (*tsaddiq*) shall live only because of their faith (*ĕmûnāh*; Hab 2:4). God's five woe oracles (*hôy*) against the temporary success of the wicked (Hab 2:6–20), as well as his theophanic imagery as a

---

115. Francis, *Laudato Si'*, no. 73.
116. Ibid., no. 73.
117. See Udoekpo ("Habakkuk's Faith," 1–26) for some of these comments on Habakkuk's faith and contributions, adapted in this study.

divine warrior (Hab 3:3–15), assure Habakkuk and his contemporaries of Yahweh's control over life's vicissitude and boost their faith. Habakkuk's faithful reaction (Hab 3:16–19) is paradigmatic for the suffering righteous today, irrespective of context and culture.

Habakkuk's theology focuses on faithfulness to God in times of trouble. Habakkuk examines how to handle a short-lived triumph of the wicked over the righteous, while the good and sovereign God seems to be indifferent.[118] Habakkuk addresses the theme of theodicy. This marks him as unique from the preceding prophets and the rest of the Twelve Minor Prophets.

Habakkuk foreshadows Pope Francis in that he is fearless in condemning the injustice of his time. Habakkuk believes that the Judean community is damaged by their sins of idolatry, as well as the injustices orchestrated from within and without Judah. Such damage breeds sin and leads to human suffering, including the inevitable invasion of the Chaldeans (Babylonians), who are presented in the book as a divine instrument to judge and punish the unrighteous. For centuries this problem has remained a hallmark of any exegetical and critical-theological discussion of evil. It troubles Habakkuk, who decisively carries the burden of his people (Hab 1:1) and engages in a dialogue with God (Hab 1:2–11). Habakkuk does not understand why and how the good, holy, just, powerful, and sovereign God of all creation would select the wicked Chaldeans to judge and repair Israel's brokenness (Hab 1:2–4, 12–17).[119] Initially, the prophet seems to think the direction things are going in this universe does not reflect a majestic and compassionate God.[120] He does not understand why the wicked would circumvent the just. Habakkuk's experience is a crisis faith.

Ultimately, it is a mystery beyond Habakkuk's or any human's comprehension. Habakkuk quickly realizes this when he experiences a vision (Hab 2:1–20). In the long run, he understands that God's

---

118. By the "sovereignty" of God in Habakkuk and in this study as whole, we mean God's superiority over all other "gods," and God as the creator of creation. Hence, God is the ruler of all nations. We are also referring to his immutability, infinity, holiness, omnipresence, omniscience, omnipotence, dominance, and control over all his creation—including human affairs and history.

119. Additional comments in the pages ahead will be made on the Chaldeans.

120. See Anderson (*Habakkuk*, 11) for his discussion of how the two realities—God and the world—sometimes do not seem to fit.

reign will always prevail despite life's vicissitudes. The prophet also comes to appreciate the truth that the just person (*tsaddiq*) shall live only because of his or her "fidelity, firmness, steadfastness, and spiritual trustworthiness" (*ĕmûnāh*; Hab 2:4) in the face of trials. Habakkuk's *ĕmûnāh* and reliability in God's plan is further expressed in his prayer (Hab 3:1–19). In this prayer, God is not only a divine warrior, but the sovereign of all creation and the giver of life—themes that resound in Francis's teachings.

Various scholars and theologians coming from different contexts and locations have offered varying approaches and interpretations of Habakkuk's themes.[121] In this section, I would like to stress the theological themes and elements in Habakkuk that Francis has imitated. Uppermost in my mind are the themes of divine sovereignty in the face of human suffering and the temporary success of the wicked—both of which are central in Habakkuk's prophecy.

Unraveling these themes and the mysterious divine place of Habakkuk's prophecy for us today demands a basic appreciation of the background, context, and setting of Habakkuk's encounter with God. A close reading of Habakkuk shows the prophet's vicissitudes, just as Pope Francis's tone would indicate the times of the church in the modern world, of the Vatican II, and perhaps beyond.[122]

Habakkuk's prophetic dialogue with God seems to date and locate the prophet's life situation (*Sitz im Leben*) in the context of suffering calamities. Grace Ko also observes that the setting of the theology of Habakkuk "is closely related to the identification of the 'wicked' and the 'righteous' in the Book."[123] Habakkuk prophesied at a critical juncture in Israel's history.[124] Many scholars have posited the time of King Jehoiakim's reign (609–598 BC) as the most likely period for Habakkuk's ministry and laments. Under these scheme, Habakkuk prophesied in the late pre-exilic period.[125]

---

121. See Dangl ("Habakkuk in Recent Research," 131–168) for past studies on themes and methodological approaches on Habakkuk, different from this new approach.

122. See Flannery, ed., (*Gaudium et spes*) and Orobator, ed., (*The Church We Want*, 1–256) for the challenges and issues facing the contemporary church addressed by Francis.

123. Ko, "Ordering of the Twelve as Israel's Historiography," 327.

124. Széles, *Wrath and Mercy*, 3.

125. Some of these scholars include: Széles (*Wrath and Mercy*, 2–5); D. W. Baker

The time of Habakkuk's ministry was a difficult period in Israel, as the people's hope for joy and restoration was dashed following King Josiah's defeat at the Megiddo battle (2 Kgs 23:28–30). As if Josiah's death were not enough, the Assyrians were not saved. Neco of Egypt also replaced Jehoahaz with Jehoiakim as the successor of Josiah, king of Judah, to gain tribute from his vassal. Jehoiakim, the newly appointed head of the Egyptian vassal, was the opposite of his father Josiah, who had embarked on reforms and had pursued pure worship of Yahweh. Injustice and the public breakdown of morality became the order of the day on Jehoiakim's watch. He was also corrupt and merciless in taxing his people, especially the poor, to pay tribute to the Egyptians (2 Kgs 23:33–36).

Habakkuk's contemporary, Jeremiah, also indicts Jehoiakim for his acts of oppression and exploitation. He criticizes Jehoiakim's decision to build his cedar place using forced labor: "Woe to him who builds his house on wrong, his terraces on injustice; who works his neighbor without pay, and gives him no wages. Who says, 'I will build myself a spacious house, with airy room,' who cuts out windows for it, panels it with cedar, and paints it with it vermillion" (Jer 22:13–14).[126] Jeremiah paid a price for this prophecy. He suffered bitterly and fled into hiding to avoid death. Jeremiah's scroll was burned (Jer 36:1–26), and those who shared his prophetic views and values were punished. For example, the prophet Uriah, son of Shemaiah, from Kiriath-Jearim was captured from Egypt, slaughtered, and buried in a common grave because he joined Jeremiah and other pre-exilic prophets in condemning the corruption and injustice Jehoiakim was perpetuating (Jer 26:20–24). It is in this atmosphere of violence and socio-economic, moral, and political deprivation that Habakkuk laments and dialogues with God concerning the mystery of such evil. He questions the whereabouts of God's divine sovereignty (Hab 1:2–2:5).

(*Nahum, Habakkuk, and Zephaniah*, 44–45); Robertson (*Books of Nahum, Habakkuk, and Zephaniah*, 36–37); Feinberg (*Minor Prophets*, 205); Roberts (*Nahum, Habakkuk, and Zephaniah*, 82–84); House ("Dramatic Coherence," 195); Barker and Bailey (*Micah, Nahum, Habakkuk, and Zephaniah*, 259).

126. Biblical quotations in the section "Effect of Habakkuk, the Prophet" are from *The Catholic Study Bible: The New American Bible*.

Questions of theodicy and divine sovereignty are of paramount importance to Habakkuk. They form the backdrop of Habakkuk's dialogue with God. He laments:

> How long, O Lord? I cry for help, but you do not listen! I cry out to you, "*violence!*" but you do not intervene. Why do you let me see *ruin*; why must I look at *misery*? *Destruction* and *violence* are before me; there is *strife*, and *clamorous discord*. This is why the law is *benumbed*, and judgment is *never rendered*: Because the wicked *circumvent* the just; this is why judgment comes forth *perverted*. (Hab 1:2–4)[127]

Several commentators have commented on this prayer (Hab 1:2–4).[128] For some it as a passionate prayer of a desperate man. Others see it as a form of an individual psalm of lament and complaint common in the Old Testament theology. This type of lament often leads to God's response. One such commentator, Claus Westermann, testifies on the important role prayerful laments played in the events of the exodus, which resulted in the liberation of God's chosen people (Exod 1–15).[129] Building on such earlier events, Habakkuk—being a man of prayer—complains in an "old fashion way" that God does not intervene to save the righteous (*tsaddiq*) nor punish the evildoers (cf. Jer 11:18–23; 12:1–4, 5–6; 20:7–18; Job 18–19).[130]

Habakkuk foregrounds Pope Francis of the modern church. Both Habakkuk and Pope Francis are clearly concerned about human and divine justice. When he looks through the window, Habakkuk sees violence/wrong (*chāmās*), ruin/disaster (*ʾāven*), trouble/misery (*ʿāmāl*), and destruction (*šōd*). He also sees strife (*rîb*) and clamorous discord (*mādôn*, Hab 1:2–3). Consequently, the law (*tôrāh*) is benumbed (*pûg*), and judgment (*mišpāṭ*) is never rendered, while the wicked (*rāšāʿ*) are busy surrounding (*maktîr*) the just (*haṣṣddîqîm*, Hab 1:4). This explains Habakkuk's specific questions and laments:

---

127. I have also highlighted in this quotation those things that troubled Habakkuk—namely, violence, ruin, misery, destruction, strife, clamorous discord, benumbed laws, denial of justice, and perverted judgment. Francis has addressed some of these themes during his pontificate.

128. See Anderson (*Habakkuk*, 123) for details.

129. Westermann ("Role of the Lament," 20–38) has additional information on the genre of lament in the Psalms.

130. See also Holmyard, "Sovereignty of God," 1–19.

"How long, O Lord" (*'ad-'ānāh 'ădônāh*)? Why (*lāmmah*) would a loving and sovereign God remain silent or indifferent in the face of pain and injustice committed against the faithful ones? Commenting on Habakkuk's complaint (Hab 1:2–4), Széles suggests that the prophet, in undergoing a crisis of faith, is not doubting God's ability to save humanity. She rightly suggests that what troubles Habakkuk is that God has taken such a long time to respond to the cries; Habakkuk is further troubled by the apparent success of the evil people in contrast to the suffering and deteriorating situation of the good people of Judah.[131] Of course, God's seeming indifference, which worries Habakkuk, had troubled other prophets and biblical figures in the past (Job 19:7). However, with his watchfulness (Hab 2:1–5), Habakkuk will live to embrace God's sovereignty in his divine response.

God is far from being indifferent. God responds to Habakkuk and invites him "to look over the nations and see, and be utterly amazed! For work is being done in your days that you would not have believed, were it told" (Hab 1:5–11). It is a mystery to Habakkuk that God announces the Chaldeans (Babylonians) as his instrument of divine justice. The prophet laments this as an act of scary injustice (Hab 1:12–14).[132] The description of these Chaldeans must have been threatening and disturbing to Habakkuk. It would have been disturbing to hear that they are bitter (*mar*) and unruly/impetuous people (*hoggôy nimhāar*, Hab 1:6). They are terrible (*'ayom*), dreadful (*nôra'*), and insubordinate (Hab 1:7). Furthermore, "nothing keeps them in check, in either a legal or moral sense. They are also a law unto themselves, a law that knows no rules."[133] Reminiscent of what we heard in Nahum, their horses are like leopards, wolves, and eagles who speed to prey on food and their perceived enemies (Hab 1:7–8), causing inevitable violence (*chamas*, Hab 1:9). This "super power" is also cynical, sarcastic, and scornful to its subjects (Hab 1:10–11). Even though the power of God, who controls national and international affairs, is hidden in this mysterious announcement and description of the Babylonians (Hos 1:6; Isa 52:15–53), this was not yet made known to Habakkuk. Because of this hiddenness of

---

131. Széles, *Wrath and Mercy*, 17; Feinberg, *Minor Prophets*, 206.

132. The Chaldeans, according to Feinberg (*Minor Prophets*, 207), "were the inhabitants."

133. Széles, *Wrath and Mercy*, 22.

the mystery of God, the prophet presses on with further complaints against the Chaldeans. Their coming, Habakkuk believes, would bring untold hardship to the righteous people.

From a theological perspective, Habakkuk's language throughout the text is fascinating. Like the questions "How long, O Lord" (*'ad-'ānāh 'ădônāh*) and "Why?" (*lāmmah*) of the earlier complaints episode (Hab 1:2-4), Habakkuk proceeds to use the interrogative particle. He asks, "Are you not . . . ?" (*hălô'*) to indirectly highlight God's attributes in comparison to the injustices committed by the Chaldeans. He laments again, "Are you not from eternity, O Lord, my holy God, immortal? O Lord, you have marked him for judgment; O Rock, you have readied him for punishment. Too pure are your eyes to look upon evil" (Hab 1:12-14).

Széles observes that this pericope of laments demonstrates that Habakkuk is sympathetic to his community. It reveals that he is a prophet who has stood his ground spiritually. It also confirms the prophet's ethical concern and deep empathy for humanity, presented in the form of a personal psalm of prayer and lament.[134] It is this combination of empathy and compassion that Pope Francis also stresses.

Habakkuk is a prophet who is aware of God's historical presence in the affairs of Israel and other nations. He is not only the sovereign of all creation, but also holy and immortal, with pure eyes that dare not admire evil (Hab 1:13). His creative acts are not limited to humankind. God is also the maker of the fish of the sea (Hab 1:14), as Francis acknowledges in his *Laudato Si'*.[135] Habakkuk uses this fish metaphor to describe how the "wicked" Babylonians mistreated other people and nations. The Babylonians dragged and snared weaker nations and the poor using hooks and nets, as fishermen would do to fish caught for their own pleasure and for their nutritional and economic benefits (Hab 1:15-16).[136] Habakkuk concludes his prophecy by wondering how God could remain silent in the face of the evil people's merciless attack of the innocent people (Hab 1:17).

---

134. Ibid., 22.

135. See Genesis 1—2:4a and Psalm 8.

136. Széles (*Wrath and Mercy*, 27-28); Roberts (*Nahum, Habakkuk and Zephaniah*, 104); and Andersen (*Habakkuk*, 189-190) have extensive comments on these verses and the fish metaphor.

Habakkuk's prophetic lament and dialogue with God also portrays him as a man of God who, amid national crises (political, socio-economic, and religious), stands on the side of the poor by defending the oppressed in the market square—a subject dear to Francis's heart. Therefore, Habakkuk serves as an intercessor, a conduit of hope, and a conscience of the people. He is not a theorist, nor does he shy away from the daily events of life. His appeal and intercession is not only heard by God, but Habakkuk's patience, endurance, and personal watchfulness for God's response is exemplary to all (Hab 2:1).

For linguists and philologists, Habakkuk's language in verse 1 is a *cohortative* language of determination and resolve.[137] Habakkuk reflexively says, "I will stand (*'e'emodhāh*) at my guard post (*mishemeret*), and station myself (*'etyatstsebāh*) upon the rampart/watchtower (*mātsōr*), and keep watch (*ătsappeh*) to see what he will say to me, and what answer he will give to my complaint." Andersen affirms that this is not only a language of resolution, but also of soliloquy because Habakkuk refers to God, to whom he is appealing, in the third person.[138] In Széles's perspective, the prophet's cohortatives, "I will stand" or "let me stand" (*'e'emodhāh*) and "station myself" (*'etyatstsebāh*), expresses his swelling emotion—his perplexity, bewilderment, and prayerful request.[139]

Nevertheless, the two nouns—"guard post" (*mishemeret*) and "rampart" or "watchtower" (*mātsōr*)—also attract scholars, who seek to highlight the unique role Habakkuk plays and his word choice in arguing with God on behalf of his suffering people. Some scholars think that *mishemeret* and *mātsōr* are the same because of their seeming euphonic resemblance or parallelism.[140] In particular, Roberts sees a certain ambiguity in the entire verse that has these two words. This

---

137. Lambdin (*Biblical Hebrew*, 118–122) and Pratico and Van Pelt (*Basics of Biblical Hebrew*, 218–218) have, for the sake of non-expert readers, noted that "*cohortative*," in biblical Hebrew grammar, is volitional verbal conjugation or imperfect, used in an indirect imperatival sense to express a wish, request, or command, either in the first persons singular or plural (1cs/1cp).

138. Andersen, *Habakkuk*, 191.

139. Széles, *Wrath and Mercy*, 28.

140. For those who hold this view, see Pinker ("Reconstruction of Matzor Habakkuk 2:1," 161–163) for some of these thoughts.

makes it difficult to decipher whether the terms are metaphorically referring to a specific waiting place or the process of waiting.[141]

Aron Pinker argues that *matzor* is a corruption of *mitzpeh*. Mitzpeh is found in Isaiah 21:8, which reads, "And I cried as a lion [*aryeh*] upon the watch-tower [*mitzpeh*], O Lord; I stand continually in the daytime, and I am set in my ward all the nights."[142] In Isaiah 21:6, the "watchman" was called *metzapeh*. He would keep watch (*etzpeh*) on his duty post. Thus, Pinker affirms that the occurrence of *matzor* in Habakkuk 2:1 is not just for orthographic changes to *atzapeh* ("watch") by a redactor, but perhaps for theological and metaphorical reasons. Habakkuk requires a *metzapeh* ("watchman") and a *mitzpeh* ("watchtower/rampart").[143]

The grammatical analysis of this ambiguous verse notwithstanding, there are antecedent theological episodes in Scripture where God's prophets and human servants retreat in solitude to discern God's will (cf. Exod 33:21; Num 23:3; 24:1; 1 Kgs 19:11; Mic 4:14; Ezek 3:17-18; 33:7-8).[144] Habakkuk is no exception. Therefore, I consider credible Széles' suggestion that, following his dialogue and laments before God, Habakkuk must have withdrawn to a certain place or room where he awaited God's response. This is not to deny the possibility that Habakkuk could have withdrawn into his inner self for contemplation, prayer, and reflection while awaiting the divine response.[145]

Habakkuk's complaints and watchfulness (Hab 2:1) must have led to two significant phenomena: First is the question of how God responds (Hab 2:2-5); second is how Habakkuk's patient waiting and questioning sheds light on the place of his prophecy in the Twelve Minor Prophets.[146] Let's begin with the second phenomena. Grace Ko observes that Habakkuk's seventh position among the Twelve speaks

---

141. Roberts, *Nahum, Habakkuk and Zephaniah*, 108.

142. Pinker, "Reconstruction of Matzor," 164.

143. Pinker ("Reconstruction of Matzor,"164-165) has additional impressive details.

144. Széles, *Wrath and Mercy*, 29.

145. Széles, *Wrath and Mercy*, 29.

146. In the MT order we have Hosea, Joel, Amos, Obadiah, Jonah, Nahum, Habakkuk (the 7th), Nahum, Zephaniah, Haggai, Zechariah, and Malachi. In the LXX we have Hosea, Amos, Micah, Joel, Obadiah, Jonah, Nahum, Habakkuk (still the 7th), Zephaniah, Haggai, Zechariah, and Malachi.

for the challenges and the unique role Habakkuk plays on behalf of his people.[147] By standing on the side of his people, Habakkuk proves himself a unique spokesman—an intercessor and a messenger. This defines a true prophet. Unlike Israel's other prophets, who usually justify divine acts by accusing and listing people's sins, Habakkuk challenges God's choice for selecting the Chaldeans as his divine instrument to judge Judah. Ko also suggests that Habakkuk is placed at the nadir of the narrative schema of the Twelve in order to tidy up from a humanistic or existential perspective the "theodic protest" of the righteous.[148] In other words, this is "why bad things happened to good people" during this terrible period of Israel's history.

Returning to the first mentioned phenomenon—the question of how God responds (Hab 2:2–5)—it is evident in the narrative that while Habakkuk waits and watches in protest, God's response is revealed in the following vision (ḥāzôn):

> Then the Lord answered me and said: Write down the vision clearly upon the tablets, so that one can read it readily. For the vision still has its time, presses on to fulfilment, and will not disappoint; if it delays, wait for it, it will surely come, it will not be late. The rash man has no integrity, but the just man, because of his faith, shall live.... He who opens with his throat like the netherworld, and is insatiable as death, who gathers to himself all the nations and rallies to himself all the peoples. (Hab 2:2–5)

It is a significant vision. Habakkuk is not only required to memorize God's answer (ʻanah), but he must also write (katabh) it down clearly on a tablet (luah) for easy reading, and perhaps for wider and universal publication (cf. Isa 30:8). Habakkuk's vision is a clear witness to God's handiwork in salvation history (heilsgeschichte). It is equally imperative to write it down since its fulfillment shall come to pass in the near future. God's promise does not fail (Hab 2:2–3).[149]

---

147. Ko, "Ordering of the Twelve," 326.

148. Ko, "Ordering of the Twelve," 329. See also Brueggemann ("Some Aspects of Theodicy," 253–268), where the "theodicy protest" particularly refers to human protest against God for not executing divine justice according to those promises made during his covenants with Israel.

149. Roberts, *Nahum, Habakkuk and Zephaniah*, 110.

The unfailing promise contained in this vision (*ḥāzôn*) is the centerpiece of Habakkuk's entire prophecy—namely, that the righteous (*tsaddiq*), because of their faith (*ĕmûnāh*), will live, but the proud, the "puffed up," and the faithless (*'uppelāh*) will perish since they have no integrity and are not upright (*yāshār*, Hab 2:4–5). It is "the most famous utterance of Habakkuk."[150] The last two concepts (*yāshār* and *'uppelāh*) evidently are used in a moral sense. Puffing up (*'uppelāh*) and not being upright (*yāshār*) bring about God's judgment and punishment, as was the case with the Babylonians.[151]

Contrary to the faithless and proud Babylonians, the righteous (*tsaddiq*) and devout find in the reliability (*ĕmûnāh*) of this vision the strength and energy to persevere in life's vicissitudes. In other words, *ĕmûnāh* in this passage communicates a righteous person's faith (firmness, steadfastness, fidelity, trust, reliability) or faithfulness that God's plan will surely come to pass.[152]

Just as Pope Francis's prophetic ministry would come to be rooted in Israel's prophets and the tradition of the church, Habakkuk's concept of faith is deeply rooted in past covenant and prophetic traditions (Gen 15:5–6; 22:1–2; Isa 7:9). In turn, these traditions are widely adapted and reinterpreted in the New Testament by Paul and the author of the Letter to the Hebrews (Rom 1:17; Gal 3:11; Heb 10:37–39), whom I appeal to in the introductory section of this work.

Paul delights in Habakkuk. He uses Habakkuk in a new context to expand his message on justification by faith. For Paul, faith means believing in Jesus Christ as the Son of God (*hios tou theou*) and the Savior of the world (*ho sōtēr tou kosmou*). For Paul, Christians are called to live by faith by believing in Jesus and experiencing a new life in Christ Jesus. Habakkuk's understanding of faith in his pre-exilic time is similar to Isaiah's; Isaiah had instructed Ahaz, "Unless your faith is firm you shall not be firm" (Isa 7:9). In Habakkuk's prophetic spirituality, faith is "trusting confidence in God who will surely fulfil his promises and bring about his plan."[153] The language of Habakkuk continues to shed light on his theology. This time, the Qal imperfect in Habakkuk's prophecy, the righteous "shall live" (*yihyeh*),

---

150. Collins, "Daniel and the Minor Prophets," 362.
151. See Széles (*Wrath and Mercy*, 31) for detailed analysis of these concepts.
152. Ibid., 32–33; Roberts, *Nahum, Habakkuk and Zephaniah*, 111.
153. Leclerc, *Prophets*, 231.

refers to the life of a wise believer in the interim between the vision and its fulfillment. It is a call to steadfastness in the face of tragedy, but with an eschatological patience and joy that only the certainty of God's coming could give to the righteous. As for the proud, the fainthearted, and the wicked, who rely on their human power and temporary wealth, Sheol and death is their final destination (Hab 2:5) This is conveyed unequivocally in the ensuing five woe oracles against the wicked (Hab 2:6-19).

This set of five woes in Habakkuk points clearly to the sovereign God who responds to Habakkuk's prayer. It includes:

1. Woe to the person who stores up what is not his or hers (Hab 2:6-8)
2. Woe to those who build their houses on ill-gotten goods (Hab 2:9-11)
3. Woe to those who build their cities on bloodshed (Hab 2:12-14)
4. Woe to those who abuse drink and the dignity of their neighbors (Hab 2:15-17)
5. Woe to those who worship stones and wood (Hab 2:18-20)

This type of woe formula (*hôy*) was not restricted to Habakkuk. Several of Israel's prophets contextually employed this formula in various circumstances to articulate misfortune, particularly their indictments against Israel and Yahweh's enemies. Several scholars have acknowledged this—and have examined the origins of the formula.[154]

In the case of Habakkuk, even though the recipients of these oracles are not specifically mentioned, it is evident that, in the first woe (*hôy*), Habakkuk is referring to the nations as well as the greedy Chaldeans who plundered them. In this section, those who grab power, treasure, and material things to the detriment of the poor may not always have the last say. This is true in the very language of

---

154. For instance, Gerstenberger ("Woe-Oracles of the Prophets," 249–263) argues that the woe oracle is a form of speech deployed by Hebrew prophets to express indictment. As a wisdom saying, its origin is traceable to wise men's reflection about the vicissitudes of life in the world. Westermann (*Basic Forms of Prophetic Speech*, 190–194) sees the woe oracles as curses. Clifford ("The Use of *Hôy* in the Prophets," 458–464) traces it to the context of laments over the dead. But I want to believe that woe oracles were used in various occasions, especially in the context of misfortunes and injustices done to the faithful. This is evident in Habakkuk. See also Udoekpo, *Day of YHWH*, 203.

the indictment: "Woe to him who stores up what is not his; how long can it last!" (Hab 2:6). This judgment speech echoes the initial question of "How long?" in the book's opening prayer (Hab 1:2). Here, the wicked are not only taunted; the prophet is assured that after the wicked have reached a certain point in their plundering, pillaging, and taking hostage (*'abṭît*) of the righteous, their creditors and victims will triumphantly turn against them.[155] The wicked will in turn become the creditors' prey (Hab 2:7–8).[156]

The second woe (Hab 2:9–11) is the result of the Chaldeans' pursuit of evil and unjust gains (*betsa'*) for the exclusive use of their household (*beth*). In this context, "household" (*bet*) clearly points to home and family interests as against the common good. While the first woe addresses ill-gotten goods, the second woe addresses the selfishness of extorting for the sake of the Babylonian dynasties' personal family security. By doing this, they have brought God's retribution and shame upon themselves. They will never gain security by threatening and burgling others' stones and wood to build their houses. Interestingly, the stolen materials (stones, sand, and wood) of the building will not only fight against each other, they will call out the building's builders (Hab 2:11).

The third woe (Hab 2:12–14) is directed against the wicked who build their cities from the bloody booty gained from exploiting weaker nations (Hab 2:12). This presents another irony: By doing this, they are toiling for the punishing flame of God, who is the sovereign of all creation. Thus, Habakkuk rhetorically asks, "Is not this from the Lord of hosts that people toil for the flame, and nations grow weary for naught?" (Hab 2:13). Different interpretations have been given for this verse. First, it could be interpreted to mean that the Babylonians' oppression of other nations was God's handiwork to punish them for their sins (cf. Isa 10:5–6). Alternatively, it could be interpreted as an echo of Psalm 127:1–2: "If Yahweh does not build the house, its builders labor in vain on it. If Yahweh does not guard a

---

155. Some scholars, particularly Roberts (*Nahum, Habakkuk, and Zephaniah*, 117–18) have curiously observed the use of *māshāl* ("saying," "wisdom saying," "figurative prophetic discourse") and *'abṭît* in verse 6 as clearly a taunting language that compares the woes that will in turn face the wicked Babylonians (cf. Isa 14:4–23).

156. See also Andersen, *Habakkuk*, 235–237; Széles, *Wrath and Mercy*, 36–37 for additional comments on these verses.

city, the guard watches in vain."[157] Either way, it points to the glory of the Lord, which is reflected in his creation, and to the evidence of his divine power, since he "keeps his finger on the pulse of history and directs all things in his sovereign style."[158] Commenting on this *hôy* (Hab 2:12–14) and its emphasis on the sovereignty of God, Charles L. Feinberg writes, "of old a kingdom had been set up in Babylon to usurp power and glory (Gen 10:10), but it must pass away and be replaced by God's kingdom and his glory (Rev 11:15)."[159]

In the fourth woe oracle (Hab 2:15–17), the oppressors in Babylon are metaphorically indicted as those who intoxicate their neighbors with the drink of their wrath while exploiting their nakedness (Hab 2:15; cf. Jer 51:7). In their human thinking, this is a glorious exercise—especially the abuse of power. But the irony here is that the sovereign God, a true king (cf. Jer 22:15–16), will divinely bring shame on the oppressors. He will reverse the fortunes of their victims, including the Lebanese, whose forests were violently exploited and mercilessly destroyed (Hab 2:16–17; cf. Isa 14:8).

The final woe (Hab 2:18–20) addresses idolatry in the form of the worship of stones, wood, and gods other than Yahweh. The prophet indicts, "Woe to him who says to the wood, 'Awake!' to dumb stone 'Arise!' . . . Of what avail is the carved image that its maker should carve it? Or the molten image and lying oracle that its very maker should trust in it, and make dumb idols?" (Hab 2:18–19). Clearly, the defense of God as the ruler and sovereign of all creation resounds in Habakkuk's rhetorical questions. For him, God remains enthroned in his holy temple. And the entire universe must remain silent and respectful of the Almighty God, who has not deserted his people despite the Babylonians' invasion (Hab 2:20; Zeph 1:7). He is never indifferent. God has a plan. While waiting for God's plan, the righteous must persevere in faith and worship. This plan of the sovereign God is poetically expanded upon in the third chapter of Habakkuk, to which we now turn.

In addition to the image of God as the ruler and sovereign of all creation, seen particularly in the debates, promises (Hab 1—2:5), and woes (Hab 2:6–20) of the preceding chapters, the central

---

157. Cf. Roberts (*Nahum, Habakkuk and Zephaniah*, 122) for fascinating details.
158. Széles, *Wrath and Mercy*, 41.
159. Feinberg, *The Minor Prophets*, 214.

theophanic image of God in the poetic prayer of Habakkuk (Hab 3:1–19) is that of a divine warrior. The prophet's prayer ($t^e pill\bar{a}h$) begins with "O Lord, I have heard your renown, and feared, O Lord, your work ... in your wrath remember our compassion" (Hab 3:2). In this prayer, Habakkuk recalls past manifestations of God's power and acts of sovereignty. He prays that God continually performs today the deeds and wonders for which he was famous in the past. Habakkuk follows this with reports of God's response, in which he receives a vision (*hazon*) of God as a divine warrior coming from Teman and Mount Paran (Hab 3:3).

Many scholars have agreed that, rooted in ancient Israel's historical antecedent (Exod 15; Judg 5), Habakkuk sees the Lord coming from the territories of the Sinai Peninsula, heading northward, and crossing over the territory of Edom to Judah.[160] God's appearance in verse 4 is as bright and dazzling (*nōgah*) as the light of the sun (*'ôr*). God's radiance overpowers human visibility, since it burst out in rays (*garnayîm*) from his hands (*miyyadô*). These are symbols of power and majesty that Pope Francis would come to embrace in his *Lumen Fidei* ("The Light of Faith").[161] God cannot be described in human language, either in his being or in his might. He can only be experienced.[162]

In the Lord's envoy are pestilence and plague (Hab 3:5). In the Exodus story, plague and pestilence are weapons used by God to punish his enemies (Exod 5:3; 9:7, 15). Habakkuk's vision personifies these phenomena, even to those referring to the demonic forces in the ancient Canaanite culture and religion that brought suffering to humanity. In Habakkuk's theology, these demons and plagues are inferior to God, who only uses them as his instrument to punish the wicked.[163] God has dominion over pestilence and plagues of all

---

160. Széles (*Wrath and Mercy*, 46) and Roberts (*Nahum, Habakkuk and Zephaniah*, 151–152) have further studies on the location of Teman and Paran.

161. This is the first encyclical letter of Francis, with the contribution of Pope Benedict XVI. It reflects the nature of belief and the need to renew our faith for a bright future of charity and love for all. With faith in God comes service, the encyclical letter stresses. Hahn ("Foreword," vii) explains further, "the encyclical letter *Lumen Fidei* is the great monument of the Year of Faith declared by Pope Benedict XVI and brought to completion by Pope Francis. It is a capstone of the year, but at the same time a milestone of a long road, a road we have only begun to travel: the road of New Evangelization."

162. Széles, *Mercy and Wrath*, 47.

163. Ibid., 48.

types. He has dominion and majesty not only over diseases, plagues, hurricanes, earthquakes, tsunamis, and typhoons—his very presence causes the earth to convulse and nations to tremble:

> He pauses to survey the earth; his looks make the nations tremble. The eternal mountains are shattered, the age-old hills bow low along his ancient ways. I see the tents of Cushan collapse; trembling are the pavilions of the land of Midian. Is your anger against the stream, O Lord? Is your wrath against the streams, your rage against the sea, that you drive the steeds of your victorious chariot? (Hab 3:6–8; cf. 10–11)

This passage presents God as a military general in battle. He is taking his stance and surveying and directing his troops in action, as does a good field marshal. His enemies are terrified at the sight of his power and manifestation of divine sovereignty. This motif of divine sovereignty found in Habakkuk was common in biblical times, as well as among people of ancient cultures (Exod 15:14–16; Deut 33; Judg 5:4–5).[164] It is also prominent among the prophetic tradition, particularly the Twelve, of which Habakkuk is a part.[165] For example, Elijah sees the God of Israel as the ruler of all nations (1 Kgs 19:15; 2 Kgs 8:13–15). Isaiah, a prophet of Zion, prophesied that all nations will come to Zion to be instructed and directed by the Lord (Isa 2:2–4). Isaiah sees Assyria as God's instrument to teach Israel and Judah a lesson (Isa 7:18–20; 10:5) and demonstrates God's sovereignty over the nations through his series of judgments (Isa 13–23). Jeremiah addresses God as the king of all the nations (Jer 10:7).

In the Twelve, of which Habakkuk is a part, there is a general and unified theological emphasis on the rapport that exists between God and his people, Israel. For instance, the prophets interpret the fall of Samaria (722 BC) and Judah (586/7 BC) in light of God's covenant with Israel. The Israelites had broken the covenant and, as a result, were sent into exile. God's judgment and deliverance reveals that he is the sovereign of all nations and creation.[166] In addition, Hosea, with his metaphor of marriage with Gomer, reminds Israel

---

164. Roberts, *Nahum, Habakkuk and Zephaniah*, 154.

165. Nogalski and Sweeney (:Preface," vii–viii) is a good place to locate recent authors who have realized the need to study the Twelve Minor Prophets, including Habakkuk, as a unified whole, especially with regard to their theological themes.

166. Ko, "Ordering of the Twelve," 331.

of God's sense of judgment and punishment of sinners. But he also stresses divine compassion, love, mercy, kindness, and restoration (Exod 34:6–7; Ps 103; 145:8; Neh 9:17; Joel 2:13; Jonah 4:2)—all themes that are familiar in the ministry of Pope Francis.

In condemning injustice and unethical worship, the prophet Amos, whom Habakkuk knew, pronounces Yahweh as the roaring Lion from Judah (Amos 1:2), who passes universal judgment over the surrounding kingdoms (Amos 1:3—2:3). For Micah, all nations will come to Zion (Mic 4:1–3). This theme of the Lion of Judah and the sovereign of all nations and creation also dominates the theology of Obadiah, Jonah, Nahum, Zephaniah (Zeph 1–3), and Zechariah (Zech 14:9). Thus, the prophetic messages in the Twelve not only remind Israel of the need to keep the covenant that God established with them, but they also remind the Israelites of God's wonders in creation—the waters and the seas. For example, in liberating Israel, God divided and took control of all nations and situations at the Red Sea and at the Jordan River (Exod 7–12; 15–18). In Habakkuk, God has done it again (Hab 3:8, 15).

Habakkuk's vision is filled with military imagery, such as horses and chariots, bows and quivers, flying arrows, and flashing spears (Hab 3:9–11). While the following actual military expedition and divine mission occurs to the prophet, Habakkuk says to God:

> You come forth to save your people, to save your anointed one. You crush the heads of the wicked, you lay bare their bases at the neck. You pierce with your shafts the head of their princes whose boasts would be of devouring the wretched in their lair. You tread the sea with your steeds amid the churning of the deep waters. (Hab 3:13–15)

Clearly, this theophanic display of God's divine control, dominion, and majesty strengthens Habakkuk's faith; additionally, his reaction is that of a joyful and righteous person who is persevering in faith amid life's calamities and challenges (Hab 3:16–19).

Habakkuk is different from other prophets, especially the rest of the Twelve. He is patient. He is human and gives voice to the suffering faithful of Judah. He is ready to wait for the day when distress will descend upon those who attack Judah (Hab 3:16). Instead of acting as God's mouthpiece in judging and condemning, like other prophets, he employs a song and lament in order to question God's sense of justice and theodicy. The prayer ends with an expression of hope—a call to have trust, faith, and confidence in the sovereign God. This conclusion echoes the messages of the preceding chapters and verses, especially Habakkuk 2:3–4. Here the prophet and the righteous are encouraged to live by faith between the time of the vision (*ḥazon*) and the time of fulfillment. Habakkuk and the righteous must rely on the only sovereign God, who saves and strengthens his faithful (Hab 3:18–19).

In sum, God has the ability to control nations and put them to work (Hab 1:6). As the creator of all creation, he has control over them (Hab 1:14–16). God can also undo the works of pseudo kings and earthly kings and kingdoms, and he brings them woe (Hab 2:6–19). He keeps his covenant with the house of David despite its national crisis (Hab 3:13). With this, Habakkuk embodies a divine message of faith, endurance, and hope, as well as a paradigm for all suffering righteous people, in every context and culture, to imitate.

Habakkuk's determination to trust God demonstrates to the Judean community that it is possible to live faithfully in times of atrocity and trouble. This, I believe, has much to offer us today and foreshadows Francis's prophetic effect. In his *Evangelii Gaudium*, Pope Francis exhorts us that the great danger in today's world is consumerism; it is the result of covetousness, pursuit of frivolous pleasure, and a blunted conscience.[167] For Francis, "whenever our interior life becomes caught up in its own interests and concerns, there is no longer room for others, no place for the poor."[168] Few will disagree that the political, social, and economic rivalries that plague and divide the globe today (including members of the United Nations) are selfishly motivated. These selfish pursuits, as with the Chaldeans, often result in wars, exchange of economic sanctions, terrorism, injustice, oppression, conflict, division, and other forms of misunderstanding. These selfish pursuits also bring about untold hardship and suffering, particularly among the poor and weak, who have been excluded, ignored, plundered, and exploited since the time of Habakkuk (Hab 2:6–19). Pope Francis defends these poor people—the excluded and the exploited.

The pain of this exclusion and exploitation transcends human control, except with Habakkuk's God, who uses humans as

---

167. Francis, *Evangelii Gaudium*, no. 2.
168. Ibid., no. 2.

his instruments to alleviate pain and suffering and restore fortune according to his appointed time and terms. Fittingly, Francis again appeals to Scripture. He calls on the church—Christians of every community—to be God's instruments in liberating and including the poor in the socio-economic and political fabric of their societies through welfare projects, employment, and minimum wage and income redistribution.[169] However, while awaiting God's time, the poor and the plundered must imitate Habakkuk's patience and faith in the sovereign God who is ever present with the righteous (Hab 2:4).

The loss of loved ones and sudden illnesses are sources of great stress and pain that afflict everyone, the poor and the rich alike. What about violence in our society, especially that which is structured and organized? What about the victims of those shootings in our nation's homes and public places? Recent earthquakes, tsunamis, hurricanes, storms, and typhoons, as well as financial and business failures, are also sources of great pain and suffering to the righteous. In all these, Habakkuk's lament framework (Hab 1:2–2:5)—its theology of theodicy (Hab 1:5–11; 2:6–19) and message for the righteous to persevere in faith (Hab 2:4), as well as the song of hope in a divine warrior (Hab 3:3–19)—serves as a paradigm for all the righteous who are suffering today.

viii. Effect of Jeremiah, the Prophet

Jeremiah of Anathoth, a celibate from a priestly family, was a late pre-exilic prophet of Israel (626–586/7 BC). In his time, Jeremiah meant so much for Israel, as does Francis today. The book bearing Jeremiah's name contains a calling narrative (Jer 1:4–19), persecution stories (Jer 36–38), responses in lamentation, dialectics of emotion, temple sermons, challenges to injustice, acts of endurance, and prophetic ministries (Jer 15:10–21; 18:18–23; 20:7–18). As such, Jeremiah is often seen as a prophetic model and the prototype of Christ, as well as a foreshadow of Pope Francis.

Like earlier prophets, Jeremiah received his calling from God, who spoke to him: "before I formed you in the womb I knew you, and before you were born I consecrated you" (Jer 1:5). Even though

---

169. Ibid., nos. 187–216.

Jeremiah thought he was too young for the mission, God promised him his divine guidance and words (Jer 1:6–8).

Jeremiah's mission was filled with controversy, challenges, and suffering in all forms. As observed by Leclerc, "Of all the prophets, Jeremiah is the one who suffered the most and who was most often publicly rejected."[170] In performing the unpopular work of denouncing sin and announcing judgment, Jeremiah was opposed, rejected, resisted, criticized, mocked, and punished. Leclerc offers the following list of Jeremiah's sufferings:

- A temple officer placed Jeremiah in stocks (Jer 20:1–2)
- He was put on trial by priests who demanded his death (Jer 26:10–11)
- He was banished from the temple (Jer 36:5)
- He and his scribe had to go into hiding (Jer 36:19)
- He was arrested, beaten, and imprisoned (Jer 37:12–16)
- He was transferred to house arrest (Jer 37:20–21)
- He was seized and thrown into a muddy cistern and left there to die (Jer 38:1–6)[171]

Jeremiah's sufferings prompted his response. Like Habakkuk, he takes his sufferings and mission directly to God in prayer, confession, and complaints in his lamentations. Jeremiah is filled with anger (Jer 6:11). Jeremiah is indignant as he thinks God has left him (Jer 15:17), and he expresses his bitterness over his enemies' plot against him (Jer 18:18–20). Jeremiah is caught up in inner tension, in a dialectics of emotion, and in prophetic consciousness of himself and God.[172] Jeremiah pushes back against his enemies. He is not only sorry for himself, but God as well. Jeremiah therefore prays:

170. Leclerc, *Prophets of Israel*, 242.
171. Leclerc, *Prophets*, 242.
172. Heschel (*Prophets*, 137–146) has a detailed comment on Jeremiah's inner tension and prophetic consciousness. For Heschel, "the call to be a prophet is more than an invitation. It is first of all a feeling of being enticed, of acquiescence or willing surrender. But this winsome feeling is only one aspect of the experience of willing surrender. The other aspect is a sense of being ravished or carried away by violence, of yielding to overpowering force against one's own will. The prophet feels both the attraction and the coercion of God, the appeal and the pressure, the charm and the stress . . . voluntary identification and force capitulation."

> Therefore give their children over to famine; hurl them out to the power of the sword, let their wives become childless and widowed. May their men met death by pestilence, their youths be slain by the sword in battle. May a cry be heard from their houses, when you bring the marauder suddenly upon them! For they have dug a pit to catch me, and laid snares for my feet. Yet you, O Lord, know all their plotting to kill me. Do not forgive their iniquity, do not blot out their sin from your sight. Let them be tripped up before you; deal with them while you are anger. (Jer 18:21-23)

Jeremiah also felt that God had seduced or dubbed him into his prophetic ministry (Jer 20:7). He felt rejected by his contemporaries as he spoke of divine judgment and justice (Jer 20:8–9). Jeremiah had to curse the day he was born (Jer 20:14–18).

Jeremiah's principal themes, some of which Francis would embrace, include:

- Israel as the bride of God (2:2)
- Israel's forgetfulness of God (Jer 2:32) and lack of knowledge of him (Jer 4:22)
- The call to conversion (Jer 4:22)
- The need for "fair judgment" and "justice" (Jer 4:2)
- God as the attacking enemy (Jer 4:1)
- The sin of social injustice (Jer 5:27–28)
- The low value of religion without justice (Jer 6:20–25; 7:3–15)
- A future Davidic king who brings salvation and security (2 Jer 3:5–6; 30:9; also see 33:15)
- The new covenant written in the heart (Jer 31:31–34; see also 32:40)[173]

In other words, Jeremiah "holds in tension divine judgement for the people's sins, divine love for the people, and divine promise of salvation . . . it highlights Israel's traditional institutions: covenant, temple monarchy, priesthood, prophecy."[174]

---

173. Branick, *Understanding the Prophets*, 157–58.
174. Cook, *Hear, O Heavens, and Listen, O Earth*, 174.

In each of these themes—beginning with the call narrative (Jer 1:4–19)—we see Pope Francis. In his *Evangelii Gaudium*, Francis exhorts us on "the church's missionary transformation" and the challenges that go with it; he appeals vehemently to Israel's prophetic calling in general, and to Jeremiah's theology of divine calling in particular. Francis says, "The word of God constantly shows us how God challenges those who believe in him 'to go forth.' Abraham received the call to set out for a new land (cf. Gn 12:1–3). Moses heard God's call: 'Go, I send you' (Ex 3:10) and led the people towards the promise land."[175] Concluding with Jeremiah, Francis says, "To Jeremiah, God say: 'To all whom I send you, you shall go: (Jer 1:7).' "[176] He also exhorts: "In our day Jesus' command to 'go and make disciples' echoes in the changing scenarios and ever new challenges to the Church's mission of evangelization, and all of us are called to take part in the new missionary 'going forth.' "[177] All of us are called to be prophetic.

One other theme of Jeremiah that Francis effectively embodies and transmits to us today is that of the covenant. This theme is connected to the concept of social justice and care for the poor and needy. Challenging oppression and exploitation of the poor and vulnerable members of his seventh-century BC society, Jeremiah calls out perpetrators of social injustice, saying:

> For scoundrels are found among my people; they take over the goods of others. Like fowlers they set a trap; they catch human beings. Like a cage full of birds, their houses are full of treachery; therefore they have become great and rich, they have grown fat and sleek. They know no limits in deeds of wickedness; they do not judge with justice the cause of the orphan, to make it prosper, and they do not defend the rights of the needy. (Jer 5:26–28)

Francis, in his prophetic ministry, classifies this aspect of preaching as "the social dimension of evangelization."[178] With this spirit of the social gospel, Francis notes the courage of the most vulnerable members of society, saying: "doubly poor are those women who endure situations of exclusion, mistreatment and violence,

---

175. *Evangelii Gaudium*, no. 20.
176. Ibid., no. 20.
177. Ibid., no. 20.
178. See Francis, *Evangelii Gaudium*, nos. 176–257.

since they are frequently less able to defend their rights. Even so, we constantly witness among them impressive examples of daily heroism in defending and protecting their vulnerable families."[179] In his writings, homilies, and pronouncements, Francis imitates Jeremiah, who prophesied to empower and lift up his suffering brothers and sisters in exile. Jeremiah exhorts such people to not despair, but rather to build houses, work hard, and be hopeful. They should conduct business, marry, plant gardens, cultivate their farms, and take care of their families and children (Jer 29:1–23).

ix. Effect of Obadiah, the Prophet

Although it is the shortest book of the Bible, composed of just twenty-one verses, Obadiah has powerful messages that inform the prophetic ministry of Pope Francis—particularly his theology of the family.

Obadiah is a review of the ancient family of Esau and Jacob (Israel and Edom); the text additionally addresses the Day of the Lord (Obad 8–18) and the sovereignty of God (Obad 19–21). Obadiah's prophesy concentrates on Edom, just as Nahum targeted Nineveh. In the text, Edom (Obad 1–7, 11–14) stands for Esau, the founding ancestor of Edom, who was the brother of Jacob. The story of these twin sons of Isaac and Rebekah is recounted in Genesis 25–27; it is the topic of daily Masses of the Fourteenth Week of Ordinary Week in the liturgical calendar of the Catholic Church. This story is a story of a family crisis, rivalry, bitterness, and jealousy. The relationship between Esau and Jacob was so bitter that Jacob had to flee for his life from Esau. Even after reconciliation, the brothers kept their distance. Leclerc notes, however, that "what may have been lacking in affection could not mitigate the obligation owed to one another as brothers."[180]

Obadiah emphasizes the sacredness of the global family and the "illustration of the tragic consequence of tensions among family members, who have both the privilege and the responsibility to care for one another." This teaching is not far from Francis's laments on

---

179. Francis, *Evangelii Gaudium*, no. 21.
180. Leclerc, *Prophets*, 275.

the "globalization of indifference" and his call to be "our brothers' and sisters' keepers."[181]

For Francis, the review of ancient family that Obadiah offers is "the first school of human values, where we learn the wise use of freedom."[182] Francis, with his familiarity with the Bible, may have been indirectly informed by Obadiah. He therefore exhorts that "the life of every family is marked with all kinds of crises, yet these are also part of dramatic beauty . . . Each crisis has a lesson to teach us."[183] I agree with Cook that the prophecy of Obadiah offers us "an opportunity to review the family beginnings of ancient Israel as they are told in Genesis. It also provides us an opportunity to reflect on the importance of caring for one another in the world family to which all people in our global society belong."[184]

x. Effect of Ezekiel, the Prophet

Ezekiel was active among the Babylonian exiles (597–570 BC). He dramatically and symbolically acted and preached judgment and hope in God, the Holy One of Israel. He suggested an alternative: hope in the future temple instead of despair. He invited the Israelites to put on a new a heart and be joyful as they await the restoration of their fortune. Ezekiel remains speechless, unable to rebuke the people or intercede to God on their behalf (Ezek 3:22–27). He enacts the siege of Jerusalem (Ezek 4:1–3), lies on his left side for 390 days and on his right side for 40 days, bearing the guilt of Israel and Judah (Ezek 4:9–11), and he bakes bread on coals made from animal dung (Ezek 4:12–15). He also burns, chops, and scatters his hair (Ezek 5:1–4) and packs his bags, digs through the wall, and leaves the city (Ezek 12:1–16). He eats bread while trembling (Ezek 4:17–20), groans aloud in the hearing of the people (Ezek 21:8–13), does not mourn the demise of his wife (Ezek 24:15–24), and ties two sticks together (Ezek 37:15–28). Ezekiel would also come to be a source of inspiration for Pope Francis, who is known for several symbolic

---

181. Cook (*Hear, O Heavens, and Listen, O Earth*, 217) has additional comments on the consequences of Esau and Jacob's rivalry.

182. Francis, *Amoris Laetitia*, no. 274.

183. Ibid., no. 232.

184. Cook, *Hear, O Heavens, and Listen, O Earth*, 218.

acts since the inception of his papacy—beginning with his taking the name "Francis."

Psalm 137 gives us a glimpse of what life in exile meant for Ezekiel and his contemporaries in Babylon:

> By the rivers of Babylon there we sat down and there we wept when we remembered Zion.
>
> On the willows there we hung up our harps.
>
> For there our captors asked us for songs, and our tormentors asked for mirth, saying,
>
> "Sing us one of the songs of Zion."
>
> How could we sing the Lord's song in a foreign land? . . .
>
> O daughter Babylon, you devastator! Happy shall they be who pay you back what you have done to us! Happy shall they be who take your little ones and dash them against the rock. (Ps 137:1–9) .

Like Jeremiah, who encouraged his contemporaries to never give up hope in the face of evil (Jer 29:1–23), Ezekiel preached hope to the exiled. He emphasized the importance of Torah. God can still be worshiped without the physical temple, which the Babylonians had destroyed. Ezekiel's invitation to preach is also presented in a very dramatic manner (Ezek 1:1–3) filled with signs and prophetic symbolism (Ezek 3:22–27; 4:4–8, 9–11, 12–15; 5:1–4; 12:1–16, 17–20; 21:8–13; 24:15–24; 33:21–22; 37:15–28). In his prophecy, Ezekiel is called the "mortal" and "the son of man" more than ninety-three times, emphasizing his simplicity and humanity as God's representative—a priest, prophet, intercessor, and mouthpiece of God. These titles place him in contrast with God, whom Ezekiel recognizes as a glorious, transcendent, and immanent God and the Holy One of Israel. Israel's sins of idolatry (Ezek 8; 16:1–52; 23) and injustice (Ezek 7:23; 22:29) have consequences—namely, the departure of the mobile Glory of the Lord (Ezek 9–11; 43:1–9). They also come with a personal responsibility (Ezek 3:16–21; 18).

Ezekiel, like Jeremiah, foregrounds Francis in challenging his contemporaries. Ezekiel offers hope for restoration (social, political, economic, and religious), and he offers hope that people of every land and culture will recognize the omnipresence of God. For Ezekiel, God is everywhere. Ezekiel draws a contrast between the good shepherd and the bad shepherd (Ezek 34). He stresses the theology of life after death or national restoration, using the famous vision of the "dry bones" (Ezek 37). Other important theological themes in Ezekiel are the theology of the new heart (Ezek 3:7; 36:26; cf. Jer 31:33), the new covenant (Ezek 6:8, 59, 61; 17:19; 44:7), and the spirituality of the new temple (Ezek 40–44).

Commenting on this new temple, Leclerc writes:

> Perhaps one of the most remarkable features of the new Temple and city is a river that starts from the sanctuary of the Temple, flows below the threshold from the east, and heads south (47:1–12). As the river flows further from the source, it grows stronger and ever mightier. It is fresh water that brings life wherever it flows. When it enters the Dead Sea, it makes those salty, dead waters fresh and teaming with fish and other creatures. . . . This river of life, coming from the sanctuary, is a potent simple of the divine life that comes from God and rejuvenates the land, the sea, creatures, plants, and humans.[185]

We can recognize Francis's gospel of hope, joy, social justice, and optimism in Ezekiel's theology of the new temple and new city, where the God of the universe has retaken his seat. Ezekiel has so much to offer our everyday life, surrounded with pain, tragedy, economic hardship, terrorism, abuse of nature and the environment, and uncertainty in boundaries and family life.[186]

Cook so well articulates the significance of Ezekiel's prophecy in the face of life's vicissitudes—seen also in the preaching of Francis's theology of mercy and optimism—in stating: "God remains faithful to us and asks for our faithfulness in return. Furthermore, God's presence is within us, not simply in our religious buildings or in any specific location. Divine in-breaking in our lives continues in unexpected ways, helping us to live faithful lives in the midst of uncertainty and alienation."[187] Similarly, Francis believes "the fruit of hope is 'apostolic courage;' It is a 'prophetic courage,' which means the willingness to transmit the gospel everywhere and always."[188]

---

185. Leclerc, *Prophets*, 298.

186. See Allen Jr. (*10 Things Francis Wants You to Know*, 38–39), where Francis is noted as saying, "let us never yield to pessimism . . . let us not yield to pessimism or discouragement, . . . let us be quite certain that the Holy Spirit bestows upon the Church, with his powerful breath, the courage to persevere and also to seek new methods of evangelization, so as to bring the gospel to the utter most ends of the earth."

187. Cook, *Hear, O Heavens, and Listen, O Earth*, 221.

188. Allen, *10 Things to Know About Pope Francis*, 39.

xi. Effect of Second Isaiah (Isa 40–55)

Pope Francis also finds an effective message in the prophecy of Second Isaiah, also known as the Book of Consolation (Isa 40–55). Written for the exiles who would return to Judah from Babylon, these chapters are meant to comfort the dispirited. Second Isaiah bears themes of the Suffering Servant of God, God as the creator of the universe, God as the sovereign of all creation, God as the cosmic God (Isa 40:12–22), and God as the mother and shepherd of his flock (Isa 40:11).[189] Second Isaiah contains promises of fertile land and restoration of fortune, water for the thirsty, and security for the poor against enemies. These things are a result of God's power and mercy. The promises in Second Isaiah would come to dominate Pope Francis's Petrine theology. Second Isaiah also stresses that there is only one God (a sense of monotheism) who is the Lord, and there is no other besides him (Isa 45:5).

Apart from his favorite theme of mercy, Pope Francis appeals passionately to Second Isaiah in many ways—especially in his theology and gospel of creation. For instance, in his *Laudato Si'*, he cites Isaiah's statement: "The Lord is the everlasting God, the Creator of the ends of the earth. He does not faint or grow weary; his understanding is unsearchable. He gives power to the faint, and strengthens the powerless" (Isa 40:28b–29).[190]

Upon close examination, Deutero-Isaiah highlights the unshakable love that God has for Israel (Isa 50:10). In Second Isaiah, God is Israel's husband (Isa 54:5–8), their comforter (Isa 40:1–2, 11; 52:9), and their redeemer and savior (Isa 41:14; 43:1, 3). In Second Isaiah, Israel's salvation and freedom will be delivered through the instrument of the Suffering Servant of Yahweh, whose songs are presented in four passages (Isa 42:1–4; 49:1–6; 50:4–10; 52:13—53:12). These passages also portray various sufferings and redemption (Isa 53:5–6, 8).

With the emergence of the Persian king Cyrus came hope that the exilic people would soon be allowed to return home. They emerged from their suffering and saw a light of joy at the end of the tunnel. In the midst of our daily challenges (economic turbulence, corrupt politicians, upheaval, threats of terrorism, war, isolation, loneliness, individualism, natural disasters, dictatorship of globalism and indifference),

---

189. See Branick, *Understanding the Prophets*, 201.
190. Francis, *Laudato Si'*, no. 73.

we, too, abide by Francis's and Deutero-Isaiah's exhortation: "Get you up to a high mountain, O herald of good tidings to Zion; lift up your voice with strength, O herald of good tidings to Jerusalem" (Isa 40:9).[191] And on this mountain, God will make Israel's religious life fruitful, as God has done for their land (Isa 55:10–11). We find the teachings of Pope Francis in the hopeful message of Deutero-Isaiah.

Effect of Post-Exilic Prophets

The post-exilic prophets include Haggai, Zechariah, Malachi, Third Isaiah, Joel, and Jonah. Common among these post-exilic prophets are the themes of the returning of the exiles, rebuilding of the temple, and settlement problems. These themes are also recounted in the book of Ezra (Ezra 1:1–11; 2:64—65:5). And as in Deutero-Isaiah and other prophetic books, we are God's instruments. In Ezra, God stirred up the spirit of King Cyrus, who issued a decree permitting the Israelites to return from exile to rebuild the temple of Jerusalem for Yahweh and teach the Torah. Some of the treasures looted from the temple were also returned (Ezra 1:2–4). Governor Sheshbazzar, a Persian imperial appointee, was among the initial group that returned to Jerusalem around 538 BC (Ezra 5:16). They were later joined by another governor, Zerubbabel, who undertook the task of laying the foundation for the new temple (Ezra 3:8–13).[192] This new temple will be the source of joy in Ezekiel 47 and in Pope Francis's *Evangelii Gaudium* ("The Joy of the Gospel").

i. Effect of Haggai, the Prophet

In Haggai, Zechariah, and Malachi we hear tones of crises, quarrels, and other challenges common in human society. In Haggai, the challenges of the post-exilic community were both external and internal. External threats came from the "people of the land"—the "Samaritans" and those who had not experienced the exile. They claimed the rightful ownership of the place and of the temple, which was under construction. Some of them opposed the returned exiles and fought against them for land. On the other hand, the returned exiles

---

191. Francis, *Evangelii Gaudium*, no. 4.
192. See the summary in Matthews, *Prophets of Israel*, 124.

thought those who had not experienced exile where unqualified to participate in the rebuilding of the new temple. These people, they thought, had not been purified by the experience of exile.[193]

Internally, the returned exiles who had married foreigners were discriminated against by Ezra, who considered them an unholy contamination to Israel's holy seed (Ezra 9:2). Additionally, abuses of corruption ensued among the returned exiles, which was against the spirit of the Torah. Haggai characteristically calls them to rebuild the temple rather than their paneled homes (Hag 1:4).[194]

Haggai reminds them of the consequences of sin. Sin and neglect of the rebuilding project breeds hardship and drought, poor harvests, and political troubles (Hag 1:9–11). If they prioritize the rebuilding project, they will experience blessing, prosperity, and fertility. For Haggai, God is the giver of fertility and prosperity (Hag 1:12—2:9).

Haggai foregrounds Francis's engagement with God, the source of life. Haggai clearly shares in the perspective of Ezekiel's new temple (Ezek 40–47). Haggai concludes his prophecy with a message of hope and a vision of the new temple, which fuels the theology of the messianic hope and expectation that is central in Pope Francis's prophetic messages. Seen through the prism of Haggai's prophecy, Francis's pastoral ministry can stimulate us today to undertake our daily challenges with hope and courage.

ii. Effect of Zechariah, the Prophet

Zechariah, a contemporary of Haggai, stresses the importance of rebuilding the temple. Both Haggai and Zechariah 1–8 contain themes centered on the proper reconstruction of worship and new life—physically, morally, politically, and religiously—after the exile. Matthews notices that, "where Zechariah differs is in the presentation of the majority of his message in eight visionary experiences (1:7–6:15)."[195] The following interrelated visions show Zechariah's understanding of God as the one in charge of the universe:

1. Horses of different colors and their horsemen (Zech 1:7–17)
2. Four horns and blacksmiths (Zech 1:18–21)

---

193. See Leclerc (*Prophets*, 334) for details.
194. Ibid., 339.
195. Matthews, *Prophets of Israel*, 125.

3. A surveyor of a city without walls (Zech 2:1–5)
4. The high priest and the branches (Zech 3:1–10)
5. The lamp stand and the olive tree (Zech 4:1–14)
6. The flying scroll (Zech 5:1–4)
7. The woman in the basket (Zech 6:1–8)
8. Four chariots (Zech 6:9–15)

Zechariah also contains a call to repentance (Zech 1:1–6), the theology of the angel, and a call to value justice, show kindness, and practice mercy—especially in respect to widows, orphans, aliens, and the poor. Pope Francis gives priority to these themes in his teachings (Zech 7:8–14; 8:14–17). For Francis, the name of God is mercy. The final section of Zechariah is a message of hope that God will return to Zion. Just as God will never abandon Zion (Zech 8:1–3, 20–23), he will not abandon us in our daily challenges.

iii. Effect of Malachi, the Prophet

The prophetic ministry of Malachi (meaning "my messenger") took place in the fifth century BC, making him a contemporary of Haggai and Zechariah. Malachi is arranged in a series of six prophecies introduced by a superscription and concluding with appendices. In Malachi, the prophet stresses God's choice of Israel and the coming judgment of Edom, which is rooted in the conflict between Esau and Jacob narrated in Genesis and addressed in the book of Obadiah (Mal 1:2–5). The good news is that this message of God's judgment has tones of divine mercy with calls for repentance. It ends with forgiveness and the restoration of fortune for family members.

Malachi also asserts God's sovereignty over all creation and people. He states, "Great is the Lord beyond the borders of Israel" (Mal 1:5). This is a favorite prophetic theme in the writings of Pope Francis. Malachi also emphasizes worship (Mal 1:6–2:9). With the rebuilding of the temple, good priests and sacrifices were needed to bring about proper worship—worship that was not devoid of ethics. Malachi identifies with Haggai and Zachariah by stressing that neglecting the temple, making unethical sacrifices, failing to tithe for the rebuilding of the temple, and failing to make wholehearted sacrifices and worship were unacceptable to God.

Malachi exhorts that priests and leaders should not cause the downfall of their subjects. He reminds them, "you have caused many to stumble by your instruction; you have corrupted the covenant of Levi, says the Lord of hosts" (Mal 2:8). Does this not echo Pope Francis's challenge of neo-clericalism?

Malachi also challenges faithlessness toward one another (Mal 2:10), God (Mal 2:11), and family members (Mal 2:16). Francis's teachings on love, mercy, and the gospel of the family in *Amoris Laetitia* is conspicuous in Malachi's prophecy of faithfulness. But for Francis, "Faith must be proposed, never imposed."[196] Notably, when Pope Francis met with media representatives on March 16, 2013, he, like his predecessors John Paul II and Benedict XVI, refused to impose his formal blessings on the mixed group of the media crew to respect the feelings of those who were not Catholic.[197]

Lastly, Malachi exhorts the community to be prepared for the Day of the Lord by respecting the dignity of the poor and the needy (Mal 2:17–3:5). God would harshly judge those who "oppress the hired workers in their wages, the widow and the orphan, against those who thrust aside the alien, and do not fear me, says the Lord of hosts (3:5)."[198] In chapter 4, Malachi sums up his theology with his message of the new covenant, which is rooted in the covenant established with Moses and promised to Elijah (Mal 4:4–5). These common prophetic themes are repeated not only in Isaiah 56–66 (Third Isaiah or Trito-Isaiah), but also in the pastoral outreach of Pope Francis.

iv. Effect of Third Isaiah (Isa 55–66)

Third Isaiah reveals the deeply divided post-exilic community of Israel. It is a prophecy addressed to a community "rife with social injustice and disorder, power politics, despair, and hopelessness."[199] According to Isaiah 61:1–3, the spirit of the Lord was given to Isaiah, and Isaiah was anointed and sent to bring good news to the poor.

196. Allen Jr., *10 Things Pope Francis Wants You to Know*, 29.
197. Ibid., 29–30.
198. See Leclerc, *Prophets*, 356.
199. Ibid., 361.

Third Isaiah is reminiscent of Second Isaiah (Isa 40:9) and foregrounds Pope Francis's love for the poor and the needy. The mission of Third Isaiah is to heal, liberate, comfort, and bring joy to the hearts of the sorrowful people. It further captures the joy of the newly rebuilt temple.

Even in the divisiveness of his society, Third Isaiah believes that God can bring healing and bridge the gaps to bring about unity. He is interested in a robust and inclusive community of eunuchs, men, women, aliens, and foreigners. This belief is apparent in the following prophecies:

> For thus says the Lord: To eunuchs who keep my Sabbaths
>
> Who choose the things that please me and hold fast my covenant, I will give, in my house and within my walls, a monument and a name better than sons and daughters; I will give them an everlasting name that shall not be cut off.
>
> And foreigners who join themselves to the Lord, to minister to him, to love the name of the Lord, and to be his servants, all who keep the Sabbath, and do not profane it, an hold fast my covenant- these I will bring to my holy mountain, and make them joyful in my house of prayer, their burnt offerings and their sacrifices will be accepted on my altar; for my house shall be call a house of prayer for all peoples. (Isa 56:4–7)

In addition to inclusiveness and the universal nature of God's love, Third Isaiah emphasizes justice, peace, and true worship (Isa 56:10–12; 59:1–15). The prophecy also portrays God as the divine warrior (Isa 59:15b–19; 63:1–13) who "puts on righteousness like a breastplate, and a helmet of salvation on his head" (Isa 59:17). Additionally, Trito-Isaiah criticizes the poor management of the temple-building project and cult centered on the temple (Isa 66:1–3). He expresses hope in the glory of the future new heaven, where there will be harmony everywhere, and he describes God as ruling and protecting the New Jerusalem (Isa 65:17–25; 66:18–23). Some of these themes (the place of Zion, the sovereignty of God, the holy one of Israel, justice, and peace) are also close to Francis's heart. Finally, in Third Isaiah we hear a voice that speaks to us today in times of regrouping, coming together again after a time of misunderstanding and stress. We hear a voice like that of Pope Francis inviting us to hold onto our basic tenets of faith, joy, love, mercy, and trust in the Lord, who in his divine nature watches over the poor and the orphans.

v. Effect of Joel, the Prophet

Like the post-exilic prophets (Haggai, Zechariah, Malachi, and Third Isaiah), Joel focuses on life in the land of promise after the exile. It was not easy for the returned exiles to reconstruct their life in the land of Judah. In fact, "life was so hard that they felt they could spare little for the building of the house for the Lord. Even when social and religious structures were reestablished, life was precarious."[200] Food was difficult to come by—even though it is something we take for granted in parts of the world today. Natural calamities like drought could quickly wipe out crops and threaten fertility, both among humans and animals. As if this were not enough, the returned exiles were not practicing fidelity to the covenant God had established with Abraham and his descendants.

Joel uses the metaphor of a plague of locusts (Joel 1:2–2:17) as a climax to these tragedies. In his view, these tragedies are God's judgment for the people's infidelity to the covenant in the new land. The locust's devastating effect on the citizens and animals of the new land was just the tip of the iceberg. In addition, the grain offering was cut off from the house of the Lord (Joel 1:9), and very little was left for sacrifices and for imploring of God's mercy, forgiveness, and blessings. In other words, standing on the traditions of Elijah and Hosea, the Prophet Joel believes in the theology of creation as the handiwork of God. God provides the crops, the land, the rain, and the harvests. The land itself, which sustains everyone, is God's gift. Our use of the land, whether for battle or cultivation, can affect the land as well. However, God is the one who blesses and gives the land its fertility. He can also withhold its fertility.

As a remedy, Joel proposes that the priests and ministers of the land practice prayer and repentance. They are to put on sackcloth, wail, mourn, lament, and devote themselves to prayer at the temple (Joel 2:13–14). Since, in Pope Francis's language, the face of God is mercy, Joel is optimistic about God's mercy and the restoration

---

200. Leclerc, *Prophets*, 274–75.

of fortune and fertility to the land and creation (Joel 2:18–29). Joel sees a river of water flowing from the sanctuary and bringing life back to the land on the Day of the Lord, reminiscent of Ezekiel 47.[201]

As Cook writes in his pastoral appreciation of Joel's ecological theology, "Our actions affect the earth for better or for worse, as the book's depictions of destruction and its far-reaching consequences show. We can work to raise consciousness of how our actions today affect the ground, the water and the air."[202] Truly, it is not difficult for us to see the influence of Joel in Pope Francis's *Laudato Si'* ("Gospel of Creation"). Additionally, Francis's encyclical *On Care for Our Common Home* is the "first in the Church's history dedicated to the environment and ecology."[203]

vi. Effect of Jonah, the Prophet

Jonah is another of Israel's classical prophets who foregrounds the fundamental themes in Pope Francis's pastoral leadership. For Francis, God's face is mercy and love. Jonah emphasizes God's merciful nature and value for justice: "you are a gracious God and merciful, slow to anger, and abounding in steadfast love, and to relent from punishing" (Jonah 4:2).

The story of Jonah is a unique story about a disobedient prophet. When the Lord commands Jonah to go east to the Assyrian city of Nineveh, Jonah goes west, toward Tarshish, because he does not want to see the people of Nineveh repent. Jonah instead wishes God would destroy his enemies. A great storm endangered the vessel upon which Jonah was fleeing westward. All the occupants, including Jonah, find their lives threatened. In need of help, they pray to the God of Jonah (Jonah 1:9). After Jonah is thrown into the sea at his request, he ends up in the belly of a fish. After three days and three nights, the fish spews Jonah onto the shore. Upon receiving another commission to go to Nineveh, Jonah reluctantly complies and preaches: "forty days more, and Nineveh shall be overthrown" (Jonah 3:4). In response to Jonah's message, "the people of Nineveh believed God; they proclaimed a fast, and everyone, great and small, put on sackcloth" (Jonah 3:5).

---

201. See Leclerc (*Prophets*, 274–81) for more details.
202. Cook, *Hear, O Heavens, and Listen, O Earth*, 283.
203. Wright, *10 Things Pope Francis Wants You to Know About the Environment*, 7.

The teaching that God's face is mercy is dear to the heart of Pope Francis's ministry. Additionally, Jonah's teaching that there is universality in God's love, inclusiveness, blessings, and mercy is the central theme of Francis's ministry.

Summary of Part I

The goal of Part I was to show how Israel's prophets emphasized the themes of ethical conduct, justice, judgment, the sovereignty of God, the people of God, Israel, Zion or Jerusalem, repentance, hope for restoration, and God's mercy.[204] I have argued that these works have directly or indirectly influenced Pope Francis's pastoral achievements.

Israel's prophets were mediators, transmitters, conduits, convoys, viceroys, and interpreters of God's will—his freedom and justice. They sought alternatives to the dominant culture. They were responsible for making known their prophecies and for proclaiming God's commandments to men, women, and children. The prophets called to order evildoers and those who engaged in unethical behaviors like infidelity, idolatry, and sin. We saw this in Nathan's actions in the David episode, in Ahijah-Jeroboam's encounter, and in Elijah's prophetic drama with Ahab.

Israel's classical prophets (Isaiah, Jeremiah, Ezekiel, Amos, Hosea, Micah, Obadiah, Jonah, Joel, Habakkuk, Nahum, Zephaniah, Haggai, Zechariah, and Malachi) also challenged bad priests, anointed and rejected kings, and held accountable the unjust ruling elite and the entire community. As watchmen and guardians of Israel's moral life, some prophets warned the people that their conduct, "if unchanged, would bring punishment."[205]

Even though this study is focused on the Old Testament texts, the gift of prophecy is also found throughout the New Testament. In many ways, Jeremiah resembles Jesus, especially in his sufferings and courage. What about Moses and the calling narratives of each of the discussed biblical prophets? Jesus, "the new Moses," appeals to and quotes the Hebrew texts—especially the prophetic narratives. A classic example is Isaiah 61, which Jesus quotes in Luke 4 at the beginning of his prophetic ministry. As if these were not enough, the

---

204. See Leclerc (*Prophets*, 108–115), where these themes are drawn.
205. Ibid., 108.

Gospel of Luke blesses us with the Cantos of Mary and Zechariah (Luke 1:46–55, 68–79). These prayers have elements of prophecies and highlight God's saving work in our lives. In Luke's Gospel, Simon and Anna served as a prophet and prophetess in the temple while Jesus was still a baby (Luke 2:1–38). John the Baptist is seen as the last of Israel's prophets in his preparing of Israel for the coming Messiah, Jesus, the "new prophet."

As mentioned in the introductory section of this study, modern-day disciples of Jesus are invited to be prophetic. We can do so by listening to and learning from Pope Francis, the Vicar of Christ. In many ways, Pope Francis has been exemplarily prophetic, acting in the vein of Israel's prophets. He has been effective, bold, courageous, and he has proclaimed the gospel with amazing simplicity. Pope Francis calls everyone—whether man or woman, rich or poor, leader, priest, religious person, politician, or scientist—to be sensitive to God's judgment, justice, mercy, sovereignty over creation, love, faithfulness, and mercy. Francis proclaims this message through his homilies, writings, pastoral visits, and other proclamations, like the synods on the year of mercy and consecrated life and family. Francis's life proclamation and the effect of his pastoral achievements form the subject of Part II.

Part II

The Life, Writings, and Ministry of Pope Francis & His Prophetic Effect

IN THE PRECEDING SECTION we examined Israel's prophets and noted how Pope Francis's pastoral activities—his preaching, homilies, writings, humors, visits, and outreach events—have drawn on the contributions, themes, motifs, and functions of Israel's prophets. We see these prophetic virtues in Francis's gestures, methods, leadership style, accomplishments, compassionate actions, gentleness, approachability, and courage.

Part II offers a review Francis's life and his major writings and messages (*Lumen Fidei, Evangelii Gaudium, Amoris Laetitia, Laudato Si' and Gaudate et Exsultate*), his synods (on family), and his proclamations (Year of Consecrated Life and the Jubilee Year of Mercy, and his New Year Messages) in light of the biblical prophets. This chapter also serves as an introduction to Part III. It pastorally expands on the "prophetic effect" of Francis and the pastoral challenges his teachings pose for contemporary society—particularly the United States of America, Africa, Asia, and other parts of the world and the church.

Life of Pope Francis (Jorge Mario Bergoglio)

Versions of Francis's biography have been printed with different perspectives. Some emphasize his birth, town, education, religious life, priestly formation, pastoral appointments, and pastoral approaches as a Jesuit priest, bishop, and pope.[1] Others graphically describe his life

---

1. See L'Osservatore Romano ("Biography of the Holy Father, Francis") for this

as a chemical technologist and nightclub bouncer before his seminary formation. Others are interested in his papacy, emphasizing the "firsts" in his life: He is the first pope from the Americas, the first pope from the Jesuit Order, and the first pope to take the name Francis.[2] Biographers have portrayed Francis as someone known to take the bus and subway, cook his own meals, have a strong devotion to Mary, visit the poor, be very spiritual, have a low-key style, and love soccer and the tango. He speaks Spanish, Italian, English, French, and German.[3] Still others have moved beyond Francis's early life, education, and priesthood to highlight his international visits, his theology of the people (missionary church, charity, mercy, options for the poor, etc.), his spiritual leadership, and his passion for the planet as an environmentalist.[4]

John Allen Jr.'s biography of Francis is short and sweet:

> Born in Buenos Aires in 1936, Bergoglio's father was an Italian immigrant and railway worker from the region around Turin, and has four brothers and sisters. His original plan was to be a chemist, but in 1958 he instead entered the Society of Jesus and began studies for the priesthood. He spent much of his early career teaching literature, psychology, and philosophy, and early on he was seen as a rising star. From 1973 to 1979 he served as the Jesuit provincial in Argentina, then in 1980 he became the rector of the seminary from which he had graduated. Although Jesuits generally are discouraged from receiving ecclesiastical honors, especially outside mission countries, Bergoglio was named auxiliary bishop of Buenos Aires in 1992 and then succeeded the ailing Antonio Cardinal Quarracino in 1998. John Paul II made Bergoglio a cardinal in 2001, assigning him the Roman church named after the legendary Jesuit Saint Robert Bellarmine. By all account, Bergoglio had strong support in the conclave of 2005 that elected Joseph Ratzinger as Benedict XVI.

---

perspective.

2. See Wikipedia ("Pope Francis,") for the description of Francis, especially as a Pope of many "firsts."

3. Cf. United States Conference of Catholic Bishops ("Pope Francis Biography Graphic"), a graphic biodata of Francis and his humble lifestyle.

4. See Scannone ("Theology of the People," 118–135), where Francis is identified with his preferential option for the poor, *teologia del pueblo* ("theology of the people"), while in the Wikipedia article ("Theology of Francis"), his life is associated with his sense of the "Church's mission," "Church leadership," "pastoral sense," "The Church's liturgy and devotions," "primacy of charity," "environmentalism," and "morality as a vehicle of God's mercy."

> Although Bergoglio wasn't on many "A" lists this time around, he was nevertheless elected in just five ballots, making his debut as the new spiritual leader of 1.2 billion Catholics around the world after the dramatic *Habemus Papam* announcement of 8:12 p.m. Rome time on March, 13, 2013.[5]

Many people have offered varying descriptions of Francis since his election. Andrea Tronielli, a Vatican reporter, sees him as the "Pope of a New World."[6] As the first Jesuit pope in this new world, he cherishes the works of his predecessors—especially John Paul II and Benedict XVI. Because of this, Father Mitch Pacwa, a fellow Jesuit, thinks that Francis has won the heart of many and "evoked another kind of pride."[7] John Allen Jr., a Vatican reporter for CNN and the National Catholic Reporter, thinks Jorge Bergoglio "has proven himself to be an 'Energizer Bunny' of a pope."[8] Francis is a "man of the people," "a Pope of Mercy," and a "cultural icon."[9]

Many of us find Francis's humility, his simple preaching style, and his evangelization strategy to be appealing. We appreciate his rich Wednesday audiences in the Vatican, his qualitative pastoral talks, his discourses, and his addresses to the nation. Additionally, we admire his relatable and engaging presentation of the faith of the church to the young and old, priests and religious, and people of diverse cultural backgrounds. We find inspiration in his visits to the poor, his Scripture-based writings (which we are about to examine), his homilies, and his critique of all forms of injustice and the "globalization of indifference."[10]

Effect of Lumen Fidei ("On the Light of Faith")

Lumen Fidei ("On the Light of Faith") is the first encyclical that Francis co-prepared with Benedict XVI. It was published on June 29,

---

5 Allen Jr., *Francis Wants You to Know*, 6–7.

6. Tornielli, *Francis Pope of a New World*, 1–18.

7. Pacwa, "Foreword," xi.

8. Allen, "Leadership of Pope Francis," 5.

9. Ibid., 15–37.

10. Francis's prophetic message of the "globalization of indifference" will be discussed in detail in Part II.

2013, during the Year of Faith.[11] Scott Hahn describes it as "the great monument of the Year of Faith declared by Pope Benedict XVI and brought to completion by Pope Francis. It is a capstone of the year, but at the same time a milestone of a long road, a road we have only begun to travel; the road of the New Evangelization."[12]

In Francis's words, his contribution to this work was meant "to supplement what Benedict XVI had written in his encyclical on faith. . . . as his brother in Christ I have taken up his fine work and added a few contributions of my own."[13] Because of their collaboration, Scott Hahn compares Francis and Benedict to Peter and Paul; they are remarkable men and model Christians and evangelizers, yet they are different from one another in style, temperament, pastoral method, and theological approach.[14]

The encyclical letter *Lumen Fidei* is composed of an introduction, four chapters, sixty paragraphs, and fifty endnotes. In the introduction, Francis describes his encyclical letter as an attempt to remind us of the importance of the great gift of faith brought to us by Christ, the light of the world, who says to us: "I have come as light into the world, that whoever believes in me may not remain in darkness" (John 12:46). Light of faith is a powerful symbol and image that philosophers like Nietzsche have attempted to ridicule as an illusion of darkness.[15] *Lumen Fidei* reminds us of the urgent need to rediscover the place of the light of faith in our Christian lives.

Popes Benedict XVI and Francis are like the biblical prophets we discussed in Part I (Amos 5:18–20; Zeph 1–3). Both men optimistically and hopefully wish that the light of faith can grow, enlighten the present, and become "a star to brighten the horizon of our journey at a time when mankind is particularly in need light."[16]

Since the inauguration of his papacy, Francis's pastoral language has reflected that of Israel's prophets in terms of judgment, repentance, hope, and joy of restoration. Francis has "startled the media (and even seasoned churchmen) with his plainspoken, spontaneous

---

11. Irwin, *Laudato Si'*, 33; Allen, Jr., *Radical Leadership of Francis*, 49.
12. Hahn, "Foreword," vii.
13. *Lumen Fidei*, no. 7
14. Hahn, "Foreword," viii.
15. Ibid., 1–3.
16. Ibid., nos. 4–6.

statements."[17] Like Israel's prophets, "he does not varnish the truth, or spin it, or gild it. He speaks it and he can deliver it bluntly and memorably."[18] Francis also demonstrates his prophetic nature by emphasizing the importance of joy in the initial pages of *Lumen Fidei*. The encyclical stresses that "Jesus Christ the Word made flesh, the Holy Spirit transforms us, lights up our way to the future and enables us joyfully to advance along that way on wings of hope."[19]

In chapter one ("We Have Believed in Love, 1Jn 4:6"), Francis recalls the importance of understanding Old Testament faith, beginning with the faith of Abraham and the promises made to him by God (Gen 13:16; 15:5; 22:7). Faith as a memorial of the future is bound up with God's hope and promises.[20] Francis wants us to appreciate that the biblical notion of faith (*ĕmûnāh*), found in several of Israel's prophets (particularly Hab 2:4), signifies "both God's fidelity and man's faith."[21] Francis devotes the remainder of chapter one to discussing Israel's faith in the book of Exodus, realized fully in Christ (John 8:56). Faith in Christ brings Christians salvation. The life of the believer, Francis insists, must be christocentric and ecclesial.[22]

In chapter two ("Unless You Believe, You Will Not Understand, Isa 7:9"), Francis appeals to Isaiah's prophecies to Ahaz, in which he stresses the unity of faith and truth while exhorting the king to serve and trust the God of truth (Isa 65:16) rather than the Assyrian, Babylonian, or Persian military might. Francis wants us to know that "we need knowledge, we need truth, because without these we cannot stand firm, we cannot move forward. Faith without truth does not save."[23] By "truth" and "knowledge," Francis does not refer to modern ways and technology; he refers to the knowledge of the truth and love, whereby one believes with the heart (Rom 10:10).[24]

For Francis, faith-knowledge also comes from hearing, *fides ex auditu* (Rom 10:17). It is a link to obedience to the covenant and

17. Hahn, "Foreword," x.
18. Hahn, "Foreword," x.
19. Francis, *Lumen Fidei*, no. 7.
20. Ibid., no. 9.
21. Ibid., no. 10.
22. Ibid., nos. 12–22.
23. Ibid., no. 24.
24. Ibid., no. 26.

the desire to see God's face. Francis goes on to discuss the interplay between faith and reason, appealing to John Paul II's *Fides et Ratio*.[25] Faith and reason are complementary. Francis also reminds us that "the light of faith in Jesus illumines the path of all those who seek God."[26] Francis is clearly very prophetic. How many times did we hear Israel's prophets—particularly Isaiah, Amos, and Zephaniah—call Israel to seek the Lord? Francis concludes this chapter by stressing the place of faith in theology, the science of faith, and a participation in God's own knowledge. Thus, "theology demands humility to be 'touched' by God. Theology also shares in the ecclesial form of faith; its light is the light of the believing subject which is the Church."[27]

In chapter three ("I Delivered to You What I Also Received, 1 Cor 15:3"), Francis discusses not only the church as the mother of our faith, but the place of the sacraments in faith transmission. He stresses faith, prayer, and dialogue, as well as the unity of the church with faith, since, according to the Blessed John Henry Newman "the unity of faith, then, is the unity of a living body."[28]

In the final chapter ("God Prepares a City for Them, Heb 11:16"), Francis ties the Old Testament prophetic stories of faith and righteousness with the Letter to the Hebrews (Heb 11:7–10). Abraham's faith journeys, Francis notes, relate to the blessings that God brought his family and descendants. From this point of view, "faith becomes a light capable of illumining all our society, in her joys and sorrows."[29] In fact, "suffering reminds us that faith's service to common good is always one of hope that ... does not disappoint" (Rom 5:5).[30]

Francis invites us to contemplate the parable of the good soil in Luke's Gospel, for blessed is she who believed (Luke 1:45). He also invites us to turn to prayer through the intercession of Mary, Mother of the Church and Mother of our faith.[31]

In sum, *Lumen Fidei* challenges us to be firm and faithful to God, as were Israel's prophets and our patriarchs and matriarchs.

25. Ibid., nos. 27–34.
26. Ibid., no. 35.
27. Ibid., no. 36.
28. Ibid., no. 49.
29. Ibid., 50–54.
30. Ibid., 57.
31. Ibid., nos. 58–60.

It challenges us to reject the evil that darkness represents and to embrace the goodness of light in Christ. It challenges us to bear suffering patiently, as did Jeremiah and Christ. It invites us to be conduits of unity and sources of dialogue and peace, as were the biblical prophets. And it calls us to do this joyfully, as stressed in Francis's Apostolic Exhortation *Evangelii Gaudium* ("The Joy of the Gospel").

Effect of Evangelii Gaudium ("The Joy of the Gospel")

Pope Francis's first Apostolic Exhortation, *Evangelii Gaudium* ("The Joy of the Gospel"), was given at St. Peter's in Rome on November 24, the solemnity of Our Lord Jesus Christ, King of the universe, during the conclusion of the Year of Faith in 2013. It consists of an extensive and impressive introduction, five chapters, 288 numbered paragraphs, and 217 endnotes. It is a core document of Francis's pontificate, charting a new path for his papacy.

As a well-trained Jesuit, Francis defines the goal of his writings in a prophetic manner. Francis wants to encourage and exhort faithful Christians throughout the world "to embark upon a new chapter of evangelization marked with joy, while pointing out new paths for the Church's journey in years to come."[32] Like Israel's prophets, who were primarily concerned with the signs of their times, Francis examines the circumstances of his time. He challenges today's dangers of covetous hearts, the feverish pursuit of pleasure, and selfish inner life with a blunted conscience. He discusses the reform of the church, her missionary endeavors, the temptations faced by pastoral leaders, the church as the people of God, homily preparation, the inclusion of the poor in society, peace and dialogue, and the spiritual motivation for mission.

In doing this, Francis, like Israel's prophets, appeals extensively to Scripture—both the Old Testament and New Testament; he also appeals to saints, church doctrine, and the Dogmatic Constitution, *Lumen Gentium*. Additionally, he seeks advice from others, especially from the Synod Fathers and his predecessors.[33] While inviting every-

---

32. Francis, *Evangelii Gaudium*, no. 1.

33. Even though Francis is not a Scripture scholar, strictly speaking, Orobator (*The Church We Want*, xvi) notes that he is a "Theologian in Chief." Therefore,

one to a new and renewed missionary spirit of evangelization, Francis speaks prophetically of "eternal newness," which breeds new ways of preaching, pastoral presence, and a transmission of faith marked by enthusiasm, joy, and vitality (Phil 4:4).[34]

In chapter one ("The Church's Missionary Transformation"), Francis stresses that evangelization grows when we are all obedient to Jesus's missionary mandate: "Go therefore and make disciples of all nations, baptizing them in the name of the Father and of the Son and of the Holy Spirit, teaching them to observe all that I have commanded you" (Matt 28:19–20).[35] For Francis, the church is that "which goes forth." If I may borrow Orobator's words, "it is not a Church that is fossilized in history."[36] Rather, it is a church on a journey—one that is aware of prophetic callings and journeys, such as those of Abraham and his descendants (Gen 12:13), Moses (Exod 3:17), and Jeremiah (Jer 1:7).

Francis then discusses the theology of church leadership. Like Israel's prophets, today's church leaders and members require obedience, courage, faith, and hope; they must be open to newness and change, and they must take joy in serving everyone—especially the poor. This requires "taking the first step, being involved and supportive, bearing fruit and rejoicing."[37] Francis also stresses the need for pastoral activities: planning, conversion, and renewal. Francis's invitation to repentance particularly echoes Israel's prophets, who constantly urged their citizens to repent from a dominant culture that did not include the poor or promote social justice. In the "prophetic" words of Francis, it is "an ecclesial renewal which cannot be deferred." This ecclesial renewal touches every aspect and component of the church—including her

---

Francis acknowledges "Scripture as the soul of theology," and impressively appeals to several scriptural passages, especially in the introductory section of his exhortation, in the following order: Matt 18:22; Isa 9:3; 12:6; 40:9; 49:13; Zech 9:9; Zeph 3:17; Sir 14:11, 14. Others are: Luke 1:28, 41, 47; John 3:29; Luke 10:21; John 15:11; 16:20, 22; John 20:20; Acts 2:46; 8:8;13:52; 8:39;16:34; Lam 3:17, 21–23, 26; 2 Cor 5:14; 1 Cor 9:16; Isa 40:31; Rev: 6; Heb 13:8; Rom 11:33; 1 John 4:19; 1 Cor 3:7; Luke 22:19; John 1:39; Heb 12:1; 13:7; 2 Tim 1:5; Luke 15:7; Phil 4:4. Francis appeals to Scripture more than forty times in the preamble of his exhortation.

34. *Evangelii Gaudium*, nos. 1–17
35. Ibid., 19.
36. Orobator, *The Church We Want*, xv.
37. *Evangelii Gaudium*, nos. 20–25.

subjects and leaders. Francis stresses that church leaders in particular must foster dialogue. They must listen to everyone "and not simply those who would tell him what he would like to hear."[38] Francis is very bold. He prefers a church that is "living in the midst of the homes of her sons and daughters."[39] He prefers a church that is "in contact with the homes and the lives of its people, and does not become a useless structure out of touch with people or a self-absorbed cluster made up of a chosen few."[40]

Francis prefers words and prophetic action. This is clear when he says, "Since I am called to put into practice what I ask of others, I too must think about a conversion of the papacy. It is my duty as the Bishop of Rome to be open to suggestions which can help make the exercise of my ministry more faithful to the meaning which Jesus Christ wished to give it and to the present needs of evangelization."[41]

Francis also stresses the need for simplicity and for relating missionary activities from the heart of the gospel, guided by faith that works through love and mercy (Gal 5:6). In this chapter, Francis exhorts that "the integrity of the Gospel message must not be deformed," and its "freshness" and "fragrance" must be maintained.[42] The missionary church must also recognize her limitations in terms of cultural changes, languages, and the diverse contexts of evangelization in the global church. She must be open to seeking new ways of evangelization, "without renouncing the truth." Francis concludes chapter one with a description of the church as a "mother with an open heart." In Francis's words, "the Church which 'goes forth' is a Church whose doors are open."[43]

In chapter two ("Amid the Crises of Communal Commitment"), the Holy Father focuses on the signs of the time. Francis mentions challenges and temptations facing the church and her pastoral workers today. This chapter is a prophetic masterpiece. With prophetic courage, Francis lists modern challenges, including

38. Ibid., no. 31.
39. Ibid., no. 28.
40. Ibid., no. 28.
41. Ibid., no. 32.
42. Ibid., nos. 38–40.
43. Ibid., nos. 43–47.

widespread disease, fear, desperation, fading joy, lack of respect for others, violence, socio-political and economic inequality, and sporadic technology.[44]

Additional challenges and temptations that Francis boldly calls us to reject include: an economy that excludes the poor, capitalism, the idolatry of money, a financial system that rules rather than serves, inequality that spawns violence, cultural challenges (indifference, relativism, fundamentalism, rationalism, secularism, consumerism, and individualism), the inculturation of faith, and challenges of urban cultures.[45]

Pastoral challenges cited by Francis include: pastoral agents' inordinate concern for the self, sterile pessimism, suspicion, habitual mistrust, broken relationships, spiritual worldliness, and warring among ourselves. Other ecclesial challenges he addresses include clericalism, the place of lay people, women, children, youth, the vocation to the priesthood, and the consecrated life.[46] For him, economic inequality kills, and "trickle-down theories" will not result in justice and inclusiveness.[47] Failing to share with the poor is equated to stealing from them—an idea defended by Amos, Isaiah, Zephaniah, Zechariah, and many of Israel's other prophets.[48] Francis calls for a change from this dominant culture and the negative behavior around us.

According to Francis, all these challenges "exist to be overcome."[49] Like every Israelite prophet who promoted ethical conduct, judgment, justice, repentance, hope, and the joy of restoration (Zeph 3:17), Francis concludes chapter two with an exhortation, saying, "let us be realists, but without losing our joy, our boldness and our hope-filled commitment."[50]

In chapter three ("The Proclamation of the Gospel"), Francis argues that "there can be no true evangelization without the explicit

---

44. Francis, *Evangelii Gaudium*, no. 52.
45. Ibid., nos. 51–75.
46. Ibid., nos. 76–108.
47. Ibid., nos. 53–54.
48. Ibid., no. 57.
49. Ibid., no. 109.
50. Ibid., no. 109.

proclamation of Jesus as Lord."[51] Francis exhorts us to be cognizant of four elements in proclaiming Jesus as the Lord: First, that the "entire people of God proclaims the Gospel." People of many faces must be encouraged to partake in evangelization, recognizing that we are all missionary disciples. There must also be room for popular piety, person-to-person encounters, recognition and use of charisma for the good of the community, and sensitivity to various cultures. Scientific, academic, and professional communities must not be ignored in the proclamation of the gospel. We must go forth with faith and courage, like the biblical prophets.[52]

Second, in preaching the homily within the liturgy, Francis exhorts pastors to be sensitive to liturgical context. Echoing John Paul II's *Apostolic Letter Dies Dominis* of May 31, 1988, Francis stresses that pastors must realize that "liturgical proclamation of the word of God, especially in the Eucharistic assembly, is not so much a time for meditation and catechesis as a dialogue between God and his people, a dialogue in which the great deeds of salvation are proclaimed and the demands of the covenant are continually restated."[53] Homilies must be approached as if a mother is having a conversation with her child, with words of love "which set hearts on fire."[54]

Third, implementation of the first two elements requires preparation, which in turn requires what Francis calls "reference for truth," "personalizing the word," "spiritual reading," "an ear to the people," and "homiletic resources."[55] All these must be geared toward positive preaching that offers hope for the present and points to the immediate future, as was the case with biblical prophets' teaching.

Fourth, we must appreciate "evangelization and the deeper understanding of the kerygma."[56] This requires ongoing formation and catechesis that leads to growth, as well as personal accompaniment in this process of growth.[57] All these must be centered on the word of God, which Benedict XVI says must "be ever more fully at the heart

---

51. Ibid., no. 110.
52. Ibid., no. 111–135.
53. See Francis, *Evangelii Gaudium*, no. 137.
54. Ibid., nos. 138–144.
55. Ibid., nos. 145–159.
56. Ibid., no. 160.
57. Ibid., nos. 163, 169.

of every ecclesial activity."[58] For Pope Francis, catechesis and preaching requires study, knowledge, and familiarity with the word of God so that all believers might be able to serve as the mouthpiece of God's word, as were his prophets.[59]

In chapter four ("The Social Dimension of Evangelization"), Francis shares his belief that "the very heart of the Gospel is life in community and engagement with others."[60] For the prophetic Francis, kerygma must have social content and bear those questions raised in the *Compendium of the Social Doctrine of the Church* and by St. Francis of Assisi and St. Teresa of Calcutta.[61] Francis goes on to stress the need for the inclusion of the poor and of migrants, the need for peace, and the need for dialogue (inter-religious and social) between faith and reason. The social dimension of the gospel is a prophetic theme that continues to unite Francis with the prophets of Israel whom we examined in Part I of this work.[62]

In chapter five ("Spirit-Filled Evangelizers"), Francis "wishes to offer some thoughts about the spirit of the new evangelization."[63] Spirit-filled new evangelizers must not only pray and work hard, but in the language of John Paul II's *Apostolic Letter Novo Millennio Inuente* of January 6, 2001, they must "reject the temptation to offer privatized and individualistic spirituality which ill accords with the demands of charity, to say nothing of the implications of the incarnation."[64] Francis recommends that Spirit-filled evangelizers have a "personal encounter with the saving love of Jesus," a recognition that we are a people of God (1 Pet 2:10), an appreciation of the "mysterious working of the risen Christ and Spirit," and the "missionary power of intercessory prayer."[65] Finally, Francis appeals to Mary, the Mother of the Church and Daughter of Zion, Star of evangelization, and Mother of the living Gospel, to pray for us.[66]

---

58. See Benedict XVI, *Verbum Domini*, no. 1; Francis, *Evangelii Gaudium*, no. 174.
59. Francis, *Evangelii Gaudium*, no. 175.
60. Ibid., 177.
61. Ibid., no. 183–184.
62. Ibid., no. 258.
63. Ibid., no. 260.
64. See Francis, *Evangelii Gaudium*, no. 262.
65. Ibid. nos. 264–281.
66. Ibid., no. 288.

The prophetic effect of this document and the challenges it poses to contemporary society cannot be over-emphasized. As we've already highlighted, this document challenges us to be joyful, to be inclusive in dealing with the poor, to be peaceful while in dialogue with one another, and to be courageous in our missionary and renewal efforts. It calls for humility, mercy, and a spirit of prayer.

The effect of this document is well captured by the multidimensional global responses to and commentaries on Francis's ministry, leadership, and writings. Some of these global responses and commentaries will be fully developed in Part III to demonstrate the prophetic effect and achievement of Francis's pontificate.

Effect of Laudato Si′ ("On Care for Our Common Home")

Another of Francis's significant and timely writings that bears the mark of significant prophetic effect is his encyclical *Laudato Si′* ("On Care for Our Common Home"). *Laudato Si'* was given in Rome at St. Peter's on May 24, the Solemnity of Pentecost, in the year 2015, the third of his pontificate. It is composed of a brilliant introduction, seven chapters, 246 paragraphs, and 172 endnotes. It is written in a very accessible style that reflects the simplicity and approachability of Francis and of St. Francis of Assisi, his inspirer, whose name he took.

Francis begins by citing the effect of the beautiful words of St. Francis of Assisi, "*Laudato Si′, mi′ Signore*" ("praise be to you, my Lord"). With this canticle, St. Francis of Assisi reminds us "that our common home is like a sister with whom we share our life and beautiful mother who opens her arm to embrace us."[67]

Francis references his predecessors and other global religious leaders (Pope John XXII, Blessed Paul VI, St. John Paul II, Benedict XVI, Ecumenical Patriarch Bartholomew, and Southern African Bishops) who have spoken about the environment and who were prophetic in their own ways. In this encyclical, Francis wants us to realize that "sister earth cries out to us because of the harm we have inflicted on her by our irresponsible use and abuse of the goods with which God has endowed her."[68] His mission is in unity with

---

67. Francis, *Laudato Si′*, no. 1.
68. Ibid, no. 2.

that of St. Francis of Assisi, the "patron saint of the environment," in whom Pope Francis finds inspiration for this encyclical. Like Israel's prophets, especially Joel, St. Francis (and his disciple, St. Bonaventure) authentically lived out care for the vulnerable and of an integral ecology; he was particularly concerned about God's creation and the "inseparable bonding that exists between nature, justice for the poor, commitment to society, and interior peace."[69] With scriptural passages, church doctrine, and Catholic social teachings, Pope Francis appeals to us to see nature as a "magnificent book in which God speaks to us and grants us a glimpse of his infinite beauty and goodness."[70] Like Israel's prophets, in this encyclical Francis further challenges us to protect our common home and be open for new dialogue while rejecting obstructionist and indifferent attitudes—nonchalant resignation to what Francis would boldly call "blind confidence in technical solutions."[71]

Apart from appealing for our response, this seven-chapter encyclical is motivational and prophetic in its tone and themes, such as:

- Intimate relationship between the poor and the fragility of the planet
- Prophetic critique of the abuse of technology
- Calls for new ways to understand markets and the economy
- Giving proper value to each creature
- Appreciation of the human dimension of ecology
- Openness for forthright and honest debate
- Renouncing a throwaway culture and the proposal of a new lifestyle
- Responsibility of international and local policies[72]

In chapter one ("What Is Happening to Our Common Home"), Francis firmly but candidly presents what he believes are scientific consensuses on climate change. He describes other threats to the environment, including threats to water, air, and biodiversity. In

---

69. Ibid., no. 10.
70. Ibid., no. 12.
71. Ibid., nos. 14–15.
72. Ibid., no. 16.

his view, environmental degradation has negatively affected human life and society at large. Francis stresses global socio-economic and political inequalities associated with environmental problems. He wants us to remember how pollution has affected us through irrational confidence in progress and human abilities, as well through what he calls "rapidification"—that is, "a more intensified pace of life and work."[73]

Francis pointedly and courageously illustrates how pollution and climate change have affected us. For example, we get sick when we breathe high levels of smoke from fuels used in cooking and heating. Transportation, industrial fumes, substances that contribute to the acidification of soil and water, fertilizers, insecticides, fungicides, herbicides, and agro-toxins also affect everyone. Additionally, we are affected by residue and industrial waste that can lead to "bioaccumulation in the organisms of the local population."[74] These problems, according to Francis, are linked to "a throwaway culture"—a culture that affects the poor and is quick to reduce things to rubbish instead of recycling them.[75]

Francis defines the climate as "a common good." By this, he means the climate not only belongs to all, but it is meant for all. The sea, the land, the trees, and the global temperature have all been affected by changes brought about by humans and by "greenhouse gases (carbon dioxide, methane, nitrogen oxides, and others)."[76] The problem is aggravated, such that Francis invites humanity to recognize the need for changes in lifestyle, production, and consumption; he invites us to alter our attitude of indifference in order to correct the human errors and protect the poor. Many of the poor, Francis notes, "live in areas particularly affected by phenomena related to warming, and their means of subsistence are largely dependent on natural reserves and exosystemic services such as agriculture, fishing and forestry."[77] Calls for changes in lifestyle and defense of the poor were typical of Israel's prophets.

---

73. Ibid., nos. 18–19.
74. Ibid., nos. 20–22.
75. Ibid., no. 22.
76. Ibid., no. 23.
77. Ibid., no. 25.

Francis also discusses what he calls "water poverty," which affects many people—especially Africans—who do not have access to safe drinking water or are experiencing droughts. Usually these droughts impede agricultural production.[78] Francis laments modern drought situations, similar to how Israel's prophets lamented droughts in biblical times (e.g., Elijah, Elisha, Haggai, Zechariah, Malachi, and Joel). He argues that "access to safe drinkable water is a basic and universal human right" that the world must defend.[79] The world must seek remedies for this lack of water by increasing funding for clean water projects and sanitary services to the poor, in addition to extending affordable educational awareness to all people.

Francis goes on to highlight the importance of biodiversity and list the threats to biodiversity. Many animals, particularly birds and insects, are extinct because of human activities, including the destruction of forests and woodlands. Their loss "entails the loss of species which may constitute extremely important resources in the future, not only for food but also for curing diseases and other uses."[80]

Francis points out that the consequences of these losses, other environmental issues, and our models of development and throwaway culture include poor transportation and urban chaos, visual pollution and noise, wasteful energy, and congested and chaotic neighborhoods. Socially, global changes affect technological innovations on employment, resulting in social exclusion which could lead to poverty, violence, drug trafficking, and loss of identity.[81]

Francis continues to show his prophetic dimension. He challenges global inequality—especially the needs of the poor and the marginalized—which we must address if we are to solve environmental degradation. Francis recalls the notion that, "whenever food is thrown out it is as if it were stolen from the table of the poor."[82] Wealthy nations must not use the debt of poor foreign countries as a means to control them or pollute their environment—particularly since wealthy countries have, in the past, offered weak responses to our environmental problems.

78. Ibid., no. 28.
79. Ibid., no. 30.
80. Ibid., no. 32.
81. Ibid., nos. 42–47.
82. Ibid., no. 50.

The combination of these problems and environmental threats have caused "sister earth, along with all the abandoned of our world, to cry out, pleading that we take another course."[83] As a possible solution, Francis suggests new leadership "capable of striking out on new paths and meeting the needs of the present (like Israel's prophets) with concern for all without prejudice toward coming generation."[84] We see in this leadership proposal Francis's prophetic dimension; he is a prophet and leader like Moses, who was called to lead God's people into the land of the Canaanites, Hittites, Amorites, Perizzites, Hivites, and Jebusites—a land flowing with milk and honey (Exod 2–3; 6:10).

In chapter two ("The Gospel of Creation"), Francis, with due respect to science, politics, and philosophy, takes the light of faith (*Lumen Fidei*) as his theological point of departure. For him, the light of faith can illumine Christians to care for the environment and for the most vulnerable of the society. As he did in his *Evangelii Gaudium*, Francis begins with the biblical account of creation and then connects it with the mystery of the universe, which Francis argues is a continuation of the revelation of God.[85] As Francis reflects on the story of creation, Adam and Eve, Cain and Abel, and Noah (Gen 1–6), he teaches us that the harmony between God, the creator, and us, the creation, was affected by humans' competing with or presuming to take the place of God by refusing to admit our limitations.

In Francis's words, "human life is grounded in three fundamental and closely intertwined relationships: with God, with our neighbor and with the earth itself . . . these three vital relationships have been broken."[86] This nature of brokenness is exacerbated by humanity's failure to recognize that Genesis 1:28 does not encourage the exploitation of nature nor its abuse and inordinate domin-

---

83. Ibid., no. 53.

84. Ibid., no. 53.

85. Scripture passages (OT & NT) cited by Francis in this chapter include, in the following order: Gen 1:31, 26; Jer 1:5; Gen 1:28, 15; 3:17—17:19; 1:28; Gen 2:15; Ps 24:1; Deut 10:14; Lev 25:23; Ps 148:5b–6; Deut 22:4, 6; Exod 23:12; Ps 104:31; Prov 3:19; Gen 4:9–11; Gen 6:13; 6:5, 6; 2:2–3; Exod 16:23; 20:10; Lev 25:1–4, 4–6, 10; Lev 19:9–10; Ps 136:6; 148:3–5; Jer 32:17, 21; Isa 40:28b–29; Rev 15:3; Ps 33:6; Wis 11:24; Matt 20:25–26; Wis 11:26; Prov 22:2; Wis 6:7; Matt 5:45; 11:25; Luke 12:6; Matt 6:26; John 4:35; Matt 13:31–32; 8:27; 11:19; 6:3; Col 1:16; John 1:1–18, 14; Col 1:19–20; 1 Cor 15:28.

86. Francis, *Laudato Si'*, no. 66.

ion. Francis calls for a proper contextual hermeneutic of faith that is sensitive also to Genesis 2:15. This text, Francis stresses, exhorts humanity to till, cultivate, plough, keep, protect, preserve, and care for the planet. These are all verbs of faith and illuminate the mutual and responsible relationship between human beings, nature, and our neighbors.[87] This mutual relationship is evident in the story of Cain and Abel in Genesis 4:9–11. Furthermore, it was through the ark of Noah that our merciful God created an everlasting path of salvation for everyone (Gen 6:6).

In this exhortative account, Francis again displays the prophetic dimension of his new leadership style and preaching by appealing to his friends, Israel's prophets Jeremiah and Deutero-Isaiah. Francis appeals to Jeremiah, who says, "Ah, Lord God! It is you who made the heavens and the earth your great power and by your outstretched arm! Nothing is too hard for you.... You brought your people Israel out of the land of Egypt with signs and wonders" (Jer 32:17, 21). Isaiah boldly acknowledges that, "The Lord is the everlasting God, the Creator of the ends of the earth. He does not faint or grow weary; his understanding is unsearchable. He gives power to the faint, and strengthens the powerless" (Isa 40:28b–29).[88]

Reflecting extensively on the mystery of the universe, Francis goes on to underscore how God's power has ordered creation and has remained the order of love (Wis 11:24). We also have a role in the universe, which is "shaped by open and intercommunicating systems" that enable everyone to participate with his or her gifts of intelligence and co-creating even through the pains of birth.[89]

But while co-creating, we must humbly view ourselves as participants who must endeavor to fit into God's plan, not our own plans, for "human beings, endowed with intelligence and love, and drawn by the fullness of Christ, are called to lead all creatures back to their Creator."[90] We must find ways to appreciate and see God in creation—in the sun, moon, stars, and trees—as did St. Francis, the patron saint of the environment. Echoes of Francis's theological and prophetic sentiments also appear in the hymn of St. Francis:

87. Ibid., nos. 67–68.
88. Ibid, no. 73.
89. Ibid., nos. 77–80.
90. Ibid., no. 83.

> Praised be you, my Lord, with all creatures
> Especially Sir Brother Sun,
> Who is day and through whom you give us light.
> And he is beautiful and radiant with great splendor; and bears a likeness of you, Most High.
> Praised be you, my Lord, through Sister Moon and the stars,
> In heaven you formed them clear and precious and beautiful.
> Praised be you, my Lord, through Brother Wind,
> And through the air, cloudy and serene, and every kind of weather
> Through whom you give sustenance to your creatures.
> Praised be you, my Lord, through Sister Water,
> Who is very useful and humble and precious chaste.
> Praised be you, my Lord, through Brother Fire,
> Through whom you light the night,
> And he is beautiful and playful and robust and strong.[91]

In addition to this canto, Francis goes on to reiterate the universal goodness of creation and nature in contrast to modern individualism and isolationism. Francis invites us to imitate Jesus's attitude or "gaze" toward creation. By this, he means the divine attitude of biblical faith—a prophetic faith of harmony and attentiveness to the beauty of creation and the divine presence therein (Matt 11:25; Luke 12:6; John 1:1–18; Col 1:19–20; 1 Cor 15:28). Francis concludes chapter two by inviting us to realize that the very flowers of the field and the birds that Jesus Christ's human eyes "contemplated and admired are now imbued with his radiant presence."[92]

In chapter three ("The Human Roots of the Ecological Crisis"), Pope Francis discusses the human origins of the ecological crisis. Francis acknowledges the benefits of science and technology, including "steam engines, railways, telegraph, electricity, automobiles, airplanes, chemical industries, modern medicine, information technology and more recently, the digital revolution, robotics, biotechnologies and nanotechnologies."[93] When well utilized, these technologies have improved humans' quality of life. They have also "given tremendous power . . . and more precisely, they have given

---

91. Ibid., no. 87. See also *Canticle of the Creatures*, 113–114.
92. Francis, *Laudato Si'*, nos. 96–110.
93. Ibid., nos. 102–103.

those with knowledge, and especially the economic resources to use them, an impressive dominance over the whole of humanity and the entire world."[94] Francis laments that "never has humanity had such power itself, yet nothing ensures that it will be used wisely, particularly when we consider how it is currently being used . . . we need to think of the nuclear bombs dropped."[95] So Francis, like Israel's prophets, calls for a change from the current situation.

Francis goes on to critique the way technological products are developed and used. Francis describes the development as an "undifferentiated and one-dimensional paradigm."[96] This paradigm exalts the concepts of the subject and tends to benefit only financiers and technological experts. Human beings and material objects are no longer friendly. Their relationship is becoming confrontational. Imposing this type of model on all has negatively affected the environment and tends to dominate economic and political life.[97]

Francis shows his prophetic characteristics by challenging technology that influences economic theories that are insensitive to the plight of the poor. Francis invites us to learn a lesson from the recent global economic crises. Modern economists seek to maximize their wealth when their market seems unable to "guarantee integral development and social inclusion."[98] For Francis, technological development alone is not an effective cure to each environmental problem, as the realities of the global system are interconnected. He therefore proposes a "liberation from dominant technocratic paradigm . . . a move forward in a bold cultural revolution."[99]

Francis observes what he calls the "crisis and effects of modern anthropocentricism." That is when human beings place themselves as the center of the world, abuse technology, and compromise the inherent dignity of the world, refusing to recognize their true place in the world by respecting the natural and moral order.[100] Francis has no doubt that the present ecological and environmental problems are a "small sign of the ethical, cultural and spiritual crisis of

---

94. Ibid., no. 104.
95. Ibid., no. 104.
96. Ibid., no. 106.
97. Ibid., no. 109.
98. Ibid., no. 109.
99. Ibid, nos. 112, 114.
100. Ibid., no. 115.

modernity."[101] The effects of anthropocentricism are practical and cultural relativism. Finally, Francis stresses the need to protect the environment and warns against new extreme biological technologies that carry out experiments using human embryos. When we do this, "we forget that the inalienable worth of a human being transcends his or her degree of development." Like Israel's prophets, Francis admonishes that technology must not be isolated from ethical conduct.[102]

In chapter 4 ("Integral Ecology"), Francis boldly argues that we are not faced with separate environmental, economic, and social problems; these problems are connected in what he calls "integral ecology." Francis recommends an integral approach in combating poverty, the exclusion of the poor, and the preservation of mother nature. In addition to preserving mother nature, Francis speaks of economic, social, and cultural ecology.[103] While addressing how the environment of our homes, workplaces, and neighborhoods might affect our quality of life, Francis speaks of the "ecology of daily life."[104] He prophetically challenges us to reflect on how poverty, overcrowded homes, lack of open spaces for sports or work, and poor housing affects the poor, as well as the principle of the common good, justice, and peace between generations.[105] Finally, Francis, like Israel's prophets, laments cultural and ethical decline and calls for ethical revival, inclusion of the poor, and intergenerational solidarity.

In chapter five ("Lines of Approach and Action"), Francis calls us to reflect on what must be done. He outlines "major paths of dialogue which can help us escape the spiral of self-destruction which currently engulfs us."[106] For him, dialogue on environmental policy must not be restricted to international communities, but must include national and local communities.[107] He challenges corruption and the exclusion of the poor in international markets. Francis says, "For poor countries, the priorities must be to eliminate extreme

---

101. Ibid., no. 119.
102. Ibid., nos. 130–136.
103. Ibid., nos. 138–146.
104. Ibid., no. 147.
105. Ibid., nos. 156–162.
106. Ibid., no. 163.
107. Ibid., nos. 164–182.

poverty and to promote the social development of their people."[108] For him, international laws must be kept, "but fragmentation and the lack of strict mechanisms of regulation, control and penalization end up undermining these efforts."[109] Of course, Francis notes the negative mindset that prevented efforts to slow the acceleration of global warming. In his view, treating global warming in isolation to social poverty is fruitless. To reduce pollution, we must take a more integral approach, including addressing issues of poverty.

Given the tendency for individuals to abuse their abilities, states must rise to the responsibility of providing security and eliminating corruption in their political capitals and institutions. Francis concedes that "the Church does not presume to settle scientific questions or to replace politics."[110] But like Israel' prophets, he encourages honest and open debate and dialogue.

Dialogue concerning politics and the economy must be for the common good and for human fulfillment. Francis writes that politics must not be "subject to the economy, nor should the economy be subject to the dictates of and efficiency-driven paradigm of technocracy."[111] So, for the prophetic Francis, there is a need to change "models of global development" by "responsibly reflecting on the meaning of the economy and its goals with an eye to correcting its malfunctions and misapplications."[112] While challenging current economic models, including the inordinate maximization of profits and mindsets that ignore the environment, Francis concludes this chapter by stressing the roles of religion and science and proposing different ways in which the two can work together.[113]

In the final chapter ("Ecological Education and Spirituality"), Francis once again demonstrates his prophetic dimension by stressing ecology and care for environment as a form of spirituality. This spirituality, he says, must be linked with care for one another—especially the poor. This form of spirituality should not applaud

---

108. Ibid., no. 172.
109. Ibid., no. 174.
110. Ibid., no. 188.
111. Ibid., no. 189.
112. Ibid., no. 194.
113. Ibid., nos. 199–201.

consumerism nor people who live a consumerist lifestyle that is self-centered and self-enclosed.[114]

Like Israel's prophets, Francis calls for changes in lifestyle, politics, the economy, and social power. By boycotting some products, consumers can help change "business as usual" in society, since "when social pressure affects their earnings, businesses clearly have to find ways to produce differently."[115]

After calling for consumers to engage in alternative social practices, Francis admonishes his readers to embrace environmental education and awareness that involves "making the leap toward the transcendent which gives ecological ethics its deepest meaning."[116] He promotes "developing an ethics of ecology, and helping people, through effective pedagogy, to grow in solidarity, responsibility and compassionate care." This forms part of Francis's ecological spirituality, which I think is prophetic as well.

In this spirituality, government and communities have roles to play in addition to individuals. They also need to experience conversions. As such, Francis invokes the rich heritage of Christian spirituality for assistance. Christianity offers a spirit of togetherness, love, and generous care. Believers look at the world not from the outside, but from within (Matt 6:3–4). Christianity calls believers to offer themselves up to God "as a living sacrifice, holy and acceptable" (Rom 12:1).[117]

At this juncture, Francis reminds readers that, throughout this encyclical, he has consistently outlined various alternatives and convictions of our faith (*Lumen Fidei*). Francis has insisted that "each creature reflects something of God and has a message to covey to us, and the security that Christ has taken unto himself this material world and now, risen, is intimately present to each being surrounding it with his affection and penetrating it with his light."[118]

Besides the light of faith, Francis recommends the light of joy and peace. Francis proposes that Christian spirituality "encourages a prophetic and contemplative lifestyle, one capable of deep

---

114. Ibid., nos. 203–204.
115. Ibid., no. 206.
116. Ibid., no. 110.
117. Ibid., nos. 220–221.
118. Ibid., no. 221.

enjoyment free of the obsession with consumption."[119] He draws readers' attention to other characteristics of Christian spirituality that "proposes a growth marked by moderation and the capacity to be happy with little."[120]

In addition, Francis teaches that love, as an important Christian virtue, must be civic, social, and political, and it must be aimed at the common good and authentic development.[121] It must be gratuitous, and "it can never be a means of repaying others for what they have done or will do for us."[122] He recommends acts of love, smiles, kind words, and gestures, which sow peace, friendship, and justice, as practiced by St. Therese of Lisieux. In other words, like Israel's prophets, Francis calls for a change from consumerism, selfishness, and indifferent attitudes toward the poor, nature, and the environment.

Francis concludes this encyclical by invoking the intercession of Mary, the Mother of God and Queen of all creation; he further stresses the role of the Trinity in relation to creation. He reminds us that the natural world, our environment, is integral to our sacramental life, as taught by St. John of the Cross. God is in charge of the universe, and the "universe unfolds in God, who fills it completely."[123] Like Israel's prophets, who faced challenges and proposed alternatives and all kinds of new models during their time, Francis concludes his encyclical by recognizing, with prayer, how joyful his thoughts could be. He recognizes all the new models and alternatives he has offered. In light of these alternatives, he recognizes the troubles and challenges facing our environment and our world today.[124]

The prophetic effect of this document cannot be overstated (this will be further explored in Part III, as will the effect of the previous documents, *Lumen Fidei* and *Evangelli Gaudium*). Many people from different parts of the globe have commented on and preached about *Laudato Si'*. Scientists and environmentalists have also reflected on it. It is used, read, and discussed in parishes, schools, seminaries, universities, and both Catholic and non-Catholic institutions. Many people have learned from Francis's *Laudato Si'* how

119. Ibid., no. 222.
120. Ibid., no. 222.
121. Ibid., no. 231.
122. Ibid., no. 228.
123. Ibid., nos. 233–242.
124. Ibid., no. 246.

to be bold, candid, simple, collegial, integral, appreciative of nature, ecumenically prophetic, and open to changes guided by faith and a deep prophetic spirituality rooted in Scripture.

In the review of *Amoris Laetitia* ("The Joy of Love") that follows, we will continue to learn about Francis's teachings on the joy and challenges of family life and spirituality.

Effect of Amoris Laetitia ("The Joy of Love")

Amoris Laetitia ("The Joy of Love") is Pope Francis's second Apostolic Exhortation. It was given in Rome, at St. Peter's, during the Extraordinary Jubilee of Mercy on March 19, 2016. It has a well-written introduction, nine chapters, and 325 numbered paragraphs. Francis begins by reminding everyone that "the joy of love experienced by families is also the joy of the Church."[125] This exhortation came after many years of discussion, examination, and input from bishops, lay people, and experts within the church.

In chapter one ("In the Light of the Word"), Francis appeals to biblical stories about families, births, and love in a refreshing and prophetic way.[126] His goal is to evoke a conscious change and to drive home his message on family, love, joy, sorrows, and values. By frequently invoking Scripture in this chapter, Francis mimics Israel's prophets, including Christ, who commonly appealed to Scripture in their prophecies and exhortations. Francis particularly draws from the prophet Hosea to demonstrate the importance of

---

125. Francis, *Amoris Laetitia*, no. 1.

126. Some of the scriptural passages cited by Francis, though not systematically, include: Gen 4; Rev 21:2, 9; Matt 7:24–27; Ps 128:1–6; Matt 19:4; Gen 2:24; 1:27, 28; 9:7; 17:2–5, 16; 23:3; 35:11; 48:3–4; 4:17–22, 25–26; 5; 10; 11:10–32; 25:1–4, 12–17, 19–26; 36; Eph 5:21–33; Gen 2:18, 20; Sir 36:24; 2:16; 6:3; Matt 19:5; Gen 2:24; Ps 128:3; 1 Pet 2:5; Ps 128; 127:1, 3–5; 1 Cor 16:19; Rom 16:5; Col 4:15; Phil 2; Rev 3:20; Ps 128, 4–5; Exod 12:26–27; Deut 6:20–25; Ps 78:3–6; Exod 13:14; Ps 148:12; Prov 3:11–12; 6:2–22; 13:1; 22:15; 23:13–14; 29:17; Exod 20:12; Mark 7:11–13; Sir 3:3–4; Luke 2:51; Matt 10:34–37; Luke 9:59–62; 2:48–50; 8:21; Matt 18:3–4; 19:3–9; Gen 3:16; Job 19:13–14, 17; Mark 1:30–31; 5:22–24, 35–43; John 11:1–44; Luke 7:11–15; Mark 9:17–27; Matt 9:9–13; Luke 19:1–10; 7:36–50; 15:11–32; Matt 21:28–31; Mark 12:1–9; John 2:1–10; Matt 22:1–10; Luke 15:8–10; Rev 21:4; Gen 2:15; Ps 127:2; 128:5–6; 31:10–31; Acts 18:3; 1 Cor 4:12; 9:12; 2 Thess 3:10; 1 Thess 4:11; Matt 20:1–16; Gen 3:17–19; 1 Kgs 21; Luke 12:13; 16:1–31; Matt 22:39; John 13:34; 15:13; 8:1–11; Ps 131; Exod 4:22; Isa 49:15; Ps 27:10; 131:2; Hos 11:1, 3–4; Matt 2:11; Luke 2:19, 51.

love, tenderness, and mercy in family relationships: "When Israel was a child, I loved him . . . I took them up in my arms . . . I led them with cords of compassion, with the bands of love, and I became to them as one who eases the yoke on their jaws, and I bent down to them and fed them" (Hos 11:1, 3–4).[127] He concludes this chapter by reiterating that "every family should look to the icon of the Holy Family of Nazareth."[128]

In chapter two ("The Experiences and Challenges of Families"), Francis examines the facts and realities of families—or in his words, the "actual situation of families." His purpose for doing so is to "keep firmly grounded in reality."[129] Throughout this chapter, Francis argues that even though families come to enjoy greater freedom "through an equitable distribution of duties, responsibilities and tasks,"[130] they need more support from the social structure so that they may have "greater emphasis on personal communication between the spouses."[131] He calls for changes in the church and state in order to respond to the challenges families face today. In his words, "anthropological and cultural changes in our times influence all aspects of life and call for an analytic and diversified approach."[132]

Francis calls on everyone to do a self-examination, since "we have been called to form consciences, not to replace them.[133] He observes that "the fear of loneliness and the desire for stability and fidelity exist side by side with a growing fear of entrapment in a relationship that could hamper the achievements of one's personal goals."[134] Francis notes that the church has done a lot to support families by offering guidance and counseling when necessary, helping families overcome conflict, and offering aid in raising children. In the church, many are also touched "by the power of grace experienced in sacramental

---

127. Ibid., no. 28.
128. Ibid., no. 30.
129. Ibid., no. 6.
130. Ibid., no. 32.
131. Ibid., no. 32.
132. Ibid., no. 32.
133. Ibid., no. 37.
134. Ibid., no. 34.

reconciliation and in the Eucharist, grace that helps them face the challenges of marriage and the family."¹³⁵

Francis notes the importance of traditional family values in parts of Africa that have resisted secularism. He further points out the common view that the church has not done enough to imitate Jesus, who would set forth demanding ideals yet show compassion and closeness to the weak, such as the Samaritan woman recorded in the Gospels. He also calls on everyone to engage in effective relationships and reject narcissism, since narcissism makes people incapable of looking beyond themselves. When it comes to relationships, he recommends patience, among many other things. The church needs to find a pastoral language appealing to the heart of new generations so that they can take up the challenges of marriage and family life.¹³⁶

Francis is clearly and truly prophetic in his approach. This is true "since prophetic ministry consists of offering an alternative perception of reality and in letting people see their own history in the light of God's freedom and his will for justice."¹³⁷ Francis continues to show his prophetic characteristics in this exhortation by drawing readers' attention to the Synod Fathers' observation that "one symptom of the great poverty of contemporary culture is loneliness, arising from the absence of God in a person's life and the fragility of relationship."¹³⁸ Francis also challenges and promotes changes regarding additional problems, including:

- Powerlessness in the face of economic hardship
- Indifference of the state, which has the capacity to pass laws and create job opportunities for families
- Lack of housing
- Economic constraints
- Childbearing outside of wedlock
- Migration issues
- Organ trafficking

---

135. Ibid., no. 38.
136. Ibid., nos. 39–41.
137. Brueggemann, *Prophetic Imagination*, 116–117.
138. Francis, *Amoris Laetitia*, no. 43.

- Prostitution
- Inattention to people or families with special needs
- Lack of respect for the elderly, single parents, and the unborn[139]
- Addiction to television
- Drug abuse
- Alcoholism
- Gambling
- Single parenthood
- Polygamy

Additionally, Francis calls attention to the challenges surrounding the conception of gender that does not respect humanity as created by God. Finally, Pope Francis prays that families may live in love with hope and joy, even though they are not perfect.[140]

In chapter three ("Looking to Jesus: The Vocation of the Family"), Francis reviews family life in light of Jesus's teachings and the teachings of the church, especially Vatican II. He quotes several New Testament texts and appeals to church documents and the writings of his predecessors.[141] The family, Francis insists, must be christocentric, cherishing love, truth, patience, and tenderness.[142] He points to the scriptural foundation of the Trinity, which reflects the structure of the family as stressed during the liturgy of the sacrament of matrimony. The family, Francis stresses, "is the image of God, who is a communion of persons."[143] This image is found in marriage, which is "not a social convention, an empty ritual or merely the outward sign of commitment. The sacrament is a gift given for the sanctification and salvation of the spouses."[144] Their "mutual belonging" reflects the relationship between Christ and the church.

139. Ibid., nos. 42–49.
140. Ibid., nos. 50–57.
141. These include *Gaudium et Spes*, nos. 47–49; *Lumen Gentium*, no. 11; *Humanae Vitae* of Paul VI as well as his *Evangelii Nuntiandi*; John Paul II's *Letter to Families Graitssimam Sane* and *Familiaris Consortio*. Others are *Deus Caritas Est* of Benedict XVI as well as his Encyclical *Caritas in Veritate*, especially no. 44.
142. *Amoris Laetitia*, nos. 58–66.
143. Ibid., no. 71.
144. Ibid., no. 71–72.

Francis points out what he calls "Seeds of the Word and Imperfect Situations."[145] The gospel of the family should nourish seeds that are still growing. Matrimony helps families to grow in the mysteries of Christ. Appreciating the mystery of Christ can also help pastors to handle imperfect situations, such as "faithful who are living together, or married civilly, or are divorced and remarried."[146] Finally, he addresses the transmission of life and childrearing as well as the relationship between the family and the church.[147] For him, a child deserves to be born of marital love—the intimate partnership of life and love.[148] He describes the church as a "family of families constantly enriched by the lives of those domestic churches."[149]

In chapter four ("Love in Marriage"), Francis emphasizes the importance of love in Christian marriage. He says, "For we cannot encourage a path of fidelity and mutual self-giving without encouraging the growth, strengthening and deepening of conjugal and family love."[150] Francis appeals to 1 Corinthians 13:2–7, especially those verses that speak of love as patient, as service to others, and as not jealous, not boastful, not rude, or resentful. "Love forgives," "love rejoices with others," "love bears all things," love believes all things, love hopes for all things, and love endures all things.[151]

Francis draws from Ignatius of Loyola, who insists that "love is shown more by deeds than by words."[152] He also quotes Dr. Martin Luther King Jr.'s "Sermon Delivered at Dexter Avenue Baptist Church, Montgomery, Alabama, on 17 November, 1957," which states that love endures and resists every negative current. In that sermon, Dr. Martin Luther King Jr said:

> The person who hates you most has some good in him; even the nation that hates you has some good in it; even the race that hates you most has some good in it. And when you come to the point that you look in the face of every man and see deep

---

145. Ibid., no. 76.
146. Ibid., nos. 78–79.
147. Ibid., nos. 80–87.
148. Ibid., no. 80.
149. Ibid., no. 87.
150. Francis, *Amoris Laetitia*, no. 89.
151. Ibid., 100–118.
152. Ibid., no. 94.

> down within what religion calls "the image of God," you begin to love him in spite of [everything]. No matter what he does, you see God's image there. There is an element of goodness that he can never sluff off. . . . . Another way that you love your enemy is this: when the opportunity presents itself for you to defeat your enemy, that is the time which you must not do it. . . . When you rise to the level of love, of its great beauty and power, you must seek only to defeat evil systems. Individuals who happen to be caught up in that system, you love, but you seek to defeat the system. . . . Hate for hate only intensifies the existence of hate and evil in the universe. If I hit you and you hit me, and I hit you back and you hit me back, and so on, you see, that goes on ad infinitum. It just never ends. Somewhere somebody must have a little sense, and that's the strong person. The strong person is the person who can cut off the chain of hate, the chain of evil. . . . Somebody must have religion enough and morality enough to cut it off and inject within the very structure of the universe that strong and powerful element of love.[153]

In addition to appealing to Ignatius of Loyola and Dr. Martin Luther King Jr., Francis briefly quotes Thomas Aquinas, who teaches that conjugal love is the "greatest form of friendship."[154] In doing this, Francis prophetically cites the prophet Malachi, who says, "The Lord was witness to the covenant between you and wife of your youth, to whom you have been faithless, though she is your companion and your wife by covenant. . . . Let none be faithless to the wife of his youth. For I hate divorce, says the Lord" (Mal 2:14–16). For him, a love that is weak cannot sustain a great commitment. The friendship of marriage must be marked with passion for union, joy, beauty, and charity.[155]

Francis spends the rest of the chapter addressing the youth about the meaning of marital love.[156] He encourages dialogue in all families.[157] He discourages violence, arrogance, and domination in a relationship and reminds contemporary families of the proper reading of Ephesian 5:22, which asks wives to be subject to their husbands. For Francis, cultural context must be kept in mind in reading

---

153. Ibid., no. 118.
154. Ibid., no. 123.
155. Ibid., nos. 124–127.
156. Ibid., nos. 131–135.
157. Ibid., no. 136–141.

this text. He invites everyone to listen to St. John Paul II, who taught us that "love excludes every kind of subjection whereby the wife might become servant or a slave of the husband.... The community or unity which they should establish through marriage is constituted by a reciprocal donation of self, which is also a mutual subjection."[158] For Francis, even when couples are aging, with prayer and the grace of the Holy Spirit, their love for each other will never fade.[159]

In chapter five ("Love Made Fruitful"), Francis stresses the importance of the fruit of marriage, which includes welcoming children. He says, "Love always gives life."[160] Francis again cites John Paul II's 1991 Apostolic Exhortation *Familiaris Consortio*: "conjugal love does not end with the couple ... The couple, in giving themselves to one another, give not just themselves but also the reality of children, who are a living reflection of their love, a permanent sign of their conjugal unity and a living and inseparable synthesis of their being a father and a mother."[161]

For Francis, a parent's love for children is like God's love for Israel (Hos 11:1–4), as he stressed in chapter one of this encyclical. In fact, it is a "reflection of the primacy of the love of God, who always takes the initiative, for children 'are loved before having done anything to deserve it.' "[162] Parents should welcome children even in large numbers, for they are a joy to the church. However, this must be done responsibly, as St. John Paul II taught.[163] Francis goes on to speak of pregnancy, which can be difficult for mothers. He therefore speaks of the love and roles of mothers, fathers, sons, and daughters; he further speaks of feminism that does not "negate motherhood," adoption with love, and the role of grandparents.[164]

In chapter six ("Some Pastoral Perspectives"), Pope Francis invites everyone—especially bishops, priests, and pastoral agents in the church—to "reflect on some more significant pastoral challenges"

---

158. See Francis, *Amoris Laetitia*, no. 156.
159. Francis, *Amoris Laetitia*, no. 164.
160. Ibid., no. 165.
161. Ibid., no. 165.
162. *Amoris Laetitia*, no. 166.
163. Ibid., no. 167.
164. Ibid, nos.168–193.

facing families today.¹⁶⁵ His intention is not to do this in detail, for "different communities will have to devise more practical and effective initiatives that respect both the Church's teaching and local problems and needs."¹⁶⁶

Francis emphasizes preaching the gospel of the family, preparing engaged couples for marriage, preparing for the celebration, accompanying and assisting the first year of married life, and providing resources needed even in the midst of challenges and crises—including marriage between Catholics and non-Catholics, old age, breakdowns, divorce, and even death of a loved one.¹⁶⁷ As a seminary professor, I thought it was interesting to hear the Holy Father, a one-time seminary professor and rector, stress the need for seminarians to "receive a more extensive interdisciplinary, and not merely doctrinal, formation in the areas of engagement and marriage."¹⁶⁸ Francis also notes that the training of the seminarians "does not always allow them to explore their own psychological and affective background and experiences. Some come from troubled families, with absent parents and lack of emotional stability. There is need to ensure that formation process can enable them to attain the maturity and psychological balance needed for their future ministry."¹⁶⁹

In chapter seven ("Towards a Better Education of Children"), Pope Francis discusses the importance of education and the moral development of children. Parents, he admonishes, "should take up this essential role and carry it out consciously, enthusiastically, reasonably and appropriately."¹⁷⁰ Parents need to know where their children are, what type of electronic devices they are using, and in what ways they are engaging with technology. In other words, Francis calls for vigilance in raising kids, but not "obsession."¹⁷¹ By this, he means parents should help their kids grow in freedom and maturity while ensuring ethical education for their children.¹⁷² He stresses the place

---

165. Ibid., no. 199.
166. Ibid., no. 199.
167. Ibid., nos. 167–253.
168. Ibid, no. 203.
169. *Amoris Laetitia*, no. 203.
170. Ibid., no. 259.
171. Ibid., nos. 260–261.
172. Ibid., nos. 263–265.

of discipline in raising kids, which requires patience and recognition that family is the "first school of human values, where we learn the wise use of freedom."[173]

Following the viewpoints of Vatican II, Pope Francis recommends "a positive and prudent sex education."[174] Sex education must be carefully conducted in a manner sensitive to the times in which we live, "when sexuality tends to be trivialized and impoverished."[175] In educating their children on these matters, parents aim at passing on the faith:

> the family is thus an agent of pastoral activity through its explicit proclamation of the Gospel and its legacy of varied forms of witness, namely solidarity with the poor, openness to a diversity of people, the protection of creation, moral and material solidarity with other families, including those most in need, commitment to the promotion of the common good and the transformation of unjust social structures.[176]

In chapter eight ("Accompanying, Discerning and Integrating Weakness"), Pope Francis courageously discusses divorce. This is a sensitive topic for anyone in the church, but especially priests, moral theologians, and divorced Catholics. Particularly sensitive is the question of whether there should be changes in the church's practices. Francis begins by citing the Synod Fathers, who said, "although the Church realizes that any breach of the marriage bond 'is against the will of God,' she is also 'conscious of the frailty of many of her children.' "[177] Rather than hurry to judgment, Francis recommends reflection and discernment, and he emphasizes the role of individual conscience. He recognizes that the role of the church "is often like that of a field hospital"[178]—that is, he wants the church to turn with love to those who share in her life in an incomplete manner. The grace of God works also in the lives of these people. Francis appeals to John Paul II, who often speaks of the "law of gradualness"—that is, a situation by which each human

---

173. Ibid., no. 274.
174. Ibid., no. 280.
175. Ibid., 280.
176. *Amoris Laetitia*, nos. 281–290.
177. Ibid., no. 291.
178. Ibid., no. 291.

being "advances gradually with the progressive integration of the gifts of God and the demands of God's infinite and absolute love in his or her entire personal and social life."[179] The church should help those in "irregular situations" by pouring out the balm of God's mercy on those who ask for it with a sincere heart. Quoting St. Thomas Aquinas and the Catechism of the Church, Francis stresses pastoral discernment, while taking into account "a person's properly formed conscience."[180] For him love covers a multitude of sins (1 Pet 4:8), and couples should be helped by the church in moments of difficulty.[181] Francis proposes a pastoral discernment of divine mercy, since "mercy is not only the working of the Father, it becomes a criterion for knowing who his true children are."[182]

In chapter nine ("The Spirituality of Marriage and the Family"), Francis discusses the "spirituality born of family life" and its characteristics.[183] This must be a spirituality of supernatural communion, whereby God has a place in our families. This spirituality requires family prayers and the Eucharist, in light of Easter, which is "a special way of expressing and strengthening this paschal faith."[184] This spirituality also requires exclusive and free love, care, consolation, incentive, and mercy, since "no family drops down from heaven perfectly formed; families need constantly to grow and mature in the ability to love."[185]

Effect of *Gaudete et Exsultate* ("Rejoice and Be Glad")

Pope Francis' third Apostolic Exhortation, *Gaudete et Exsultate* ("Rejoice and Be Glad"), is biblical and prophetic in title (Gen 17:1). It is drawn from Matthew 5:12, the Sermon on the Mount delivered by the new Moses, Christ (Matt 1—7:27). *Gaudete et Exsultate* ("Rejoice and Be Glad") was delivered in Rome on March 19, 2018, the Solemnity of St. Joseph. As the subtitle implies, the work focuses "on

---

179. Ibid. no. 295.
180. Ibid., nos. 301–302.
181. Ibid, no. 306.
182. Ibid., nos. 310–312.
183. Ibid., no. 313.
184. Ibid., nos. 317–318.
185. Ibid., nos. 321–325.

the call to holiness in today's world," a subject that was equally dear to the hearts of Israel's prophets in all periods (pre-exilic, exilic, and post-exilic). Francis's five-chapter work, composed of 177 concise paragraphs, is not "a treatise on holiness, containing definitions and distinctions helpful for understanding this important subject,"[186] but a prophetic reproposal of the call to holiness "in a practical way for our time, with all its risks, challenges and opportunities."[187]

In chapter one ("The Call to Holiness"), which is rooted in Scripture as well as in the lives of the saints, the "great cloud of witnesses" (Heb 12:1),[188] Francis stresses Vatican II's theme of the universal call to the holy life. He acknowledges "the saints next door"[189] and the humble parents who raise their children with love and work hard to support the families that is "the middle class of holiness."[190] In addition to this "middle class of holiness," he exhorts everyone, irrespective of culture and continent, to "be spurred on by the signs of holiness that the Lord shows us through the humblest members of that people which 'shares also in Christ's prophetic office, spreading abroad a living witness to him, especially by means of a life of faith and charity.' "[191] Our identification with Christ's mission, which sanctifies, includes not only love, justice, and universal peace, but also "an ecological spirituality" and "a spirituality of family life" stressed in his earlier documents (*Laudato Si'* and *Amoris Laetitia*).[192] For Francis, we should not be afraid, since holiness in no way makes us less human. Rather, it is an encounter between our weaknesses and the power of God's grace, "for in the words of León Bloy, when all is said and done, 'the only great tragedy in life, is not to become a saint.' "[193]

In chapter two ("Two Subtle Enemies of Holiness"), Francis identifies Gnosticism and Pelagianism as two heresies of early Christian times that continue to plague and threaten holiness of life in our time. The former presumes "a purely subjective faith whose only

---

186. Francis, *Gaudete et Exsultate*, no. 2.
187. Ibid., no. 2.
188. Ibid., no. 3.
189. Ibid., no. 6.
190. Ibid., no. 7.
191. Ibid., no. 8.
192. Ibid., nos. 25–28.
193. Ibid., nos. 32–34.

interest is a certain experience or a set of ideas and bits of information which are meant to console and enlighten, but which ultimately keep one imprisoned in his or her own thoughts and feelings."[194] Those who yield to the later "ultimately trust only in their own powers and feel superior to others because they observe certain rules or remain intransigently faithful to a particular Catholic style."[195] In other words, in this chapter he generally exhorts against:

- an intellect without God
- doctrine without mystery
- unlimited reason
- a will lacking humility
- an often overlooked Church teaching on God's grace
- obsession with law
- forgetting that there is a hierarchy of virtues[196]

In chapter three ("In the Light of the Master"), Francis proceeds to teach prophetically about the Gospel Beatitudes (Matt 5:3-12; Luke 6:20-23). He addresses these as a positive model of holiness presented "in the light of the Master" rather than as vague religious ideology. For Francis, in light of the master, holiness means:

- being poor of heart
- reacting with meekness and humility
- knowing how to mourn with others
- hungering and thirsting for righteousness
- seeing and acting with mercy
- keeping a heart free from all that tarnishes love
- sowing peace all around us
- accepting daily the path of the Gospel, even though it may cause us problems[197]

---

194. Ibid., no. 36.
195. Ibid., no. 49.
196. Ibid., nos. 36–62.
197. Ibid., nos. 63–94.

Francis concludes chapter three by reminding everyone of "the great criterion" by which we will be judged worthy or unworthy of the Kingdom of Heaven. This great criterion will include faithfulness to the master, Jesus, and respect for the dignity of every human, especially the poor, for "I was hungry and you gave me food, I was thirsty and you gave me drink, I was a stranger and you welcomed me, I was naked and you clothed me, I was sick and you took care of me, I was in prison and you visited me" (Matt 25:35–36). He also stresses that our worship and prayer life must be authentic since "the powerful witness of the saints is revealed in their lives, shaped by the Beatitudes and the criterion of the final judgment."[198]

In chapter four ("Signs of Holiness in Today's World"), Francis describes some characteristics of holiness in this world, which include:

- patience and meekness
- joy and a sense of humor
- boldness and passion
- community life[199]

In fact, for him, "The prayerful reading of God's word, which is 'sweeter than honey' (*Ps* 119:103) yet a 'two-edged sword' (Heb 4:12), enables us to pause and listen to the voice of the Master," Jesus. Encountering Jesus in Scripture also leads us to the Eucharist, "where the written word attains its greatest efficacy."[200]

In chapter five ("Spiritual Combat, Vigilance and Discernment"), Francis pastorally exhorts Christians to not take the devil for granted by dismissing Satan as a myth. Rather, we should abide by God's word by being alert and trustful in God, who "delivers us from evil," which we must stand against (Eph 6:11).[201] In the final section, while warning us against spiritual corruption, Francis stresses the importance of discernment. According to Francis, this is not about "discovering what more we can get out of this life, but about recognizing how we

---

198. Ibid., nos. 95–109.
199. Ibid., nos. 112–139.
200. Ibid., nos. 140–57.
201. Ibid., nos. 158–161.

can better accomplish the mission entrusted to us at our baptism. This entails a readiness to make sacrifices, even to sacrifice everything."[202]

Finally, Francis concludes his third Apostolic Exhortation, *Gaudete et Exsultate* ("Rejoice and Be Glad"), which is dedicated to holiness, its enemies, models, signs, and the spiritual life, by praying that his reflections will be "crowned by Mary," who lived the Beatitudes, who rejoiced in the presence of the Lord, and who treasured everything in her heart. Mary, Francis affirms, is that saint who teaches us the way of holiness.

Effect of Other Letters, Messages, and Visits

Francis's prophetic effects are not only felt through his challenging yet simple homilies, gestures, visits, apostolic exhortations, and encyclicals, but also through his letters and New Year messages, which are usually read in churches and shared in Catholic schools, seminaries, colleges, and universities all over the world. Some of these letters and messages include:

- "Fraternity, the Foundation and Pathway to Peace" (2014)
- "Apostolic Letter to Consecrated People" (2014)
- "No Longer Slaves, but Brothers and Sisters" (2015)
- "Overcome Indifference and Win Peace" (2016)
- "Apostolic Letter *Misericordia et Misera*" (2016)/"Letter According to Which an Indulgence is Granted" (2015)
- Francis's "Letter to the Bishops of Nigeria" (2015)
- "Nonviolence as a Style of Politics for Peace" (2017)
- "Migrants and Refugees: Men and Women in Search of Peace" (2018)

i. "Fraternity, the Foundation and Pathway to Peace"

In his January 1, 2014 message celebrating the World Day of Peace, "Fraternity, the Foundation and Pathway to Peace," Francis courageously and prophetically offers everyone his best wishes for a life

202. Ibid., nos. 174–78.

filled with joy and hope. He argues for the importance of global fraternity, which we share as an essential human quality among relational beings. He believes that the sooner we become aware of our relatedness, the sooner we will be able to look upon and treat each other as true sisters or brothers. For him, the family is a school of fraternity. In line with Benedict XVI, Francis warns that globalization could make us neighbors, but not brothers.[203]

Drawing from the story of Cain and Abel, which asks the pointed question, "Where is your brother?" (Gen 4:9), Francis discusses at length the importance of being our brother's keeper.[204] He also cites Matthew's Gospel, which says, "and you will all be brothers" (Matt 23:8).[205] While appealing to the work of his predecessors, such as Paul VI's *Populorum Progressio* and John Paul II's *Caritas in Veritate*, he stresses that fraternity is not only the foundation and pathway to peace, but a prerequisite for fighting poverty.[206] Francis insists that the challenges the economy poses could be an avenue for rediscovering fraternity:

> The grave financial and economic crises of the present time—which find their origin in the progressive distancing of man from God and from his neighbors, in the greedy pursuit of material goods on the one hand, and in the impoverishment of interpersonal and community relations on the other—have pushed man to seek satisfaction, happiness and security in consumption and earnings out of all proportion to the principles of a sound economy.[207]

Current economic crises can lead us to rethink models of economic development as well as provide us opportunities to learn prudence, temperance, justice, and strength.[208] Francis also notes that fraternity can extinguish war. He warns that corruption and

---

203. Francis, "Fraternity," no. 1.
204. Ibid., no. 2.
205. Ibid., no. 3.
206. Ibid., nos. 4–6.
207. Ibid., no. 6.
208. Ibid., no.6.

organized crime threaten fraternity.²⁰⁹ Finally, he says that fraternity needs to be discovered, loved, experienced, proclaimed, and witnessed.

ii. "Apostolic Letter to Consecrated People"

On November 21, 2014, the date of the Feast of the Presentation of the Blessed Virgin Mary, Pope Francis sent an Apostolic Letter to all Consecrated People, in line with the Post-Synodal Exhortation of John Paul II, *Vita Consecrata*. This tripartite document was very timely, and its language is prophetic in nature. Part I discusses the aims of the Year of Consecrated Life. Part II takes up the expectations for the Year of Consecrated Life, while Part III discusses the horizons of the Year of Consecrated Life.

In Part I, Francis explains the three aims of the Year of Consecrated Life, which include "looking to the past with gratitude, living the present with passion, and embracing the future with hope."²¹⁰ In Part II, he addresses the expectations for the Year of Consecrated Life and recalls the saying, "where there are religious, there is joy." He hereby reminds us that we are all called to show that "God is able to fill our hearts to the brim with happiness; that we need not seek our happiness elsewhere; that the authentic fraternity found in our communities increases our joy."²¹¹ For Francis, the joy of the religious rather than proselytization will attract young people to join religious orders. Francis believes that "we can inspire others through witness so that one grows together in communicating. But the worst thing is religious proselytism, which paralyzes: 'I am talking with you in order to persuade you' No. Each person dialogues, starting with his and her own identity. The church grows by attraction, not proselytizing."²¹²

Francis calls on the religious "to wake up the world," since the distinctive sign of consecrated life is prophecy. He believes that "radical evangelical living is not only for religious: it is demanded of everyone.

---

209. Ibid., nos. 7–9.
210. Francis, "Consecrated People," Part I, nos. 1–3.
211. Ibid., Part II, no. 1.
212. See Glatz ("In Latest Interview, Pope Francis") for details of Francis's views on proselytization, which he strongly discourages consecrated people from doing.

But, religious follow the Lord in a special way, in a prophetic way."[213] For Francis, this is the priority that is needed now: "to be prophets who witness to how Jesus lived on this earth . . . a religious must never abandon prophecy."[214] He explains:

> Prophets receive from God the ability to scrutinize the times in which they live and to interpret events: they are like sentinels who keep watch in the night and sense the coming of the dawn (cf. Is 21:11–12). Prophets know God and they know the men and women who are their brothers and sisters. They can discern and denounce the evil of sin and injustice. Because they are free, they are beholden to God alone, and they have no interest other than God. Prophets tend to be on the side of the poor and the powerless, for they know that God himself is on their side.[215]

In line with Brueggemann, who sees prophets as those who search for alternatives, Francis reminds religious people that "rather than living in some utopia, you will find ways to create 'alternate spaces,' where the gospel approach of self-giving, fraternity, embracing differences, and love for one another can thrive."[216] Even when prophetic ministry seems demanding, frustrating, wearisome, or fruitless—as it seemed to Elijah, Jonah, and many of Israel's prophets—religious people today should remember that they are never alone. The same God who was with Jeremiah encourages us today, saying, "Be not afraid of them, for I am with you to deliver you" (Jer 1:8).[217]

In Part III, aside from calling the religious to pursue prophetic behavior and seek alternative ways of bearing witness to the gospel in place of proselytization, Francis invites the laity to live this Year of Consecrated Life "as a grace which can make you more aware of the gift you yourselves have received" from God.[218] Francis stresses the importance of the Year of Consecrated Life for the entire church. He rhetorically asks: "What would the Church be without Saint Benedict and Saint Basil, without Saint Augustine and Saint Bernard, without Saint Francis and Saint Dominic, Saint Ignatius of Loyola

---

213. Ibid., no. 2.
214. Ibid., no. 2.
215. Ibid., no. 2.
216. Ibid., no. 2.
217. Ibid., no. 2.
218. Francis, "Consecrated People," Part III, no. 1.

and Saint Teresa of Avila, Saint Angelica Merici and Saint Vincente de Paul... Saint John Bosco and Blessed Teresa of Calcutta."[219]

In his usual and cherished ecumenical style, Francis addresses consecrated men and women as well as members of fraternities, monasticisms, and church communities outside the Catholic tradition.[220] Finally, he addresses his brother bishops. He prays that this year may be an opportunity for them to accept Institutes of Consecrated Life "readily and joyfully, as a spiritual capital which contributes to the good of the whole body of Christ (cf. *Lumen Gentium*, 43)."[221] He also urges pastors to promote within their communities the different charisms, whether long-standing or recent.

iii. "No Longer Slaves, but Brothers and Sisters"

In January 1, 2015, Francis delivered the New Year message "No Longer Slaves, but Brothers and Sisters." Its tone, style, and content are prophetic and timely. In it, Francis builds on his 2014 message on fraternity. In so doing, he is moved by what he calls "the growing scourge of man's exploitation by man [which] have gravely damaged the life of communion and our calling to forge interpersonal relations."[222] In this message, Francis addresses "the abominable phenomenon, which leads to contempt for the fundamental right of others and to the suppression of their freedom and dignity."[223] Scripturally, Francis draws from St. Paul's Letter to Philemon, in which Paul asks his co-workers to welcome Onesimus, who was no longer a slave, but a Christian. Francis cites the Old Testament story of creation in Genesis 1:27–28, where God made male and female, Adam and Eve; he further cites the challenges of old creation till the new creation in Christ (cf. Gal 3:28c).[224]

Francis then goes on to discuss the many faces of slavery yesterday and today. Even though slavery has been formally abolished, and the international community adopted numerous agreements,

---

219. Ibid., no. 2.
220. Ibid., nos. 3–4.
221. Ibid., no. 5.
222. Francis, "No Longer Slaves," no. 1.
223. Ibid., no. 1.
224. Ibid., no. 2; see also Uzukwu (*Unity of Male and Female in Jesus Christ*) for additional reflection on these texts (Gen 1:27–28; Gal 3:28c).

millions of people today are deprived of freedom and are forced to live in conditions akin to slavery. Francis notes that many children, woman, and men of all ages are subjugated to modern slavery in domestic and agricultural workplaces and industries. What about the many migrants who face hunger? He also points to those who are forced into prostitution as well as those who are made objects of trafficking for the sale of organs, for recruitment as soldiers, for begging, for illegal activities such as the production and sale of narcotics, or for disguised forms of cross-border adoption; he also cites those who are kidnapped and held for terrorist groups.[225]

A deeper cause of slavery is the notion of the human person that allows that person to be treated as an object—a rejection of another person's humanity. Other root causes include poverty, underdevelopment, exclusion, lack of education, and lack of employment opportunities. Francis also identifies corruption, armed conflicts, violence, criminal activities, and terrorism as causes of slavery.[226]

We all have a shared responsibility to end slavery, whether as part of a religious congregation, institution, intergovernmental organization, or business. Francis also exhorts civil organizations to play a role in awakening consciences and promoting steps to end and uproot slavery.[227] Finally, he calls on everyone to participate in globalized fraternity—to be our brothers and sisters' keepers rather than allowing our brothers and sisters to be subjected to modern slavery or adopting an attitude of indifference to their needs.[228]

iv. "Overcome Indifference and Win Peace"

In 2016, Francis continues with his theme of "indifference," which he had begun in the previous years, through his "Overcome Indifference and Win Peace."[229] For him, God is not indifferent. He cares about humankind. Even though the past years have been marked with kidnappings, ethnic and religious persecution, and the misuse of power, Francis encourages everyone to maintain reason and hope.[230]

225. Ibid., no. 3.
226. Ibid., no. 4.
227. Ibid., no. 5.
228. Ibid., no. 6.
229. Francis, "Overcoming Indifference," no. 1.
230. Ibid., no. 2.

Francis goes on to cite types of indifference, including personal indifference—that is, neighbors closing their hearts to the needs of others or closing their eyes to what is happening in the world. Another type of indifference takes a global dimension. Francis calls this type the "globalization of indifference." He further warns against "indifference to God, which then leads to indifference to one's neighbor and to the environment." What leads to these forms of indifference, Francis stresses, is a false sense of humanism, materialism, relativism, and nihilism. We must be sensitive to God, our neighbors, society, and our environment, as Francis had mentioned in *Laudato Si'*. Otherwise, he warns, indifference could lead to self-absorption and lack of commitment. It can also lead to absence of peace with God, with our neighbors, and with the environment.[231] For him, when we are not at peace with God, we easily become prey to relativism and find it difficult to be at peace with one another.[232]

Francis strongly recommends mercy and conversion of the heart, "For mercy is the heart of God. It must also be the heart of the members of the one great family of his children."[233] In addition to mercy, Francis suggests we practice solidarity as a moral virtue to overcome indifference. The fruit of solidarity is mercy and compassion. In the spirit of the Jubilee Year of Mercy, Francis calls on everyone to work courageously and concretely to minimize indifference of all kinds in their families, neighborhoods, and workplaces.[234]

v. Misericordia et Misera ("Mercy with Misery")

In his letter *Misericordia et Misera*, issued at the conclusion of the Extraordinary Jubilee of Mercy on November 20, 2016, Francis referenced the phrase used by St. Augustine's commentary on Jesus's encounter with the woman caught in adultery in John 8:1–11:

> Then each of them went home, while Jesus went to Mount of Olives. Early in the morning he came again to the temple. All the people came to him and he sat down and began to teach them. The scribes and the Pharisees brought a woman who

---

231. Ibid., no. 3.
232. Ibid., no. 4.
233. Ibid., no. 5.
234. Ibid., nos. 7–8.

had been caught in adultery; and making her stand before all of them, they said to him, "Teacher, this woman was caught in the very act of committing adultery. Now in the law Moses commanded us to stone such women. Now what do you say?" They said this to test him, so that they might have some charge to bring against him. Jesus bent down and wrote with his finger on the ground. When they kept on questioning him, he straightened up and said to them, "Let anyone among you who is without sin be the first to through a stone at her." And once again he bent down and wrote on the ground. When they heard it, they went away, one by one, beginning with the elders; and Jesus was left alone with the woman standing before him. Jesus straightened up and said to her, "Woman, where are they? Has no one condemned you?" She said, "No one, sir." And Jesus said, "Neither do I condemn you. Go your way, and from now on do not sin again."

Francis believes the mystery of God's love lies in this text when it touches the sinner: "the two of them alone remained: mercy with misery." John's Gospel serves as an icon of that Holy Year of Mercy, of which continuous celebration constitutes the church's existence.[235] Francis points out that, in this story, the misery of sin was clothed with the mercy of God's love, which Jesus sought to reveal during life and ministry. Francis's *Misericordia et Misera* is also based on the text of Exodus, which expresses the very nature of God as just, kind, merciful, and righteous: "The Lord passed before him and proclaimed, 'The Lord, the Lord, a God merciful and gracious, slow to anger, and abounding in steadfast love and faithfulness, keeping steadfast love for thousandth generation, forgiving iniquity and transgression and sin'" (Exod 34:6–7).[236]

Francis points prophetically to the consummate expression of divine mercy recorded in various passages of the Old Testament, especially the Prophetic Books (Pss 85:1–2; 103:8–12; Neh 9:17; Joel 2:13; Jonah 4:2; Isa 38:17; Mic 7:18–20). In the Year of Mercy, the church listens to and attentively experiences the presence and closeness of God; the end of the Jubilee calls on the church to look to the future and figure out how best to continue with joy, fidelity, and

---

235. Francis, *Misericordia et Misera*, no. 1
236. Ibid., no. 2.

enthusiasm and experience and celebrate the richness of the nature of God, which is full of divine mercy (*Misericordiae Vultus*).[237]

This could be accomplished during liturgy, during Lent, at every aspect of the Eucharistic celebration, and in every sacramental life of the church.[238] Divine mercy can also be celebrated by attentively listening to and reading the word of God; in God's word, we "trace the history of salvation through the proclamation of God's tireless work of mercy."[239] Francis singles out the Sacrament of Penance and Reconciliation as a unique place where the celebration of God's mercy takes place. In this, we "feel the embrace of the Father, who comes forth to meet us and grant us the grace of being once more his sons and daughters . . . God shows us the way to turn back to him and invites us to experience his closeness anew."[240] He also acknowledges with gratitude the role of the "Missionaries of Mercy," whose pastoral role sought to emphasize the boundless love of God for those who seek him with a contrite heart.[241] Additionally, Francis prophetically gave permission to the priest of the Priestly Fraternity of St. Pius X to validly and licitly receive the sacramental absolution of those faithful who attend churches officiated by them.[242]

With reference to Second-Isaiah, Francis stresses "Consolation or Comfort" to families, the poor, the bereft, and to everyone as another face of mercy (Isa 40:1). The doors of basilicas and cathedrals that were opened and closed during this Jubilee Year symbolized God's doors of mercy. They represent our own paths as the doors of mercy of our hearts, which must continue to remain open with charity, love, and forgiveness toward our fellow brothers and sisters.[243] Francis also invites us to continue to live out the corporal

---

237. This means "The Face of Mercy."
238. Francis, *Misericordia et Misera*, nos. 4–5.
239. Ibid., no. 6.
240. Ibid., no. 8.
241. These were qualified priests made available to forgive sins normally reserved to the Holy See's Apostolic Penitentiary.
242. Francis, *Misericordia et Misera*, no. 12. See also Francis ("Letter According to Which an Indulgence Is Granted to the Faithful"). Normally, the priests of the Fraternity of Pius X do not possess the jurisdiction needed to confer this sacrament. Francis prophetically sought alternatives. For Francis, "the Jubilee Year of Mercy excludes no one."
243. Francis, *Misericordia et Misera*, no. 16.

works of mercy (Matt 25) and promote what he calls a "culture of mercy based on the rediscovery of encounter with others, a culture in which no one looks at another with indifference or turns away from the suffering of our brothers and sisters."[244] Finally, he recommends that the church might celebrate on the Thirty-Third Sunday of Ordinary Time the World Day of the Poor, trusting in the intercession of Mary, the Holy Mother of God, who always looks upon us with her eyes of mercy.

We should recall that Francis's passion and theology of divine mercy did not begin with his papacy. In the 1990s, he was promoted as the Auxiliary and the Coadjutor Archbishop of Buenos Aires, and he chose "*Miserando Atque Eligendo*" ("because he saw him through the eyes of mercy and chose him") as his episcopal motto. His choice was based on the Gospel account of "The Call of St. Matthew," the tax collector, in a homily of St. Bede the Venerable (cf. Matt 9:9–13).[245] Francis, the first Latin American pope, has proven to be a pope and a prophet of mercy whose impact has reached the four corners of the earth.

vi. Francis's "Letter to the Bishops of Nigeria"

Francis wrote to the Nigerian bishops in March of 2015. In this letter, Francis assures the bishops and his readers of his closeness and prayerful support for the suffering faithful in Nigeria (compare Jer 29). Historically, when Nebuchadnezzar of Babylon captured Zion in 598 BC, he also took King Johoiachin, priests, nobles, members of the royal family, and the elite of the community with him as prisoners. He replaced Johoiachin with his uncle Zedekiah as the new puppet ruler—someone he could control—to the dislike of Israel's prophets (2 Kgs 24:12–17).

Jeremiah was one of those prophets who spoke up against oppression and encouraged the exiles that their sufferings and humiliation would not be forever (Jer 27–28). The Israelites needed to recognize that they would remain in exile for generations (Jer 29:10), therefore they need to settle into their new condition by building houses for their families. Jeremiah also encouraged them to go about

---

244. Ibid., no. 20.
245. Glatz, "Episcopal Motto," 1.

their business and engage in regular activities, such as marriage (Jer 29:5–6). Importantly, Jeremiah emphasized the importance of praying in their new cities, since prayer was never to be restricted to the Jerusalem temple. Jeremiah assured Israel that, with prayer, hope, and trust in the Lord, who is ever faithful, Israel could survive in and after their exile and the ugly predicament their leaders had led them into (Jer 29:21–23).[246]

Like Jeremiah, Pope Francis not only recognizes the many blessings God has blessed Nigeria with, but he entrusts the many problems that Nigeria has had to deal with into God's hands—problems such as "new and violent forms of extremism and fundamentalism on ethnic, social and religious grounds."[247] Francis prays for those Nigerians who have "been killed, wounded or mutilated, kidnapped and deprived of everything: their loved ones, their land, their means of subsistence, their dignity and their rights."[248] He also unites in prayer with Christian and Muslim believers who "have experienced a common tragic outcome, at the hands of people who claim to be religious, but who instead abuse religion, to make of it and ideology for their own distorted interests of exploitation and murder."[249]

The Holy Father's letter, like Jeremiah 29, confers a message of hope and peace and communicates his closeness to all suffering Nigerians. He expresses appreciation for the Nigerian church, priests, religious people, and catechists, who, despite what they have gone through, do "not cease to witness hospitality, mercy and forgiveness."[250] He also encourages Nigerian bishops to continue in their good works of promoting peace by accompanying the victims of violence and the Nigerian poor with love and compassion. Finally, Francis reassures the nation of his love and the intercession of Mary, Queen of Africa.

---

246. See Matthews, *Prophets*, 97–99.

247. See Francis ("Bishops of Nigeria") for details of his prophetic message to the church in Nigeria.

248. Ibid.

249. Ibid.

250. Ibid.

vii. "Nonviolence as a Style of Politics for Peace"

On the occasion of the Fiftieth World Day of Peace in 2017, Francis reflects on "Nonviolence: A Style of Politics for Peace."[251] Francis notes that the last century saw two devastating world wars, the threat of nuclear war, and a great number of other conflicts; today, sadly, we still find ourselves engaged in a horrifying world war, albiet one that is fought piecemeal.[252] Piecemeal violence, he says, causes all forms of suffering, such as wars in different countries and continents, terrorism, and abuse of immigrants. Even though we live in a broken world, violence is not a cure to our brokenness.

Francis recommends that we learn from Jesus, who also lived in a violent time. He teaches us that the battlefield where violence and peace meet is the human heart. Francis cites many passages of Scripture to demonstrate Jesus's nonviolent approach, and he also cites the nonviolent approach of St. Francis of Assisi. Appealing to Mother Teresa's approach, Francis notes that loving one another nonviolently is more powerful than guns, bombs, and all kinds of evil.[253] Francis praises the effort and achievements of Mahatma Gandhi, Khan Abdul Ghaffar Khan of India, and Dr. Martin Luther King Jr. in combating racial discrimination and violence. Francis further mentions the role of Leymah Gbowee and thousands of Liberian women, who organized pray-ins and nonviolent protests that resulted in high-level peace talks to end the second civil war in Liberia.[254]

Pointing back to his *Amoris Laetitia*, Francis exhorts families to cultivate nonviolent behavior. He says, "the family is the indispensable crucible in which spouses, parents and children, brothers and sisters, learn to communicate and to show generous concern for one another, and in which frictions and even conflicts have to be resolved not by force but by dialogue, respect, concern for the good of other, mercy and forgiveness."[255] In the spirit of St. Therese of Lisieux's "little way of love," a culture of nonviolence must begin little by little, starting in our homes and then spreading to the entire

---

251. Francis, "Non Violence," no. 1.
252. Ibid., no. 2.
253. Ibid., nos. 3–4.
254. Ibid., no. 4.
255. Ibid., no. 5.

larger human family.[256] Francis, borne into a home with parents and siblings, believes that "Nothing is impossible if we turn to God in prayer. Everyone can be an artisan of peace."[257]

viii. "Migrants and Refugees; Men and Women in Search for Peace"

In his 2018 message for the celebration of the Fifty-First World Day of Peace, Francis timely reflects on the plight of "Migrants and Refugees: Men and Women in Search of Peace."[258] He invites everyone to embrace those "fleeing from war and hunger, or forced by discrimination, persecution, poverty and environmental degradation to leave their homes."[259] There are also those who migrate for various reasons, including the desire for a better life.[260] Francis recommends that with a contemplative gaze fostered by wisdom and faith we must recognized that all belong to one family with a common destination and right to enjoy the blessings the Lord has blessed the earth with. Such contemplative gaze would also assist us find God in our homes and cities. It would help us to nature not only peace, and "workshops of peace" on earth, but appreciate the gifts and talents brought by immigrates and refugees to those cities and nations that receive them.[261]

Francis appeals to scripture passages (Heb 13:2; Ps 146:9; Deut 10:18–19), recommends four milepost for action: welcoming, protecting, promoting and integrating immigrants. He invites international community to accept his proposed "two Global Compacts, one for safe, orderly and regular migration and the other for refugees."[262] In the spirit of Saint John Paul II, Francis believes "if the dream of peaceful world is shared by all, if the refugees' and migrants' contribution is properly evaluated, then humanity can become more and more a universal family and on earth a true common home."[263]

256. Ibid., no. 6.
257. Ibid., no. 7.
258. Francis, "Migrants and Refugees," no.1.
259. Ibid., no.1.
260. Ibid., no.2.
261. Ibid., no.3.
262. Ibid., nos.4–5.
263. Ibid., no.6

Summary of Part II

In Part II, we have examined Francis's life, visits, writings, and other pastoral ministries, as well as their effect on society and the church. From the time of his birth in Buenos Aires, Argentina, his life and ministry has been marked with humility and simplicity, even as a pope. In his *Lumen Fidei*, Francis challenges readers to resent and reject the darkness of evil and embrace the light of faith that Christ represents. Through *Lumen Fidei*, Francis invites everyone to serve as conduits of love, unity, dialogue, and peace despite our daily challenges, as did the biblical prophets.

In his *Evangelii Gaudium*, Francis calls on the church to joyfully reach out to the marginalized and be inclusive in dealing with the poor. Like Israel's prophets, he reminds the church and her members of the importance of good leadership and membership characterized by obedience, listening, courage, faith, hope, compassion, and openness to the newness of life in the service of the neighbor. He prefers active evangelization and the proclamation of the gospel in context. He prophetically recommends peace and dialogue as well as courageous missionary efforts that are accompanied by humility, mercy, and prayer.

Apart from his humility, emphasis on God's mercy, concern for the poor, and commitment to interfaith dialogue, Francis's papacy is also marked by a theology of climate change and care for our common home planet, as expressed in his *Laudato Si'*. In this document, Francis rejects bridled capitalism, isolationism, modern individualism, anthropocentricism, throwaway culture, consumerism, irresponsible development, and the dominant modern technological paradigm. Like Israel's prophets, Francis prefers taking action in addressing issues of climate change; he adopts a Christlike attitude toward creation that includes harmony and integral-ecological spirituality that does not economically, politically, socially, and technologically exclude the poor.

In his *Amoris Laetitia*, Francis, among other things, discusses challenges facing modern families and marriages. In *Gaudete et Exsultate*, Francis invites everyone to a life of holiness. The New Year messages ("Fraternity, the Foundation and Pathway to Peace"; "No Longer Slaves, but Brothers and Sisters"; "Overcome Indifference and Win Peace"; "Nonviolence: A Style of Politics for Peace",

"Migrants and Refugees: Men and Women In Search for Peace") and letters ("Apostolic Letter to Consecrated People"; Francis's "Letter to the Bishops of Nigeria"; *Misericordia et Misera*; "Letter of the Holy Father According to Which an Indulgence Is Granted") further comprised a major portion of our discussion in Part II. Throughout this section, we highlighted the prophetic nature of Francis's ministry (Part I).

In Part III, we will discuss the detailed global effect and challenges that Francis's pastoral paradigmatic achievement poses for modern society.

Part III

Prophetic Effect of Francis and Challenges to Contemporary Society

THIS FINAL PART EXPANDS on the preceding two parts by discussing the impact of Francis's prophetic ministry. In what follows, we will offer specific examples of his effect and impact on the globe, especially on the contemporary United States of America, Africa, and Asia, as well as the challenges he poses to these regions.

Francis's Prophetic Effect on the U.S.A.

Many people from the United States have written about and responded to Francis's election and ministry. Some of these responses evidence Francis's effect on the church and society. One such responses is that of a Jesuit priest, Fr. Thomas Reese, a senior analyst for National Catholic Reporter (NCR) and author of *Inside the Vatican: The Politics and Organization of the Catholic Church*. In an article reacting to Francis's effect on the church and society published on March 16, 2014, he observes that Francis is the most discussed person in the world and points out how the Holy Father has dominated the cover of almost every magazine. Francis makes the news every week and has become a sensation on Twitter and Facebook.[1]

Reese cites views gathered from a February 2014 survey by the Pew Research Center on Religion & Public Life to demonstrate the impact Francis has had on the life of the church in the United States. According to this survey, people in the U.S. overwhelmingly like

1. Reese ("Francis Effect") has details of this.

Pope Francis. Eighty-five percent of Catholics and 60 percent of non-Catholics view Francis favorably. Francis has given the young and old, liberals and conservatives alike in the U.S. something to think about. In fact, "many conservative commentators have argued that Francis does not represent significant change in church. Seventy-one percent of Catholics disagree. The young and the old are more likely (73 percent) to see major change than the middle cohort (40–59 years; 67 percent). And of those Catholics who see major change, 68 percent see it as change for the better."[2]

Reese also notes that, in terms of marriage and family issues, "Francis has urged more compassion for Catholics unable to observe the church's teachings on marriage; he has noted that celibacy is a matter of law not doctrine; and has ruled out women priests but called for a greater role for women in the church. Catholics want more, but they still like Pope Francis."[3]

Again, even though church attendance has not changed, it has not gone down since the papacy of Francis—an indication of a positive effect on the church in the U.S. With Francis, a good number of Catholics in the U.S. are more excited about their faith (26 percent). Additionally, 40 percent are praying more, and 20 percent are reading their Bible. Francis's impact challenges people in the U.S.—particularly bishops, priests, and the faithful—to join in his mission of rejecting consumerism, capitalism, and individualism and instead reaching out with love and compassion to the poor and the planet.

i. The Prophetic Effect of Francis's Visits

Francis, like his predecessors, is a pope on a mission. His missionary travels after his election point to where his heart lies and to what type of missionary he is. Even though he came to the United States in 2015, his prophetic ministry prior to the U.S. visit took him to places like Lampedusa (July 2013), Brazil (2013), Israel, South Korea, Albania, Turkey (2014), Sri Lanka, the Philippines, Bosnia-Herzegovina, Bolivia, Ecuador, Paraguay, Cuba, Poland, Mexico, Egypt, and Columbia (2017). Others which have been scheduled include Chile, Peru, Ireland, Estonia, Latvia, Lithuania, India, Romania Panama etc (2018).

2. Ibid.
3. Ibid.

In his article "Pope Francis the Prophet," Reese describes the pontiff's 2015 visits to the United States as truly prophetic.[4] He bases this conclusion on the way the Holy Father "exercised his prophetic office by comforting the afflicted and afflicting the comfortable, but he did it in a soft and respectful voice."[5] Reese points out that during the pope's visits to Congress, he confounded his critics by demonstrating his prophetic love for the American people. Pope Francis reached out with love and warmth to people of all ages and to everyone he encountered. That the Holy Father called America "the land of the free and the home of the brave" demonstrates that Francis, like Israel's prophets, was familiar with his environment and had done his homework in studying America, including America's founding documents, especially the Declaration of Independence. Pope Francis repeatedly quoted this document, both before Congress and at Independence Hall, saying, "We hold these truths to be self-evident, that all men are created equal, that they are endowed by their Creator with certain unalienable rights that among these are life, liberty and the pursuit of happiness."[6] In doing this, Francis was not there to lecture Congress but to "dialogue with all of you."[7]

Showing his characteristic love for the poor and commitment to interfaith and cultural dialogue, Francis spoke for the middle class during this visit. He emphasized "the many thousands of men and women who strive each day to do an honest day's work, to bring home their daily bread, to save money . . . one step at a time . . . to build a better life for their families."[8] Francis also exercised his prophetic office by the way he spoke of business as a noble vocation directed at producing wealth and improving the world as an essential service to the common good. Like Israel's prophets, Francis urged the U.S. Congress not to ignore the plight of the poor. Politics, Francis stressed, must not be a slave to the economy and finances; politics must build the common good and sacrifice "particular interest in order to share, in justice and peace, its goods, its interest, its social life."[9]

4. See Reese, "Pope Francis the Prophet," 1–4.
5. Ibid., 1.
6. Ibid.
7. Ibid.
8. Ibid.
9. Ibid., 2.

Reese observes that, in addressing the United Nations, the Holy Father was prophetic in condemning "a selfish and boundless thirst for power and material prosperity" that "leads both to the misuse of available natural resources and to the exclusion of the weak and disadvantaged."[10] Throughout his U.S. visits, Francis defended the immigrants and the need to observe the Golden Rule—doing to others what we would want done to us. For him, there should also be a global abolition of the death penalty. He also spoke in defense of our environment. Climate change, he said, "is a problem that cannot no longer be left for a future generation."[11] Francis called on the United Nations to work toward a world free from nuclear weapons—one that instead promotes diplomacy and dialogue. Pope Francis, Reese concludes, was prophetic in his visit to the United States. He effectively challenged the American government and the people on the issues of immigration, refugees, poverty, and the environment.

ii. Pew Research Center Report & Francis's Effect

A Pew Research Center survey determined that, in the wake Francis's visit to the United States, Francis has generated a lot of goodwill toward the Catholic Church among people across the political spectrum.[12] In the survey, both liberal and moderate Democrats say that Francis has impacted them positively and changed their views of the Catholic Church. About 28 percent of adults in the U.S. say they have a more positive view of the Catholic Church because of Pope Francis. Six out of every ten Americans (58 percent) are impressed by Francis's prophetic ministry.

The same Pew Research Center survey determined that nearly four out of ten liberals (39 percent) have a positive impression of Francis, against the 4 percent who have a negative view of the church. And among ideological moderates, 31 percent view Francis positively, while only 5 percent remain negative. That is a six to one ratio. Among the conservatives, by contrast, 20 percent remain negative. A similar split is seen among Democrats and Republicans. While 27 percent of Republicans say Francis has had a positive effect

10. Ibid., 2.
11. Ibid.
12. Pew Research Center, "Positive Impact of Pope Francis."

on them, only 10 percent remain negative. The survey concludes that with Francis's prophetic visits, his favorability has jumped from 64 percent to 68 percent between June and October 2015.

In the same Pew Research Center survey, positive views toward Francis are found among non-Catholics. About 65 percent of non-Catholics say they love Francis and what he does, while 81 percent of Catholics view Francis positively. In the same survey, of the 97 percent of Catholics who attend daily Masses, 84 percent view Francis positively. With Francis's visit in 2015, Mass-attending Catholics have not changed their positive views about Pope Francis, and neither has Mass attendance dropped.

Apart from offering questions about people's views of Pope Francis and his effect on the church, the survey also asked what one word would best describe their impression about Pope Francis. Most people responded with words such as "good," "humble," "kind," and "compassionate."[13] In 2017, most Catholics and non-Catholics continue to view Pope Francis and his effect positively.[14]

iii. Publication of John Gehring & Francis's Effect

In 2015, John Gehring published a lengthy volume entitled *The Francis Effect: A Radical Pope's Challenge to the American Church*. In this text, Gehring outlined the effect of Francis's ministry on society and the church. The title of this text accurately captures Gehring's subject matter. In this volume, Gehring broadly identifies Francis's symbolic gestures that resemble those of the biblical prophets (Isaiah and Ezekiel).

In Isaiah 20, for instance, the prophet Isaiah symbolically fasted, clothed himself in sackcloth, and walked around naked and barefoot in Jerusalem for three years (Isa 20:2) as a sign of mourning for the nation and an expression of his rejection of Judah's military alliance with foreign nations, which Isaiah believed would only lead to doom. Additionally, Isaiah gave symbolic names to his children.[15] Ezekiel also acted out some of his prophecies. Examples include:

---

13. Pew Research Center, it must be noted, is a nonprofit, tax-exempt 501(c)(3) organization and subsidiary of the Pew Charitable Trusts, its primary funder.

14. See Gecewich ("View Pope Francis Favorably") for details.

15. These symbolic names include: *Shear-jashub* (Isa 7:3), meaning "remnants

- Remaining speechless, unable to rebuke or intercede on behalf of exiled Israel (Ezek 3:22–27)
- Enacting the siege of Jerusalem (Ezek 4:1–3)
- Lying on his left side for 390 days and on his right side for another 40 days, bearing the guilt of Israel and Judah (Ezek 4:4–8)
- Eating the meager rations apportioned to a person under siege (Ezek 4:9–11)
- Baking bread on coals made of animal dung, symbolizing how the exiled people will eat unclean food when they are in exile (Ezek 4:12–15)
- Shaving his hair and beard and scattering all but a small remnant, which he hides in the hem of his garment, to symbolize the people's faith after Jerusalem's fall (Ezek 5:1–4)
- Acting the part of an exile by packing his bags and digging through the wall to leave the city, portraying the fate of Israel (Ezek 12:1–6)
- Eating bread while trembling and drinking water anxiously, as will the exiles (Ezek 12:17–20)
- Groaning aloud in the hearing of the people, indicating how they will respond when they hear bad news (Ezek 21:8–13)
- Refusing to mourn the death of his wife (Ezek 24:15–24)
- Regaining his speech when he hears the news that "the city is taken" (Ezek 33:21–22)
- Tying two sticks together to symbolize the future reunification of Israel and Judah (Ezek 37:15–28)[16]

Comparing Ezekiel's prophetic pantomime with the prophetic signs and symbols in Francis's papacy, Gehring notices specific visible signs that a new era is on the way. One example is that, soon after his election, Pope Francis broke with centuries of tradition by declining to move into the Apostolic Palace, instead preferring a simple apartment in the Vatican guesthouse (*Domus Sanctae Marthae*)—the

---

shall return", and *Maher-shalal- hash-baz* (Isa 8:1–4), meaning, "quick spoil," and perhaps Immanuel, "God is with us" (Isa 7:14; 8:8).

16. See Leclerc, *Prophets*, 286.

same guesthouse that his brother cardinals resided in during the papal election. What could be the meaning of Francis's choice of a simple house? Perhaps it speaks to his identification with the poor. Perhaps it demonstrates his prophetic dimension in the likes of Ezekiel, the priest and prophet. For instance, Ezekiel was expected to keep to the tradition of ritual purity (Lev 21), but to pass on his message more actively, Ezekiel "plays in the dirt using an inscribed clay brick and stick figures to portray the siege of Jerusalem."[17]

Other effective prophetic pantomimes Gehring attributes to Francis include:

- Bowing to receive blessings from the people after his election
- Referring to himself as the "Bishop of Rome"
- Cancelling his newspaper subscription in Buenos Aires
- Calling a pregnant Italian woman whose fiancé wanted her to have an abortion
- Encouraging an engineering student who wrote to him about his fears of not finding a job
- Washing the feet of prison inmates, including two Muslim women, on Holy Thursday/Mass of the Last Supper
- Ordering showers to be installed in St. Peter's square for the homeless and having breakfast with the homeless
- Arranging a private tour of the Sistine Chapel for those who sleep in the streets around the Vatican
- Greeting his guests individually[18]

In addition to the prophetic images, symbols, and practices in which Francis engaged even as a cardinal of Buenos Aires, Gehring reiterates Francis's blueprint—albeit one that is challenging to the church in the United States and beyond. In the beginning of his ministry, Pope Francis expressed his preference for

> A Church which is bruised, hurting and dirty because it has been out on the streets, rather than a Church which in unhealthy from being confined and from clinging to its own

---

17. Matthew, *Prophets of Israel*, 107.
18. Gehring, *Francis Effect*, 2–3.

security. I do not want a Church concerned with being at the center and then ends by being caught up in a web of obsessions and procedures. More than by fear of going astray, my hope is that we will be moved by the fear of remaining shut up within structures which give us a false sense of security, within rules which make us harsh judges, within habits which make us feel safe, while at our door people are starving and Jesus does not tire of saying to us, "Give them something to eat."[19]

Francis's "blueprint" calls for an alternative approach. It challenges the current "dominant culture" in the United States and around the world, which does not effectively respond to the urgency of the gospel command, "give them something to eat." Rather, the dominant culture is marked by unfettered capitalism, exploitation, idolatry of money, a growing economy of exclusion and inequality, consumerism, and neglect of nature and the mother planet.[20]

Francis consequently calls for spiritual renewal and institutional reforms. His prophetic effect is reflected in his new appointments and shifting of priorities, which have already impacted the church in the United States. For example, two American cardinals who sat on the Congregation for Bishops, the thirty-plus-member Vatican Committee that nominates new candidates for the episcopacy, have been replaced. Cardinal Donald Wuerl of the Archdiocese of Washington has replaced Cardinal Raymond Burke. Cardinal Wuerl is widely regarded for a pastoral style that is in line with Francis's own. As I write this work, Cardinal O'Malley of Boston is the only American on the Pope's select council tasked with reforming church governance. He also leads the pope's clergy abuse watchdog commission.[21]

Additional themes covered in Gehring's work include:

- "The Making of a Cultural Warrior Church"
- "Catholic Progressivism on the March: The New Deal to Vatican II"
- "The Rise of the Religious Right and a Power Struggle in the Church"
- "The Battle for Catholic Identity"

19. See Gehring, *Francis Effect*, 11.
20. Gehring, *Francis Effect*, 11–12.
21. See Gehring (*Francis Effect*, 15–18) for details of Francis's new appointments and reshuffling as it affects the church in the United States.

- "The Francis Era in America"
- "A 'Francis Effect' on U.S. Politics?"
- "The Search for Common Ground."
- "Millennials, Latinos and the future of the U.S. Church"[22]

Gehring's discussion is marked with extensive notes and arranged in chapters. It echoes the idea that Francis is a modern-day prophet who has affected the U.S. church and society.

In his foreword to Gehring's work, Tom Robert expresses well Francis's engaging pastoral ministry, prophetic effect, and significant achievements:

> In the brief time since his election, Pope Francis has firmly supplanted a rigidly legalistic approach to evangelism and Catholic identity with a far more pastoral style. The "art of accompaniment" has become the leading edge of Catholic engagement with the world, the phrase evoking something less precise than law, a skill requiring practice as well as flexibility and, above all, a willingness to journey with the other ahead of listing "non-negotiable" conditions for the journey.[23]

Israel's prophets were engaging, and Francis is likewise engaging. According to Tom Robert, if a word-cloud of Francis's papacy were to be displayed on San Pietro's Basilica in Rome, the terms competing for dominance "would be *mercy* and *poor*."[24] Francis's emphasis on serving the poor and reaching out to the marginalized, Tom Robert stresses, "recalibrates both the theological and political conversation that emanates from the church today. It is appropriate to speak of a 'Francis effect' and to attempt to understand how it will alter the way the Catholic Church moves in society and deals with the issues of this edge. . . . he challenges us almost daily in his homilies and public exhortation, and especially by his example, to understand that the call to holiness must move beyond self-concern."[25]

---

22. Gehring, *Francis Effect*, 19–229.
23. See Robert, "Foreword," xi.
24. See Robert, "Foreword," xi.
25. See Robert, "Foreword," xi.

iv. Center for Climate Change & Francis's Effect

In November 2015, the Center for Climate Change Communication published "The Francis Effect: How Pope Francis Changed the Conversation About Global Warming."[26] This work is a direct response to Francis's *Laudato Si´: On Care for Our Common Home,* reviewed in the preceding chapters. The document heightens Francis's prophetic effect and achievements and underscores the challenges his ministry poses for the United States and beyond.

Edward Maibach and his fellow investigators begin by conceding that they engaged in this survey in order "to draw Christians into dialogue with one another, and with all humanity about the implications of climate change and other forms of environmental destruction."[27] Maibach and his friends also confirm that, in the encyclical, "Francis presents a strong moral call to action: people and nations should come together and take the actions necessary to protect the Earth-and thereby protect the world's poorest and most vulnerable people from climate change."[28] Francis's calling is not far from the task of prophetic ministry discussed in the preceding chapters.

Francis is a pope who loves to travel, as did his immediate predecessors Benedict XVI and John Paul II. Francis "visited the United States for five days to meet with President Obama, address a joint session of the U.S. Congress, address the General Assembly of the United Nations, and meet, talk, pray and hold Mass with ordinary Americans. During several of these events, he urged the nations of

---

26. According to its introduction, "this report is based on findings from nationally representative panels' survey—Climate Change in the American Mind—conducted by the Yale Program on Climate Change Communication (http://environment.yale.edu/climate-communication) and the George Mason University Center for Climate Change Communication (http://www.climatechangecommunication.org). First interview dates (n=1,273 adults): February 27–March 10, 2015. Final interview dates (n=905): September 30-October 19, 2015. Average margin of error: +/-3 percentage points at the 95% confidence level. The research was funded by the 11th Hour Project, the Energy Foundation, the Grantham Foundation, the V.K. Rasmussen Foundation, the Sierra Club, and the Nature Conservancy." The six principal investigators of this ninety-two page work, which I would love to describe as "echoes of the effect and achievements of Francis in the United States," include: Edward Maibach, Anthony Leiserowitz, Connei Roser-Renouf, Teresa Myers, Seth Rosenthal, and Geoff Feinberg.

27. Maibach, et al., *Francis Effect,* 3.

28. Ibid., 3.

the world to come together to address climate change. His views were covered broadly in American news media.[29]

Francis's theology of the environment, which he expressed during his visit, impacted many in the United States, especially the Catholic Climate Covenant and the U.S. Conference of Bishops, who widely disseminated the message of *Laudato Si'* and held several press conferences at the National Press Club and five diocesan press events. These events "generated more than 3,000 news stories and more than 500 downloads of a free parish program."[30]

Maibach's report, which basically aims at assessing the effect of Francis's *Laudato Si'* on Americans' (particularly Catholics') understanding, opinions, and dialogue about climate change, is an ambitious undertaking:

> The report examines a large, representative cohort of American adults who were first surveyed in spring of 2015, and then again in early October—a within-subject study of changes in public responses. In the two surveys, we assessed the same respondents' global warming beliefs, attitudes, risk perceptions, behaviors and policy preferences, and their views of Pope Francis—so that we could determine who, if anyone, had change their opinions, and if so, in what ways.[31]

The survey also focuses on change among American adult Catholics, non-evangelicals, and Protestants, as well as born-again/evangelical Christians. In all this, the goal remains the same: to discern the effect of Francis's teachings on global warming and the theology of creation. Maibach's study concludes that American Catholics became more engaged in and concerned about global warming because of Pope Francis's teachings and writings on the subject.[32] Francis conducts his teaching on this subject with prophetic courage by appealing to Scripture and to Israel's prophets, as discussed in the preceding chapters.

In 2016, Kevin W. Irwin joined Maibach and his principal investigators in stressing the effect of Francis's *Laudato Si'* on Americans and society in general. His work is entitled *A*

29. Ibid., 3.
30. Ibid., 3.
31. Ibid., 3.
32. Ibid., 3.

Commentary on Laudato Si´: Examining the Background, Contributions, Implementation, and Future of Pope Francis's Encyclical. As the lengthy title implies, Irwin examines the background, contributions, implementation, and future of Pope Francis's encyclical. He concludes by acknowledging that Francis's papacy will be "a game changer both in style (living quarters) and content (daily homilies and interviews online)."[33]

Irwin acknowledges Francis's positive effect and wonders, "is counting the number of people who participate in sacraments or increase their weekly church offerings the real measure of 'the Francis effect'?"[34] Irwin encourages everyone to embrace, welcome, and take advantage of the general goodwill that the first Jesuit Pope has shared with the world. For him, Francis has uplifted the credibility of the Catholic Church, which has had "its share of scandals."[35]

Considering *Laudato Si´*, which Maibach and many others have responded to, Irwin is convinced that Francis, through his achievements, has truly affected the church and society. He invites his readers to respond positively by:

> Appreciating the way that Pope Francis welcomes dialogue with all peoples from all parts of the world. It would mean taking stock of the way he has weighed into controversial issues with pastoral sense and sensitivity. These include, but are not limited to, marriage and the family, ecumenism, and ecology viewed from a number of issues like immigration, economics, politics, spirituality, and so on. While none of these are measurable the way that counting the number of communicants can be measured, all of these—and more—cannot help but put a new face on the Catholic Church in our day. If "we all drink from our own wells," then Pope Francis offers us a deep well to drink from to gain insight, knowledge, and wisdom.[36]

In other words, the prophetic effect of Francis's theology and integral spirituality of creation in the United States and beyond cannot be over-emphasized.

---

33. Irwin, *Laudato Si´*, 254.
34. Ibid., 254.
35. Ibid., 254.
36. Ibid., 254.

v. Michael Wright & Francis's Prophetic Effect

In addition to Maibach's and Irwin's acknowledgement of the positive and prophetic effect of Francis's theology concerning the environment and creation on the American people, Michael Wright, in his *10 Things Pope Francis Wants You to Know About the Environment*, confirms the immeasurable extent to which Francis has impacted the world. Ten things Francis has communicated, with his typical simple style, to everyone in the pews include:

- The agony in the garden: What's happening to our home
- Everything's connected: God, environment, life
- Let it be: the intrinsic value of creation
- The common good: now and later
- Buy now, pay later: our throwaway culture of consumerism
- Stop and smell the roses: discerning the spirit
- The techno kingdom: using technology responsibly
- Home is where the heart is: development and culture
- We're all in this together: a "culture of care"
- Our calling: what we can do[37]

Wright acknowledges that these ten things are not new in the social teachings of the Catholic Church. Throughout the "Church's history, Jesus, Scripture, saints, and popes have spoken about creation and its connection to earthly and spiritual existence."[38] What is new is the fact that "*Laudato Si'* . . . is arguably the most comprehensive, outspoken, and timely statement for the faithful, and indeed the entire world."[39]

In the last paragraph of *Laudato Si'*, Francis acknowledges that his encyclical has prophetic dimensions in that it is joyful yet troubling. This is the prophetic dimension of Francis. He offers a timely and radical alternative to the dominant culture.[40] Francis

---

37. Wright, *Environment*, 10–46.
38. Ibid., 8.
39. Ibid., 8.
40. Ibid., 47.

"comes across as the preeminent prophet of today, expressing grave issues and wise solutions with such authority that they must be taken seriously."[41]

vi. John Allen Jr. & Francis's Prophetic Effect

In 2013, John L. Allen Jr., a senior Vatican analyst for CNN, author, and senior correspondent for the National Catholic Reporter, wrote from Rome about a few things that Francis wants the church and the world to know about his papacy. His writings reflect both intimacy and clarity. Francis is not new to the leadership role. Like some of Israel's prophets, he is a seasoned leader "who has thought long and carefully about the kind of pope he intends to be. This is a man, in other words, whose style reflects real substance."[42]

This man of substance wants the world to know and be affected by the following topics:

- Inclusiveness of the poor in the church
- Place of humility in Christian life
- That the priest and church leaders stay close to the people
- That we never give up on God's mercy
- That we know that we are all Franciscan now
- That Christian faith must be proposed to people, but never imposed on anyone
- That we understand that we are not a NGO; church leaders should not act like company CEOs
- That we never give in to pessimism
- That we have a sense of humor
- That we realize the importance of unity[43]

In 2014, John Allen Jr. reacted to the prophetic effect of Francis's Apostolic Exhortation *Evangelii Gaudium* ("The Joy of the Gospel"). In *Against the Tide: The Radical Leadership of Pope Francis*, he

---

41. Ibid., 8.
42. Allen Jr., *Francis Wants You to Know*, 6.
43. Ibid., 9–48.

discusses the effect of Francis's achievements on different sections of the world. Allen rightly suggests that Francis has left on the world "an indelible impression."[44] He lists six images of Francis in action that have already impacted the world and which I consider prophetic and have mentioned elsewhere in this study:

- In November 2013, Francis embraced Vinicio Riva, an Italian whose face and body are scarred by a genetic disorder and who says people normally go out of their way to avoid him. Riva later said the encounter restored his faith.
- In June of 2013, Francis invited a seventeen-year-old boy with Down syndrome named Alberto di Tullio to join him for a ride in his papal vehicle. The moment left Alberto and his father in tears.
- During Holy Week in March of 2013, Francis visited Rome's Casa del Marmo incarceration center for juvenile offenders, where he washed the feet of twelve inmates during Holy Thursday service. In a break from tradition, two of the inmates he served were Muslims, and two were women.
- In August of 2013, Francis met with a group of youngsters from two Italian dioceses and posed for a picture with several of them afterward. The shot was taken by one of youngsters with a cell phone held at arm's length. It quickly went viral as the first papal "selfie."
- In October of 2013, another shot of Francis became a global sensation when a little boy wandered onstage during a Vatican ceremony and clung to the pope when officials tried to gently steer him away. Francis embraced the boy and took his presence in stride, at one point reaching down to pat him on the head while he continued to deliver his talk.
- In December of 2013, Francis welcomed three homeless men and their dog, Marley (named after the music icon Bob Marley), into the Vatican to share his birthday breakfast.[45]

These gestures of divine mercy and solidarity with the poor and common-day people are not without precedent in Scripture and in

---

44. Allen Jr., *Leadership of Pope Francis*, 6.
45. Ibid., 6–7.

the teachings of the church; however, Francis performs these gestures with an alternative style, simple language, and prophetic courage that proves him to be a modern prophet.

vii. McElwee Joshua & Francis's Effect

The effects of Francis's *Amoris Laetitia* ("The Joy of Love") are also felt globally, as discussed in the preceding chapter. Considering *Amoris Laetitia*, Joshua J. McElwee sums up Francis's prophetic effect in the United States with profound simplicity in his work *10 Things Pope Francis Wants You to Know About the Family*. In this book, he challenges everyone in the United States and around the world:

- To be prophetic—opt for the alternatives and go against the dominant culture, as Brueggemann would put it, knowing that family life today is in crisis
- To realize that mothers are the joy of the church
- To appreciate the fact that fathers need to "waste time" with their children
- To know that grandparents possess the richness of memory and are treasures
- To make sure that children have courage to move forward
- To be conscious of the fact that there are no closed doors
- To be aware of ideological colonization
- To opt for responsible parenthood
- To cherish this time of mercy
- To keep eyes cleansed through our tears[46]

Echoes of Francis's Prophetic Effect in Asia

The effects of Francis's papacy on Asia are well expressed by the Philippine author Earnest L. Tan in his simple and readable work, *Why I Love Pope Francis*.[47] In his foreword to Tan's work, Socrates

---

46. McElwee, *Francis Wants You to Know*, 10–48.

47. I have chosen this as a case study. This does not mean there are not many other

B. Villegas, the Archbishop of Lingayen-Dagupan, acknowledges the challenges Francis's prophetic ministry has brought to modern society, as well as the effect of the many values and expressions of goodwill he promotes. He writes:

> Pope Francis is a challenge. He shakes us up to make us better. He disturbs us from our complacency and status attitude. He humbles us with his humility. He has slowly moved the Church from being dogmatic, self-engrossed and authoritative institution to being gentle, outreaching, compassionate and persuasive Church through the power of love and mercy.[48]

Asians have also felt the impact of Francis's ministry. He is a pope who does not cling onto the "dominant culture" and "hierarchical thinking."[49] Francis is a pope of many firsts, as we mentioned earlier. Throughout his papacy, Francis is not afraid to do things differently, like Israel's prophets. He is the first pope who comes from a non-European country, and he prefers a simple lifestyle patterned on that of St. Francis of Assisi. As a cardinal, he would even "take public transport in place of having his own car."[50] Tan cites the following outstanding gestures that set Francis apart from "dominant culture" or "hierarchical thinking":

- Right after his proclamation, he personally made a call to the office of the Superior General of the Jesuit. He wanted to show courtesy to his superior and teach the world humility by making his own calls.

- As a cardinal, he was already known to be austere. He lived in a small apartment. He took the bus. He cooked his own meals. As a pope, he continues to practice this by residing in a small villa rather than the usual palatial ground of the Vatican. He drives an old car. He refuses to use the papal vehicle, which distances him from the crowd. He prefers to mingle with people.

- He cues up for confession like any other person.

- He sometimes eats his lunch in the Vatican cafeteria.[51]

---

writings, reactions, and responses to Francis's pontificate in different parts of Asia.

48. See Tan, *Why I love Pope Francis*, 7–8.
49. Ibid., 13–22.
50. Ibid., 18.
51. Ibid., 19–20.

Francis is like Israel's prophets, a "Shepherd with a heart for the poor and marginalized."[52] Tan further describes Francis's love for the poor and the people by sharing the following story about Francis:

> One early morning, Pope Francis reportedly took the time to step out of his residence to speak to the man who is guarding him. Normally, they were taken for granted. He made efforts to inquire about him—his background and condition. Then, knowing how exhausted he might be, he proceeded to prepare him a sandwich. While eating, the pope asked him to sit, as he had been standing the whole night. But the guard refused because this was against the protocol of his job. The pope humorously used his authority and said: "Since I am your boss, I command you, sit."[53]

Tan notes that, besides recognizing Francis's heart for the poor, Asians recognize him as a leader who calls for authentic witnessing and challenges capitalism.[54] He is also seen in Asia and beyond as "a hero with feet of clay disposed to show mercy." He cherishes his predecessors' contributions and promotes collegiality and synodality.[55] Francis's prophetic dimension is clear in that he does not cling to the "dominant culture" but prefers alternatives with courage, faith, love and hope for a better future.

Echoes of Francis's Prophetic Effect in Africa

Apart from the United States, Asia, and other locations, Francis's "prophetic effect" on the African church and society cannot be overemphasized. The impact of Francis's achievements and ministry can be seen in families, churches, schools, and on streets across the continent of Africa, and they are a topic of discussion among African theologians in particular. The latter is evident in the recent publication *The Church We Want: African Catholics Look to Vatican III*, which I will use as a case study for Francis's prophetic effect in Africa.

This tripartite volume is a compendium of eighteen essays (six in each part) written by notable male and female African scholars

---

52. Ibid., 23.
53. Ibid., 25.
54. Ibid., 42–51.
55. Ibid., 53–68.

and theologians. As a product of a three-year Theological Colloquium on Church, Religion, and Society in Africa (TCCRSA), issues addressed in these essays cover the theology of Vatican II and the prophetic effect of Francis's papacy, and they point metaphorically into the future to "Vatican III." The text has a well-written introduction, an indexed guide for further scholarship, and a beautiful "matriarchal" epilogue, "*Vade mecum*: Come Walk with Me," penned by Mercy Amba Oduyoye.

The general editor, Agbonkhianmeghe E. Orobator, remains an inspiring and brilliant Jesuit scholar of Nigerian descent, who has served as a missionary in different parts of the world, including Hekima College Jesuit School of Theology in Nairobi, Kenya, where he served as principal. In his "Introduction: Reading the Times for Signs of the Future," Orobator displays his theological skills, his Jesuit's power to synthesize volumes of essays, and his love for Francis, a fellow Jesuit. In particular, Orobator agrees with Francis's description of the church as a community that "goes forth."[56] Francis's description of the church as a community that examines its historical past in light of present reality puts this Vicar of Christ in line with Israel's prophets, who were primarily concerned with the present.

Francis's era is a new era for the world church, Orobator declares. That Francis elicits such a global and fascinating effect "owes not only to his bold and creative ideas but also to his singular capacity to personify these ideas in powerful actions and striking gestures."[57] Some of these gestures are prophetic in nature, which we have already discussed in the preceding chapters.

Essays in this volume affirm the prophetic effect of Francis on African society and in the African church. They testify that "Francis incarnates a sort of living theology, where text takes flesh in context, challenges and spurs 'readers' into action . . . his exercise of pastoral leadership permits critical inquiry and encourages further analysis, debate, and conversation about issues of critical importance in the church."[58] Essays in this volume also remind us of Francis's prophetic actions and his refreshing interpretation of the basic and pastoral

---

56. Orobator, "Signs of the Future," xv. Cf. Francis, *Evangelii Gaudium*, no. 46.
57. Ibid., xv.
58. Ibid., xvi.

meaning of synod, which promotes a listening dialogue and sensitivity to the *sensus fidelium* ("sense of the faithful").

Part one ("The Francis Effect and the Church in Africa") "takes an incisive look" at "the Francis effect" and its challenges for the church in Africa and beyond.[59] Contributors in this section include:

- Bishop Kevin Dowling ("Bishops as Theologians: Listening, Discerning, and Dialogue")
- Stan Chu Ilo ("The Church of Pope Francis: An Ecclesiology of Accountability, Accompaniment, and Action")
- Josée Ngalula ("Milestones in Achieving a More Incisive Feminine Presence in the Church of Pope Francis")
- Bienvenu Mayemba ("Reviving a Church of the Poor and for the Poor," and "Reclaiming Faith Doing Justice and Seeking Liberation: Convergence between Pope Francis and Jean-Marc Ela")
- Anne Arabome ("When a Sleeping Woman Wakes . . . : A Conversation with Pope Francis in *Evangelii Gaudium* about the Feminization of Poverty")
- Bishop Antoine Kambanda ("'If You Want Cows, You Must Sleep Like a Cow': The Bishop in the Church of Pope Francis")[60]

In his essay, bishop Dowling shows that he and his flock have been impacted by the ministry of Francis. Like Francis, Dowling calls on everyone—priests, religious people, and bishops—in Africa to listen to the call of the poor. Church leaders "should work with the sheep and smell like them."[61] Bishop-theologians in particular are called to listen, discern, and engage in dialogue with the people of God entrusted to their care. In Dowling's words, an African bishop-theologian or teacher

> needs to respond to the actual lived reality in the spirit and practice of listening deeply, discerning what the Spirit seems to be saying to the churches, and engaging in a dialogical process with the people to promote and build a *sensus fidelium* that will allow God's Word and the mission of Jesus to be

---

59. Ibid., xviii.
60. Orabotor, *Church We Want*, 3–76.
61. Dowling, "Bishops as Theologians," 3–6.

incarnated anew in the unfolding reality of people's lives and especially the most vulnerable members of our communities and societies.[62]

In other words, the African church must imitate Francis's spirit in caring for and reaching out to the poor and to the general population.

Stan Chu Ilo's essay builds on Dowling's. Ilo hypothetically wonders what kind of pope an African pope would have been if one was elected in place of Francis. Would he have chosen alternative prophetic paths, as Francis has done in challenging consumerism and capitalism, reaching out to the poor, smelling the sheep, preaching the content of *Lumen Fidei, Evangelii Gaudium, Laudato Si'*, or *Amoris Laetitia*?[63] Impacted by Francis's pontificate and his achievements, Ilo believes that an African pope would "seek a more centrist approach to church governance and would be cautious about embracing any changes dictated by Western social pressures."[64] An African pope would not only emphasize rigorous interpretation of church authority and unquestionable obedience, he would also not be amenable to granting greater autonomy to local churches. Ilo also speculates that while an African pope might preach against poverty, secularism, materialism, neoliberal capitalism, and the rough ages of globalization, he doubts he would denounce the papal palace and its associated trappings, as does Francis. An African Pope, Ilo thinks, would likely take advantage of those trappings to validate his power and authority.[65]

Ilo notes that Francis's teachings are not completely new; they are all embedded in the spiritual treasures and the documents of the church (*Lumen Gentium*, no. 8, and *Gaudium et Spes*, no. 1), especially in the teachings of Vatican II. What is new is Francis's prophetic approach. Ilo, who is greatly impacted by Francis's spirit, invites Africans to embrace "an ecclesiology of accountability," "a pastoral theology of accompaniment," and "a spirituality of action."[66] Ilo proposes that Africans be open to Francis's prophetic style of witnessing the gospel.

62. Dowling, "Bishops as Theologians," 10.
63. See Ilo, "Church of Pope Francis," 11.
64. Ibid.
65. Ibid., 11–12.
66. See Ilo ("Church of Pope Francis," 19–30) for interesting details.

Josée Ngalula's article, written originally in French and translated into English by Andrew Setoafia, SJ, is another testimony to Francis's prophetic effect on the Church in Africa. Francis's teachings on inclusiveness and the indispensable contribution of women in the church and society foregrounds Ngalulas's essay.[67] In "Reviving a Church of the Poor and for the Poor, and Reclaiming Faith Doing Justice and Seeking Liberation: Convergence between Pope Francis and Jean-Marc Ela," Bienvenu Mayemba highlights not only the effects of Francis but also those of Jean-Marc Ela, a humble peasant priest from Cameroon, in West Africa. After an extensive review of the theologies and lives of Francis and Ela, Mayemba concludes that:

> Pope Francis and Jean-Marc Ela are both men of God, of the church, of their countries, and of the poor. They both believe in the power of compassion and the power of love. They both believe in interaction between love and faith, between faith and compassion, between community and solidarity, and faith and justice. Their lives, theologies, and their ecclesiology are committed to reviving a church of and for the poor and to reclaiming faith doing justice and seeking liberation. For them, theology is not only faith seeking understanding or faith concerned with its intelligibility in a rational sense. Theology is an active quest for and concrete practice of love and mercy, faith and compassion, and liberation and justice.[68]

In Anne Arabome's essay, "When a Sleeping Woman Wakes...: A Conversation with Pope Francis in *Evangelli Gaudium* about the Feminization of Poverty," she highlights the prophetic effect of Francis in Africa and for women in particular, who are often excluded, degraded, and discarded after being used. Arabome argues for the joys and hope of African women that are often suppressed. With Francis on the stage, Arabome brings to everyone's consciousness that "the life of an African woman is filled with struggles and challenges. She is the caregivers and bearers of children. In spite of these roles, she often faces subordination, hard work, family, limited economic resources and opportunities: her joys and hopes are very dim, as she has to depend most often solely on men."[69] Relying heavily

---

67. Ngalula, "Feminine Presence in the Church of Pope Francis," 31–41.
68. Mayemba, "A Church of the Poor," 43–54.
69. Arabome, "Feminization of Poverty," 56–59.

on the prophetic effect and doors Francis has courageously opened throughout the course of his papacy, Arabome poses the following questions for additional reflection:

- Are women present in the decision-making process of the African church?
- Why were African women largely absent in the preparation for the Synod on the Family? Are they included in the conversations regarding family and the role of women in the church?
- What is the church teaching in regard to issues of rape and domestic violence?
- What is the church teaching regarding female genital mutilation, early childhood marriage, and polygamous marriages?
- Where are the conversations with women about the use of prophylactics to protect them against death at the hands of a partner who brings home HIV/AIDS?
- In what way will the "Francis effect" impact men in the hierarchy, leaders in parish communities, and husbands in families, and transform them to become more compassionate and humble learners?[70]

The good news is that Francis's teachings—his prophetic search for alternative paths that encourage dialogue, understanding the *sensus fidelium,* the *sensus populi,* defense of the poor, challenges to "dominant culture" and "hierarchical thinking," inclusion of women, and integral spirituality—have been heard globally.

In his final essay of this section, "'If You Want Cows, You Must Sleep Like a Cow': The Bishop in the Church of Pope Francis," Antoine Kambanda identifies African problems and stresses the role of an African bishop for an African church. He does this in light of the prophetic effect of Francis.

The church in Africa is confronted with violence, political instability, divisiveness, religious extremism, fundamentalism, corruption in nations' capitals, syncretism, and all types of scandals. Thankfully, there is a new spirit in this African church brought by Francis. It is a prophetic spirit of compassion, courage, love, and concern for

---

70. Arabome, "Feminization of Poverty," 60–62.

the poor and environment. It is a pastoral spirit whereby the pope encourages church leaders to reach out to the flock and smell them. This new spirit should guide everyone in the church, especially bishops as they exercise their pastoral leadership.[71]

In part two of this book ("Critique of Theological Methodology and Ecclesial Practice"), six theological heavyweights and exegetes stress Christian identity in the church in Africa, African theological method, and leadership. Some of these discussions demonstrate the impact Francis's pontificate has had on the African church. Contributors include:

- Laurenti Megesa ("Truly African, Fully Christian? In Search of a New African Christian Spirituality"),
- Teresa Okure ("Becoming the Church of the New Testament")
- Elochukwu Uzukwu ("A Theology of Christian Unity for the Church in Africa")
- Paul Béré ("Scripture Studies and African Theology: A Critical Overview from an Old Testament Perspective")
- Nader Michel ("The Coptic Church: A Long Heritage with New Challenges")
- Philomena N. Mwaura ("The Gospel of the Family: From Africa to the World Church")

Part three ("A Church That Goes Forth with Boldness and Creativity") offers hopeful and inspiring contributions by:

- Emmanuel Katongole ("The Church of the Future: Pressing Moral Issues from Ecclesia in Africa")
- Tina Beattie ("Maternal Well-Being in Sub-Saharan Africa: From Silent Suffering to Human Flourishing")
- Joseph G. Healey ("Beyond Vatican II: Imagining the Catholic Church of Nairobi I")
- Nontando M. Hadebe ("'Advocate for Life!' A Kairos Moment for the Catholic Church in Africa to be a Guardian, Sustainer, and Protector of Life")

---

71. Kambanda, "Bishop in the Church of Pope Francis," 65–76.

- Peter Knox ("*Laudato Si'*, Planetary Boundaries, and Africa Saving the Planet")
- Marguerite Akossi-Mvongo ("The Church We Want: Ecclesia of Women in Africa?")

Discussion of all the essays in parts two and three of this text are beyond the scope of this work. However, we will take a closer examination of the contributions by Teresa Okure and Peter Knox, as representative of each section.

In "Becoming the Church of the New Testament," Okure demonstrates Francis's prophetic effect not only on her but on the church in Africa. She appeals to two significant documents that address the mission of the church in Africa: (1) the *Ecclesia in Africa* (EIA), the Post-Synodal Apostolic Exhortation of the First African Synod, and (2) the *Africae Munus* (AM), the Post-Apostolic Exhortation of the Second African Synod. The themes underlying these two documents are expressed in the New Testament verses "you shall be my witnesses" (Acts 1:8)" and "you are the salt of the earth . . . You are the Light of the world" (Matt 5:13–14).[72] With these initial appeals, Professor Okure focuses the rest of her work "on the church in Africa as an entity and examines the NT in reference to it."[73] She concludes by acknowledging that "the universal attraction of Pope Francis derives from his witness to the gospel or his Jesus-centered life."[74] Significantly, she demonstrates the effect of Francis's *Evangelii Gaudium* ("The Joy of the Gospel") on her and on the church in Africa by noting that Pope Francis has reminded us that the church of the New Testament, and of the new covenant, is "a church that goes forth" (cf. Matt 28:16–20) joyfully.[75]

In his article "*Laudato Si'*, Planetary Boundaries, and Africa Saving the Planet," Knox bears witness to the prophetic effect of Francis's theology of the environment and integral spirit on African society and the church. Knox concludes that Francis's Encyclical Letter "is an example of theology that takes scientific discourse seriously and is neither exclusively Christian nor exclusively African." Francis

---

72. Okure, "Church of the New Testament," 93.
73. Ibid., 93.
74. Ibid., 104.
75. Ibid., 104–105; Francis, *Evangelii Gaudium*, nos. 20–24.

challenges African Christians and Catholics to embrace the ecological crisis as a matter of urgency and faith. Every Christian theologian "must include western science in our discourse. This will allow us to fashion a culturally aware, relevant, effective, and prophetic response to the ecological crisis facing our common home."[76]

Summary of Part III

Thus far, we have offered specific examples of Francis's prophetic effect on the United States of America as well as Asia and Africa. Views gathered by the Pew Research Center on Religion and Public Life in 2014 clearly show that people in the U.S. overwhelmingly love Pope Francis, particularly his humility, his emphasis on divine mercy, his concern for the poor and the middle class, his theology of the people, his concern for climate change, and his commitment to interfaith and intercultural dialogue. His pontificate has impacted people in the U.S. in many ways. Eighty-five percent of Catholics and 60 percent of non-Catholics appreciate Francis's pastoral achievements. Francis has given food for thought to the young and the old, the liberal and the conservative in the U.S. Even though church attendance has not dramatically changed in the U.S., it has not gone down throughout Francis's papacy—an indication of Francis's positive effect on the U.S. church. During his visits in 2015, he confounded his critics by demonstrating his prophetic love for the American people, who live in the "land of the free and the home of the brave." Views and reactions gathered from the publications of Gehring, the Center for Climate Change, Michael Wright, John Allen Jr., and Joshua J. McElwee also attest to the impact of Francis's writings, visits, and pastoral ministry on the American people.

Views gathered from Ernest L. Tan and Socrates B. Villegas are good examples of how Francis's life and pastoral ministry are perceived in Asia. Francis, among other things, challenges everyone and the dominant status quo in the Philippines. He also teaches everyone humility, gentleness, love, and mercy, as well as skills for pastoral outreach—especially to the poor and marginalized.

In Africa, echoes of Francis's effect are heard in families, schools, churches, and streets across the continent. Views drawn from *The*

---

76. Knox, "Saving Planet," 229–242.

Church We Want: African Catholics Look to Vatican III cover not only the theology of Vatican II, but also the prophetic effect of Francis's papacy. Essays in this volume, edited by Orobator, touch on issues of faith, hope, love, marriage, divine mercy, women, contextual theology, family, economic and socio-political problems, leadership, climate change, pastoral humility, and New Testament witnessing; they also affirm the prophetic effect of Francis's pontificate on African society, and the church in particular. The eighteen essays of this compendium testify that "Francis incarnates a sort of living theology, where text takes flesh in context, challenges and spurs 'readers' into action."[77] Francis's "exercise of pastoral leadership permits critical inquiry and encourages further analysis, debate, and conversation about issues of critical importance in the church."[78]

---

77. Orobator, "Signs of the Future," xvi.
78. Ibid.

Summary and Conclusion

With his election, and throughout his public life, Pope Francis has been noted for his pastoral courage, humility, emphasis on God's mercy, and deep love for the poor, as well as his concern for families, the mother planet, and commitment to cultural and interfaith dialogue. As a pope of many "firsts"—the first Jesuit pope, the first pope from the Americas, and the first pope to take the name Francis—he has been seen as the "Pope of a New World."[1] He has won the heart of many and "evoked another kind of pride."[2] Francis has also proven himself an "energizer bunny" of a pope," "a man of the people," "a pope of mercy," and a "cultural icon."

Pope Francis also has his critics. However, many of us have become endeared to Francis through his humility, pastoral simplicity, evangelization strategies, rich Wednesday Vatican audiences, high quality and memorable pastoral talks, homilies, discourses, addresses, and visits, and his relatable presentation of the faith of the church to people across the socio-religious, cultural, and political spectrum. His Scripture-based writings, apostolic letters, exhortations, symbolic language, and symbolic gestures have also been seen as both appealing and prophetic.

Given that Francis is such a popular global religious leader, the preceding sections have discussed Francis's pastoral achievements in light of Israel's prophets and its effect on contemporary society.

---

1. See Tornielli (*Francis Pope of a New World*) and his description of Pope Francis.

2. See Pacwa ("Foreword," xi).

In Part I, we historically and theologically examined the meaning, nature, and function of Israel's prophets to demonstrate how the biblical prophets' charisma, courage, and ministries anticipate, foreground, and foreshadow the ministry of Pope Francis.

As divine agents, prophets and prophetesses were fundamentally the mouthpieces, messengers, mediators, transmitters, conduits, convoys, and interpreters of God's divine will, his freedom, and his justice. They were divinely called to preach and reinterpret the covenant theology for their day, time, and culture. This included God's acts in Israel's past, his dealings with them in the present, and his continuing interactions with them in the immediate future.

While engaged in their role as divine representatives, prophets were sensitive to evil (Amos 8:4–8; Jer 2:12–13). They recognized the importance of trivialities. They were luminous and explosive, pursuing the highest good. They sought alternatives from or radical breaks away from the dominant culture and unethical status quo. Their preaching was dominated by the themes of ethical conduct, justice, judgment, God's sovereignty, the people of God, Israel, Zion or Jerusalem, sin, idolatry and punishment, suffering, endurance, repentance, hope for the remnant, faith, authentic leadership, fertility, covenant, courage, true worship, intercession, appointment and rejection of kings, and divine mercy.

Israel's prophets are classified as pre-classical (Abraham, Moses, Miriam, Balaam, Deborah, Samuel, Nathan, Ahijah, Shamaiah, Elijah, Elisha, Micaiah ibn Imlah, and Huldah) and classical. The classical prophets are further subdivided into the categories of the Major Prophets (Isaiah, Jeremiah, and Ezekiel) and Minor Prophets (Hosea–Malachi). Viewed as watchmen and guardians of Israel's moral life, prophets frequently exhort and warn the people against bad conduct that may result in divine judgment. Each of these prophets, whose ministries Francis is familiar with, effectively challenge us to be prophetic and pose unique questions for us in matters of contemporary ethical conduct, justice and peace, dialogue and unity. Prophets promote courage to preach and lead by example.

In Part II, we examined Francis's life in detail, beginning with his birth in Buenos Aires, Argentina, and his origins as a chemist prior to his studying for the priesthood through the Jesuit Order. This section also seeks to establish the influence of Israel's prophets on Francis and argues that elements of the biblical prophets are hidden treasures in Francis's pastoral ministry. We explored the many ways in which Francis has been prophetic in his homilies, humors, gestures, visits, preaching, proclamations, messages, pastoral outreach, and writings (including *Lumen Fidei, Evangelii Gaudium, Amoris Laetitia,* and *Laudato Si'*).

Francis's *Lumen Fidei* challenges us to be firm and faithful to God, rejecting the evil represented by darkness while embracing the goodness of light in Christ. It also invites us to be conduits of unity and sources of dialogue and peace, as were the biblical prophets. For Francis, this must be done joyfully—the very theme of *Evangelii Gaudium* ("The Joy of the Gospel").

Like Israel's prophets, who were primarily concerned with the signs of their times, in *Evangelii Gaudium* Francis prophetically examines the circumstance of his time. From there he fearlessly challenges today's dangers, which include covetous hearts, feverish pursuits of pleasure, and selfish inner life with a blunted conscience. He identifies pastoral challenges facing the church today, including her missionary endeavors, homily preparations, inclusion of the poor in society, peace and dialogue, and spiritual motivation for mission. He prefers the poor church that goes forth and reaches out to the sheep, feeling and smelling them. He boldly expresses his preference for a church that is in contact with the homes and lives of its members—a church that does not become a useless structure out of touch with people or a self-absorbed cluster made up of a chosen few. He does not support unbridle capitalism, an economy that excludes the poor, consumerism, the idolatry of money, and a financial system which rules rather than serves. Francis promotes peace and dialogue as well as courageous missionary efforts accompanied by humility, mercy, and prayer.

In addition to his humility, concern for the poor, commitment to interfaith dialogue, and emphasis on prayer and God's mercy, Francis is noted for his theology of climate change and care for our common home. This theology is well-articulated in his *Laudato Si'*—a writing that has significantly marked his papacy. In *Laudato Si'*, Francis teaches with prophetic courage. He devotes seven chapters to presenting his theology of the environment and the integral spirituality of ecology, modeled after the lifestyle of St. Francis of Assisi. His writing is marked by a simple and accessible style that reflects the simplicity and approachability that are the hallmarks of his pontificate. Our common home, Francis says, is like our sister, with whom we share our life, and our beautiful mother, who opens her arms to embrace us.

Francis, like Israel's prophets, promotes alternatives to the global socio-economic and political inequalities associated with environmental problems. He searches for an alternative to what he calls "rapidification"—that is, an intensified pace of life and work. Climate change has affected us negatively as we get sick from breathing high levels of smoke from fuels used in cooking and heating. He also searches for alternatives to "water poverty," the ecological crisis, dominant technocratic paradigms, and modern anthropocentricism. He rejects a throwaway culture, consumerism, irresponsible development, and the dominant modern technological paradigm. Francis admonishes all to embrace environmental education that involves making the leap toward the transcendent, which gives harmony, ecological ethics, and integral ecological spirituality its deepest meaning and which does not economically, politically, socially, and technologically exclude the poor.

We also examined Francis's *Amoris Laetitia*. In this text, Francis discusses and offers solutions to problems facing modern families and marriages. In his *Gaudete et Exsultate*, as noted, Francis calls us to pursue holiness of life. Discussion also focused on the prophetic effect of Francis's New Year messages ("Fraternity, the Foundation and Pathway to Peace"; "No Longer Slaves, but Brothers and Sisters"; "Overcome Indifference and Win Peace"; and "Nonviolence: A style of Politics for Peace") and letters ("Apostolic Letter to Consecrated People," "Francis's Letter to the Bishops of Nigeria," "*Misericordia et Misera*," and "According to Which an Indulgence Is Granted"). This discussion highlighted the prophetic aspects of Francis's writings (Part I) and anticipated the global effects and challenges that Francis's pastoral achievements pose for contemporary society (Part III).

In the final part, we discussed Francis's prophetic effect—underlying the proposal that this entire volume serve as a pastoral companion to the Prophetic Books and pastoral ministry. Before arriving at such a proposal, we offered specific examples of Francis's prophetic effect in the United States of America, Asia, and Africa.

We discussed how views gathered by the Pew Research Center on Religion and Public Life in 2014 clearly show that people in the U.S. overwhelmingly love Pope Francis because of his humility, emphasis on divine mercy, concern for the poor and the middle class, theology of the people, concern for climate change, and commitment to interfaith and cultural dialogue. In the United States, 85 percent of Catholics and 60 percent of non-Catholics appreciate Francis's pastoral achievements.

In the United States, Francis has given food for thought to the young and the old, the liberal and the conservative. Even though church attendance in the United States has not dramatically changed, it has not gone down throughout Francis's papacy—an indication of Francis's positive effect on the U.S. church. During his visits in 2015, Francis confounded his critics by demonstrating his prophetic love for the American people, who live in the "land of the free and the home of the brave." Finally, the publications of Gehring, the Center for Climate Change, Michael Wright, John Allen Jr., and Joshua J. McElwee also evidence the impact of Francis's writings, visits, and pastoral ministry on the American people.

In Asia, views gathered from Ernest L. Tan and Socrates B. Villegas serve as case studies of how Francis's life and pastoral ministry are perceived in Asia. Francis, among other things, challenges everyone and the dominant status quo, particularly in the Philippines. People in the Philippines feel Francis's humility, gentleness, exercise of love and mercy, and his emphasis on pastoral outreach, especially to the poor and marginalized. In Asia, Francis is seen as "a shepherd with a heart for the poor and marginalized."[3] This is well summarized in the following story:

> One early morning, Pope Francis reportedly took the time to step out of his residence to speak to the man who is guarding him. Normally, they were taken for granted. He made efforts to inquire about him—his background and condition. Then, knowing how exhausted he might be, he proceeded to prepare him a sandwich. While eating, the pope asked him to sit, as he had been standing the whole night. But the guard refused because this was against the protocol of his job. The pope

---

3. See Tan (*Why I love Pope Francis*, 23) for details.

humorously used his authority and said: "Since I am your boss, I command you sit."[4]

Like in the United States and Asia, Francis's prophetic effect in Africa cannot be over-emphasized. Echoes of his effect are heard in families, schools, churches, and on streets across the continent of Africa. Views drawn from *The Church We Want: African Catholics Look to Vatican III* are representative. As an anthology of essays edited by Orobator, this volume covers not only the theology of Vatican II, but also the prophetic effect of Francis's papacy. The essays touch on issues of faith, hope, love, marriage, divine mercy, women, contextual theology, family, economic and socio-political problems, leadership, climate change, pastoral humility, and New Testament witnessing, and they affirm the prophetic effect of Francis's pontificate on African society—and the church in particular.

These eighteen essays, despite being focused on Africa, testify that "Francis incarnates a sort of living theology, where text takes flesh in context, challenges and spurs 'readers' into action."[5] Francis's "exercise of pastoral leadership permits critical inquiry and encourages further analysis, debate, and conversation about issues of critical importance in the church."[6]

In summary, this three-part theological survey challenges us to actively be prophetic in our daily lives. It also serves as a prophetic paradigm for contemporary evangelizers, exegetes, leaders, pastors, preachers, ministers, seminarians, teachers, theologians, and members of all faith communities.

---

4. Tan, *Why I Love Pope Francis*, 25.
5. Orobator, "Signs of the Future," xvi.
6. Ibid.

Bibliography

Aihiokhai, Simon Mary A. "The Need for Prophetic Voices in the African Catholic Churches: The Nigerian Context." *IJAC* 5 (2014): 7–27.
Allen, John L., Jr. *Against the Tide: The Radical Leadership of Pope Francis*. Quezon City, Philippines: Claretian Publications, 2014.
———. *10 Things Pope Francis Wants You to Know*. Liquori, Missouri: Liquori Publications, 2013.
Anderson, Bernhard W. *Understanding the Old Testament*. New Jersey: Prentice-Hall, 1986.
———. "'God with Us'—In Judgement and in Mercy: The Editorial Structure of Isaiah 5–10 (11)." Pages 230–45 in *Canon, Theology and Old Testament Interpretation: Essays in Honour of Brevard S. Childs*, edited by Gene M. Tucker, David L. Petersen, and Robert R. Wilson. Philadelphia: Fortress, 1988.
Anderson, Francis I. *Habakkuk: A Translation with Introduction and Commentary*. AB 25. New York: Doubleday, 2001.
Arabome, Anne. "When A Sleeping Woman Wakes . . . : A Conversation with Pope Francis in *Evangelii Gaudium* about Feminization of Poverty." Pages 55–63 in *The Church We Want: African Catholics Look to Vatican III*, edited by Agbonkianmegehe E. Orobator. Maryknoll, NY: Orbis, 2016.
Auld, A. Graeme. "Prophets Through the Looking Glass: Between Writings and Moses." *JSOT* 27 (1983): 3–23.
Barton, John. "Postexilic Hebrew Prophecy." *ABD* 5:489–95.
Béchard, Dean P. "Pontifical Biblical Commission Document on the Interpretation of the Bible in the Church." Pages 224–317 in *The Scripture Documents: An Anthology of Official Catholic Teachings*, edited and translated by Dean P. Béchard. Collegeville, MN: Liturgical, 2002.
Benedict XVI. *The Word of God (Verbum Domini): Post-Synodal Apostolic Exhortation of the Holy Father Benedict XVI*. Vaticana: Libreria Editrice, 2010.
Binz, Stephen J. *Introduction to the Bible: A Catholic Guide to Studying Scripture*. Collegeville, MN: Liturgical, 2007.
"Biography of the Holy Father, Francis." *L'Osservatore Romano*, Year LXIII, number 12. Accessed August 29, 2017. http://w2.vatican.va/content/francesco/en/biography/documents/papa-francesco-biografia-bergoglio.html.
Birch, Bruce C. "Review of *The Role of the Micaiah Narrative (1 Kings 22) in the Development of Early Prophetic Tradition* by Simon J. De Vries." *JBL* 98 (1979): 594–95.

Bibliography

Boda, Mark J., and Lissa M. Wray Beal, eds. *Prophets, Prophecy, and Ancient Israelite Historiography.* Winona Lake, IN: Eisenbrauns, 2013.

Boda, Mark J. "Recycling Heaven's Words: Receiving and Retrieving Divine Revelation in the Historiography of Judges." Pages 43–67 in *Prophets, Prophecy, and Ancient Israelite Historiography*, edited by Mark J. Boda and Lissa M. Wray Beal. Winona Lake, IN: Eisenbrauns, 2013.

Boring, M. Eugene. "Early Christian Prophecy." *ABD* 5:495–502.

Branick, Vincent. *Understanding the Historical Books of the Old Testament.* New York: Paulist, 2011.

———. *Understanding the Prophets and Their Books.* New York: Paulist, 2012.

Brueggemann, Walter. *The Prophetic Imagination.* Second Edition. Minneapolis: Fortress, 2001.

Chinitz, Jacob. "Were the Prophets Opposed to Sacrifice?" *JBQ* 37 (2009): 53–56.

Clements, Ronald E. "Patterns in the Prophetic Canon: Healing the Blind and the Lame." Pages 189–200 in *Canon, Theology and Old Testament Interpretation: Essays in Honour of Brevard S. Childs*, edited by Gene M. Tucker, David L. Petersen, and Robert R. Wilson. Philadelphia: Fortress, 1988.

Cliford, R. J. "The Use of *Hôy* in the Prophets." *CBQ* 28 (1966): 458–464.

Cook, Joan E. *Hear, O Heavens and Listen, O Earth: An Introduction to the Prophets.* Collegeville, MN: Liturgical, 2006.

Craigie, C. *The Problem of War in the Old Testament.* Grand Rapids, MI: Eerdmans, 1978.

Cross, Frank M. *Canaanite Myth and Hebrew Epic: Essays in the History of the Religious of Israel.* Cambridge, MA: Harvard University Press, 1973.

Dangl, Oskar. "Habakkuk in Recent Research." *Current Research* 9 (2001): 13–168.

Dawes, Gregory W. *Introduction to the Bible.* New Collegeville Bible Commentary, Vol. I. Collegeville, MN: Liturgical, 2007.

Dowling, Kevin. "Bishops as Theologians: Listening, Discerning, and Dialogue." Pages 3–10 in *The Church We Want: African Catholics Look to Vatican III*, edited by Agbonkianmeghe E. Orobator. Maryknoll, NY: Orbis, 2016.

Feinberg, Charles L. *The Minor Prophets.* Chicago: Moody Press, 1991.

Flennery, Austin. *Vatican Council II: The Basic Sixteen Documents, Constitutions Decrees, Declarations.* A Completely Revised Translation in Inclusive Language, edited by Austin Flannery. Dublin: Dominican, 1996.

Gehring. John. *The Francis Effect: A Radical Pope's Challenge to the American Catholic Church.* New York: Rowman & Littlefield, 2015.

Hays, J. Daniel. *The Message of the Prophets: A Survey of the Prophetic and Apocalyptic Books of the Old Testament.* Grand Rapids: MI: Zondervan, 2010.

Gersternberger, Erhard. "The Woe-Oracles of the Prophet." *JBL* 81 (1962): 249–263.

Gecewicz, Claire. "U.S. Catholics, Non-Catholics Continue to View Pope Francis Favorably." *Pew Research Center.* Accesses August 28, 2017. http://www.pewresearch.org/fact-tank/2017/01/18/favorable-u-s-views-pope-francis/.

Glatz, Carol. "Pope's Episcopal Motto Comes from Homily by English Doctor of the Church." *Catholic News Service.* March 15, 2013. http://www.catholicnews.com/services/englishnews/2013/pope-s-episcopal-motto-comes-from-homily-by-english-doctor-of-church.cfm.

———. "In Latest Interview, Pope Francis Reveals 10 Top Secrets to Happiness." *Catholic News Service.* July 29, 2014. http://www.catholicnews.com/services/

englishnews/2014/in-latest-interview-pope-francis-reveals-top-10-secrets-to-happiness.cfm.

Gordon, R. P. "Where Have All the Prophets Gone? The 'Disappearing' Israelite Prophet Against the Background of Ancient Near Eastern Prophecy." *BBR* 5 (1995): 67–86.

Hann, Scott. "Foreword." In *Lumen Fidei: The Light of Faith*. New York: Image, 2013.

Harrington, Wilfred J. *Record of Promise*. Chicago, IL: The Priory, 1965.

———. *Record of Revelation*. Dublin: Helicon, 1966.

Hays, J. Daniel. *The Message of the Prophets: A Survey of the Prophetic and Apocalyptic Books of the Old Testament*. Grand Rapids: MI: Zondervan, 2010.

Healy, Mary. "Verbum Domini and the Renewal of Biblical Preaching." Pages 109–122 in *Verbum Domini and the Complementarity of Exegesis and Theology*, edited by Scott Carl. Grand Rapids, MI: Eerdmans, 2015.

Heschel, Abraham J. *The Prophets*. New York: Haper & Row, 1962.

Huffmon, H. B. "Prophecy." *ABD* 5:477–82.

Holmyard, Harold. "The Sovereignty of God in the Book of Job: God Used Job to Change Theology." *Testamentum Imperium* 2 (2009): 1–19.

House, Paul R. 'Dramatic Coherence in Nahum, Habakkuk, and Zephaniah." Pages 194–208 in *Forming Prophetic Literature: Essays on Isaiah and the Twelve in Honor of John D. W. Watts*, edited by James W. Watts and Paul R. House. JSOTSup 235. Sheffield: Sheffield Press, 1996.

Irwin. Kevin W. *A Commentary on Laudato Si´: Examining the Background, Contributions, Implementation, and Future of Pope Francis's Encyclical*. New York: Paulist Press, 2016.

Jeremias, Jörg. "Amos 3–6: From the Oral Word to the Text." Pages 217–229 in *Canon, Theology and Old Testament Interpretation: Essays in Honour of Brevard S. Childs*, edited by Gene M. Tucker, David L. Petersen and Robert R. Wilson. Philadelphia: Fortress, 1988.

John Paul II. *Encyclical Letter of John Paul: Redemtor Hominis (The Redeemer of Man)*. Boston: Pauline Books, 1979.

———. *Encyclical Letter of John Paul II: Dominum et Vivificanem (The Holy Spirit in the Life of the Church and the World)*. Boston: Pauline Books, 1986.

———. *Encyclical Letter of John Paul II: Redemtoris Missio (Mission of the Redeemer)*. Boston: Pauline Books: 1990.

Kambanda, Antoine. "'If You Want Cows, You Must Sleep Like a Cow': The Bishop in the Church Pope Francis." Pages 65–76 in *The Church We Want: African Catholics Look to Vatican III*, edited by Agbonkianmeghe E. Orobator. Maryknoll, NY: Orbis, 2016.

Kastfelt, Niels. "African Prophetism and Christian Missionaries in Northeast Nigeria: A Healing Prophet among the Mbula of Adamawa 1927-c. 1932, as seen by Danish Missionaries." *Journal of Religion in Africa* VIII (1976): 175–88.

Kim, Hyun Chul Paul. "Review of *Prophets Male and Female: Gender and Prophecy in the Hebrew Bible, the Eastern Mediterranean and the Ancient Near East*, edited by Jonathan Stökl and Corrine L. Carvalho." *CBQ* 76 (2014): 584–86.

Knox, Peter. "*Laudato Si´*, Planetary Boundaries, and Africa: Saving the Planet." Pages 229–242 in *The Church We Want: African Catholics Look to Vatican III*, edited by Agbonkianmeghe E. Orobator. Maryknoll, NY: Orbis, 2016.

Ko, Grace. "The Ordering of the Twelve as Israel's Historiography." Pages 315–332 in *Prophets, Prophecy, and Ancient Israelite Historiography*. Edited by Mark J. Boda and Lisa M. Wray Beal. Winona Lake, IN: Eisenbrauns, 2013.

Bibliography

Lambdin, Thomas O. *Introduction to Biblical Hebrew*. New Jersey: Prentice Hall, 1971.

Leclerc, Thomas L. *Introduction to the Prophets: Their Stories, Sayings and Scrolls*. New York: Paulist, 2007.

Lee, Bernon. "'Face to Face': Moses as Prophet in Exodus 11:1–12:28." Pages 3–21 in *Prophets, Prophecy, And Ancient Israelite Historiography*, edited by Mark J. Boda and Lissa M. Wray Beal. Winona Lake, IN: Eisenbrauns, 2013.

Leuchter, Mark. "The Prophets and the Levites in Josiah's Covenant Ceremony." *ZAW* 121(2009): 31–47.

Luciani, Rafael, and Felix Palazzi. "Pope Francis' theology begins with the people' faith." *American Magazine*. April 14, 2016. https://www.americanmagazine.org/issue/popular-voice.

Maibach, E., et al. *The Francis Effect: How Pope Francis Changed the Conversion about Global Warming*. George Mason University and Yale University. Fairfax, VA: George Mason University Center for Climate Change Communication, 2015.

Mayemba, Bienvenu. "Reviving A Church of the Poor and for the Poor, and Reclaiming Faith Doing Justice and Seeking Liberation: Convergence between Pope Francis and Jean-Marc Ela." Pages 43–54 in *The Church We Want: African Catholics Look to Vatican III*, edited by Agbonkianmegehe E. Orobator. Maryknoll, NY: Orbis, 2016.

McElwee. Joshua, J. *10 Things Pope Francis Wants You to Know About Family*. Liquori, Missouri: Liquori Publications, 2016.

McKane, W. "Prophet and Institution." *ZAW* 94 (1982): 251–266.

Meddleton, J. Richard. "Samuel Agonistes: A Conflicted Prophet's Resistance to God and Contribution to the Failure of Israel's Frist King." Pages 69–91 in *Prophets, Prophecy, and Ancient Israelite Historiography*, edited by Mark J. Boda and Lissa M. Wray Beal. Winona Lake, IN: Eisenbrauns, 2013.

Meko, Tim. "Pope Francis Biography Graphic." *United States Conference of Catholic Bishops*. Accessed August 29, 2014. http://www.usccb.org/about/leadership/holy-see/francis/pope-francis-biography-graphic.cfm.

Oeste, Gordon. "The Shaping of a Prophet: Joshua in the Deuteronomistic History." Pages 23–41 in *Prophets, Prophecy, and Ancient Israelite Historiography*, edited by Mark J. Boda and Lissa M. Wray Beal. inona Lake, IN: Eisenbrauns, 2013.

Okure, Teresa. "Becoming the Church of the New Testamenet." Pages 93–105 in *The Church We Want: African Catholics Look to Vatican III*, edited by Agbonkianmegehe E. Orobator. Maryknoll, NY: Orbis, 2016.

Orobator, Agbonkhianmeghe E., ed. *The Church We Want: African Catholics Look to Vatican III*. Maryknoll, NY: Orbis, 2016.

———. "Introduction: Reading the Times for Signs of the Future." Pages xv–xxxi in *The Church We Want:African Catholics Look To Vatican III*, edited by Agbonkianmegehe E. Orobator. Maryknoll, NY: Orbis, 2016.

Oswalt, John N. "Is There Anything Unique in the Israelite Prophet?" *BS* 172 (2015): 67–84.

Nogalski, James D., and Marvin A. Sweeney. "Preface." Pages vii–viii in *Reading and Hearing the Book of the Twelve*, edited by James D. Nogalski and Marvin A. Sweeney. Symposium Series 15. Atlanta: SBL, 2000.

Pacwa, Mitch. "Foreword." Pages ix–xiii in *Jorge Mario Bergoglio: Francis Pope of a New World* by Andrea Tornielli. San Francisco: Ignatius, 2013.

Paul VI. *Dogmatic Constitution on Divine Revelation, Dei Verbum*. Boston: Pauline Books and Media, 1965.

Petuchowski, Jakob J. "Faith and Works in the Biblical Confrontation of Prophets and Priests." *Judaism* 39 (1990): 184–191.

Pew Research Center. "Positive Impact of Pope Francis on Views of the Church, Especially Among Democrats and Liberals." *Pew Research Center: Religion and Public Life*. October 7, 2015. http://www.pewforum.org/2015/10/07/following-visit-two-thirds-in-u-s-view-pope-francis-favorably/.

Pinker, Aron. "A Reconstruction of *Matzor* (Habakkuk 2:1)." *Jewish Bible Quarterly* 31 (2003):161–163.

Pontifical Biblical Commission. *The Interpretation of the Bible in the Church*. Boston: Pauline Books and Media, 1993.

Pontifical Biblical Commission. *The Inspiration and Truth of Sacred Scripture*. Collegeville, MN: Liturgical, 2014.

Pope Francis. *The Joy of the Gospel, Evangelii Gaudium: Apostolic Exhortation*. Vatican City: Libreria Editrice Vaticana, 2013.

———. *On Care for Our Common Home, Laudato Si': Encyclical Letter*. Vatican City: Libreria Editrice Vaticana, 2015.

———. *Amoris Laetitia, The Joy of Love: On Love in the Family, Post-Apostolic Exhortation*. Vatican City: Libreria Editrice Vaticana, 2016.

———. "Apostolic Letter Misercordia et misera of the Holy Father Francis at the Conclusion of the Extraordinary Jubilee of Mercy." November 20, 2016. https://w2.vatican.va/content/francesco/en/apost_letters/documents/papa-francesco-lettera-ap_20161120_misericordia-et-misera.html.

———. "Letter of His Holiness Pope Francis According to Which an Indulgence is Granted to the Faithful on the Occasion of the Extraordinary Jubilee of Mercy." September 1, 2015. https://w2.vatican.va/content/francesco/en/letters/2015/documents/papa-francesco_20150901_lettera-indulgenza-giubileo-misericordia.html.

———. "Pope Francis: '*Miserando atque Eligendo*.'" *Vatican Radio*. March 22, 2013. http://www.news.va/en/news/pope-francis-miserando-atque-eligendo.

———. "Letter of His Holiness Pope Francis to the Bishops of Nigeria." 2015. http://w2.vatican.va/content/francesco/en/letters/2015/documents/papa-francesco_20150302_lettera-vescovi-nigeria.html .

———. "Message of His Holiness Francis for the Celebration of the World Day of Peace: Fraternity, the Foundation and Pathway to Peace." January 1, 2014. https://w2.vatican.va/content/francesco/en/messages/peace/documents/papa-francesco_20131208_messaggio-xlvii-giornata-mondiale-pace-2014.html.

———. "Apostolic Letter of His Holiness Pope Francis to All Consecrated People on the Occasion of the Year of Consecrated Life." November 21, 2014. https://w2.vatican.va/content/francesco/en/apost_letters/documents/papa-francesco_lettera-ap_20141121_lettera-consacrati.html.

———. "Message of His Holiness Pope Francis for the Celebration of the World Day of Peace: No Longer Slaves, But Brothers and Sisters." *January 1, 2015*. https://w2.vatican.va/content/francesco/en/messages/peace/documents/papa-francesco_20141208_messaggio-xlviii-giornata-mondiale-pace-2015.html.

———. "Message of His Holiness Pope Francis for the Celebration of the XLIX World Day of Peace: Overcome Indifference and Win Peace." January 1, 2016. http://w2.vatican.va/content/francesco/en/messages/peace/documents/papa-francesco_20151208_messaggio-xlix-giornata-mondiale-pace-2016.html.

———. "Message of His Holiness Pope Francis for the Celebration of the Fiftieth World Day of Peace: Nonviolence: A Style of Politics of Peace." January 1, 2017. https://w2.vatican.va/content/francesco/en/messages/peace/documents/papa-francesco_20161208_messaggio-l-giornata-mondiale-pace-2017.html.

———. "Message of His Holiness Pope Francis for the Celebration of the Fifty-First World Day of Peace. January 1, 2018. Vatican: Libreria Editricce Vaticana.

Pratico, Gary D., and Miles V. Van Pelt. *Basics of Biblical Hebrew Grammar.* Grand Rapids, MI: Zondervan, 2007.

Prichard, James B. *Ancient Near Eastern Texts Relating to the Old Testament.* Third Edition with Supplement. Edited by James B. Pritchard. Princeton, NJ: Princeton University Press, 1969.

Reese, Thomas. "The Francis Effect." *National Catholic Reporter.* March 6, 2014. https://www.ncronline.org/blogs/faith-and-justice/francis-effect.

———. "Pope Francis the Prophet." *National Catholic Reporter.* October 1, 2015. https://www.ncronline.org/print/blogs/faith-and-justice/pope-francis-prophet.

———. "A Readers' Guide to 'Laudato Si.'" *National Catholic Reporter.* June 26, 2015. https://www.ncronline.org/blogs/faith-and-justice/readers-guide-laudato-si.

———. "Study Guide for 'Amoris Laetitia.'" *National Catholic Reporter.* April 21, 2016. https://www.ncronline.org/blogs/faith-and-justice/study-guide-amoris-latitia.

Robert, Tom. "Foreword." Pages ix–xii in *the Francis Effect: A Radical Pope's Challenge to the American Catholic Church,* by John Gehring. New York: Rowman & Littlefield, 2015.

Robertson, O. P. *The Books of Nahum, Habakkuk, and Zephaniah.* NICOT. Grand Rapids, MI: Eerdmans, 1990.

Roberts, J. J. M. *Nahum, Habakkuk, and Zephaniah.* OTL. Louisville: Westminster John Knox, 1991.

Rofé, Alexander. "How Is the Word Fulfilled? Isaiah 55:6–11 within the Theological Debate of Its Time." Pages 246–61 in *Canon, Theology and Old Testament Interpretation: Essays in Honour of Brevard S. Childs,* edited by Gene M. Tucker, David L. Petersen, and Robert R. Wilson. Philadelphia: Fortress, 1988.

Scannone, Juan Carlos. "Pope Francis and the Theology of the People." *Theological Studies* 77 no. 1 (2016): 118–135.

Schmitt, John J. "Preexilic Hebrew Prophecy." *ABD* 5:482–89.

Smith-Christopher, Daniel L. "Returning to the Sources: The Hebrew Bible." Pages 24–44 in *The College Student's Introduction to Theology,* edited by Thomas P. Rausch. Collegeville, Minnesota: Liturgical Press, 1993.

Széles, Eszenyei Maria. *Wrath and Mercy: A Commentary on the Books of Habakkuk and Zephaniah.* Grand Rapids, MI: Eerdmans, 1987.

Sheppard, Gerald T. "True and False Prophecy within Scripture." Pages 262–82 in *Canon, Theology and Old Testament Interpretation: Essays in Honour of Brevard S. Childs,* edited by Gene M. Tucker, David L. Petersen, and Robert R. Wilson. Philadelphia: Fortress, 1988.

Skehan, Patrick W. "Review of *The False Prophets of the Old Testament: Summary of a Dissertation Submitted to the Faculty of Sacred Sciences of the Catholic University of America* by Edward F. Siegman." *CBQ* 1 (1939): 281.

Sklba, Richard J. *Pre-Exilic Prophecy: Words of Warning, Dreams of Hopes, Spirituality of Pre-Exilic Prophets.* Collegeville, MN: Liturgical, 1990.

Bibliography

Tan, Earnest L. *Why I Love Pope Francis*. Quezon City, Philippines. Claretian Publications, 2014.

Tornielli, Andrea. *Jorge Mario Bergoglio: Francis, Pope of a New World*. San Francisco: Ignatius, 2013.

Tucker, Gene M., David L. Peterson, and Robert R. Wilson, eds. *Canon, Theology and Old Testament Interpretation: Essays in Honour of Brevard S. Childs*. Philadelphia: Fortress, 1988.

Tucker, Gene M. "The Law in the Eighth-Century Prophets." Pages 201–16 in *Canon, Theology and Old Testament Interpretation: Essays in Honour of Brevard S. Childs*, edited by Gene M. Tucker, David L. Petersen, and Robert R. Wilson. Philadelphia: Fortress, 1988.

Turner, H. W. "Review of *Prophetism in Ghana: A Study of Some "Spiritual" Churches* by C. G. Baëta." *International Review of Mission* 53 (1964): 94–96.

Udoekpo, Michael Ufok. *Re-thinking the Day of YHWH and Restoration of Fortunes in the Prophet Zephaniah: An Exegetical and Theological Study of 1:14–18; 3:14–20*. Das Alte Testament Im Dialog, vol. 2. Bern: Peter Lang, 2010.

———. "Review of *Prophets, Prophecy, and Ancient Israelite Historiography*, edited by Mark J. Boda and Lissa M. Wray Beal." *CBQ* 76 (2014): 165–67.

———. "Habakkuk's Faith and God's Sovereignty: A Paradigm for the Suffering Righteous Today." *American Journal of Biblical Theology* 15 (2014): 1–26.

———. "The Theological Functions of 'Seek the Lord' (*băqqaš ʾădōnāy*) in Zephaniah 2:1–3 for Contemporary Society." *International Journal of African Catholicism* 6 (2015): 77–91.

Uzukwu, Gesila Nneka. *The Unity of Male and Female in Jesus Christ: An Exegetical Study of Galatians 3.28c in Light of Paul's Theology of Promise*. New York: Bloomsbury T&T Clark, 2015.

Vawter, Bruce. "Introduction to Prophetic Literature." Pages 186–200 in *The New Jerome Biblical Commentary*, edited by Raymond E. Brown, Joseph A. Fitzmyer, and Roland E. Murphy. Englewood Cliffs, NJ: Prentice Hall, 1990.

Von Rad, Gerhard. *Der Heilige Krieg im Alten Israel*. AThNT 20. Zurich: 1951.

———. *Old Testament Theology*. Vol. II. Translated by D. M. G. Stalker. New York: HarperCollins, 1965.

———. *Holy War in Ancient Israel*. Translated and edited by Marva J. Dawn. Grand Rapids, MI: Eerdmans, 1991.

Wifall, Walter. *Israel's Prophets: Envoys of the King*. Chicago: Franciscan Herald, 1974.

Westermann, Claus. *Basic Forms of Prophetic Speech*. Translated by H. C. White. Philadelphia: Westminster, 1967.

———. "The Role of Lament in the Theology of the Old Testament." *Interpretation* 28 (1974): 20–38.

Wikipedia. "Pope Francis." Accessed August 29, 2017. https://en.wikipedia.org/wiki/Pope_Francis.

Wikipedia. "Theology of Pope Francis." Accessed September 14, 2017. https://en.wikipedia.org/wiki/Theology_of_Pope-Francis.

Wilson, Robert R. *Prophecy and Society in Ancient Israel*. Philadelphia: Fortress, 1980.

Wright. Michael. *10 Things Pope Francis Wants You to Know About the Environment*. Liquori, Missouri: Liquori Publications, 2016.

Wolff, Hans Walter. "Prophets and Institutions in the Old Testament." *Current in Theology* 13 (1986): 5–12.

Bibliography

Wray Beal, Lissa M. "Jerobaom and the Prophets in I Kings 11–14: Prophetic Word for Two Kingdoms." Pages 105–124 in *Prophets, Prophecy, and Ancient Israelite Historiography*, edited by Mark J. Boda and Lissa M. Wray Beal. Winona Lake, IN: Eisenbrauns, 2013.

Wuerl, Cardinal Donald. *The Gift of Saint John Paul II: A Celebration of His Enduring Legacy*. Fredrick, MD: The Word Among Us, 2011.

Author Index

Allen, John L., Jr., 64n186, 69n196, 76, 77, 78n11, 140–141, 152, 158
Anderson, Bernhard W., 3, 4, 5n17, 20, 21n67–68, 22n70, 24n74, 26n79
Anderson, Francis I., 40n120, 43n128
Arabome, Anne, 146, 148, 149
Beal, Lissa M. Wray, 16n59
Benedict XVI, xxii, 53n161, 69, 76–78, 85, 86n58, 87, 102n141, 113, 136
Binz, Stephen J., 7n27
Boda, Mark J., 11n42
Branick, Vincent, xxiiin3, 7n29, 16n58, 18n60, 24n73, 26n80, 27n82, 33, 36n104, 37n107, 59n173, 65n189
Brueggemann, Walter, xxiiin3, 6, 8, 48n148, 101n137, 115, 142
Cook, Joan E., xxiiin3, 33n96, 59n174, 62, 64, 72
Craigie, C., 12n47
Cross, Frank M., 12n47, 98
Dangl, Oskar, 41n121
Dawes, Gregory W., 7n27
Dowling, Kevin, 146–147
Feinberg, Charles L., 41n125, 44n131, 52
Gehring. John, 131–135, 158
Glatz, Carol, 114n212, 121n245
Hays, J. Daniel, xxiiin3, 4, 9n37
Heschel, Abraham J., xxiiin3, 5, 16n56, 58n172
Huffmon, H. B., xxiiin3, 2
Holmyard, Harold, 43n130
House, Paul R., 41n125
Irwin, Kevin W., xxiiin4, 30n90, 78n11, 137–139

John Paul II, xxii, 13–15, 69, 76–77, 80, 85–87, 102n141, 105, 107, 113–114, 124, 136
Kambanda, Antoine, 146, 149, 150n71
Knox, Peter, 151, 152n76
Ko, Grace, 41, 47–48, 54
Lambdin, Thomas O., 46n137
Leclerc, Thomas L., xxiiin3, 1n1, 2, 3n8, 7n29, 8n32, 9n35, 10n39, 11n43, 12n46, 13n48, 15n54, 16n57, 18n62, 21n66, 22n70, 24n72, 25n77, 26n79, 27n81, 31n91, 36n103, 37n107, 38n110, 49n153, 58, 61, 64, 67n193, 69n198, 71n200, 72n201, 73n204, 132n16
Lee, Bernon, 10
Maibach, E., xxiiin4, 136–139
Mayemba, Bienvenu, 146, 148
McElwee, Joshua, J., 142, 152, 158
Oeste, Gordon, 10
Okure, Teresa, xx, 150–151
Orobator, Agbonkhianmeghe E., xxiiin4, 41n122, 81n33, 82, 145, 153, 159
Nogalski, James D., 54n165
Pacwa, Mitch, 77, 154n2
Paul VI, 14n52, 87, 102n141, 113
Pew Research Center, 127, 130–131, 152, 158
Pinker, Aron, 46n140, 47
Pratico, Gary D., 46n137
Reese, Thomas, xxiiin4, 127–130
Robert, Tom, 135
Robertson, O. P., 42n125

Author Index

Roberts, J. J. M., 42n125, 45n136, 46, 47n141, 48n149, 49, 51n155, 52n157, 53n160, 54n164
Scannone, Juan Carlos, 76n4
Smith-Christopher, Daniel L., 5n18
Széles, Eszenyei Maria, 41n124, 44–45, 46n139, 47, 49n151, 51n156, 52n158, 53n160
Sklba, Richard J., 24n75, 25n76
Sweeney, Marvin A., 54n165
Tan, Earnest L., 18n61, 142–144, 152, 158, 159n4
Tornielli, Andrea, 77n6, 154n1
Udoekpo, Michael Ufok, xxiiin3, 7n28, 12n47, 15n55, 29n84, 30n88, 37n105, 39n117, 50n154
Uzukwu, Gesila Nneka, 116n224, 150
Van Pelt, Miles V., 46n137
Vawter, Bruce, xxiiin3, 1, 2n4
Von Rad, Gerhard, 1n2, 12n47
Wifall, Walter, xxiiin3, 4–5, 28n83
Westermann, Claus, xxiiin3, 43, 50n154
Wilson, Robert R., xxiiin3
Wright, Michael, 72n203, 139, 152, 158
Wuerl, Cardinal Donald, 14n50, 134

Subject Index

Aaron, 8–9
Abraham, 8–9, 28, 60, 71, 79–80, 82, 155
Accompanying, 106–107, 122
Accountability, feminine perspective, 146
Africa, 101, 144, 148, 152, 159
African Catholics, 152–153
African church, 144–151
African pope, 147
African scholars, 144–145
African theological method, 150
African woman, 148–149
Ahijah, 16–20, 28, 73, 155
Alternatives, xxi, 6, 37, 73, 97, 98, 115, 120, 142, 144, 155, 157
Amoris Laetitia, xvii, xxii, 32, 62, 69, 75, 99–109, 123, 125, 142, 147, 156–157
Amos, 2, 4, 7, 26, 28–32, 35, 55, 73, 80, 84
Ancient near east, 1–3, 38
Anthropocentricism, 94–95, 125, 157
Asia, 75, 127, 142–144, 152, 157–159
Asians, 143–144
Assyrian Empire, 29, 35, 39, 54, 72, 79
Assyrians, 1, 34, 42
Assyrian texts, 2
Babylonian Empire, x, 2, 52, 63, 65, 79, 121
Babylonians, 1, 39–40, 44–45, 49, 51–52, 63
Balaam, 9, 155
Beatitudes, 110–112
Benedict XVI, xxii, 53, 69, 76–78, 85–87, 113, 136
Biblical prophecy, 3, 9, 10

Biblical prophet, x, xxii, xxiii, 4, 73, 75, 78, 81, 85, 125, 131, 155, 156
Biblical stories, 9, 19, 24, 57, 80, 99
Biodiversity, 88, 90
Biography, ix, 75–76
Brothers and sisters, 61–62, 112–117, 120–121, 123, 125, 157
Cain and Abel, 91–92, 113
Canaanites, 11, 22, 38, 53, 91
Capitalism, 6, 84, 125, 128, 134, 144, 147, 156
Cardinals, 16, 133–134, 143
Catechesis, xiv, 85–86
Catechism of the church, 108
Catholic church, 61, 130, 135, 138–139
Catholic climate conference, 137
Catholics, 8, 77, 106–107, 128, 131, 137, 152, 158
Catholic tradition, 116
Center for Climate Change, 136
Chaldeans, 40, 44–45, 48, 50–51, 56
Challenges, xxi, xxiii, 18, 22, 28, 30–31, 48, 55, 58, 60, 65–69, 75, 83–84, 87, 98–102, 105–106, 109, 113, 116, 125–127, 136, 143, 148–149, 157
Changes, xxiii, 9, 18, 37, 47, 83, 89–90, 97, 99–101, 107, 137, 147
Christ, 13–14, 37, 49, 57, 78–83, 86, 92–93, 97, 99, 102–103, 108–109, 116, 125, 156
Christ's mission, 109
Christian and Muslim, 122
Christian theologian, 152
Christian virtue, 98

Subject Index

Church's missionary activity, 13-14
Church attendance, 128, 131, 152, 158
Church leaders, 15-16, 82-83, 140, 146, 150
Classical prophets, 7, 26, 28, 72
Climate change, 88-89, 125, 130, 136-137, 152-153, 156-159
Comfort, 65, 70, 120, 129
Coming messiah, 74
Commentary, 35, 118-119, 138
Common good, 3, 51, 80, 89, 95-96, 98, 107, 129, 139
Community, 9, 40, 45, 56-57, 66, 69-70, 73, 85-86, 105, 111, 113, 116, 121, 124, 145, 148
Compendium, 86, 144, 153
Complaints, 45, 47, 58
Conscience, 46, 56, 81, 100, 107-108, 117, 156
Consecrated life, 74-75, 84, 114-116
Consecrated people, 112, 114, 126, 157
Contemporary society, 13, 75, 87, 127, 154, 157
Conversion, 59, 82-83, 97, 118
Corruption, 29, 31, 36, 42, 47, 67, 95-96, 111, 113, 117, 149
Covenant, xxi, 5, 10-11, 17, 24, 32, 48-49, 54-56, 59, 64, 69-71, 79, 85, 104, 151, 155
Covenant theology, 155
Criteria, 10, 31, 111
Cultural context, xi, 104
Cultural icon, 77, 154
Daily lives, xxiii, 159
David, 4, 13-20, 29, 34, 56, 59, 73
Day of the Lord, 31, 34, 37, 61, 69, 72
Deborah, 11, 27-28, 155
Despair, 6, 61-62, 69
Deutero-Isaiah, 65-66, 92
Deuteronomistic History, 10, 24
Deuteronomistic historians, 19-20
Dialogue, xxiii, 18, 28, 40, 42-43, 46-47, 80-81, 83, 85-87, 95-96, 114, 125, 129-130, 136-138, 146, 149, 152, 154-156, 158
Discerning, 2, 107, 139, 146
Discernment, 107-108, 111
Disciples, xiv, xv, 60, 74, 82, 85

Disobedient prophet, 72
Divine agents, 19, 28, 155
Divine judgement, xxi, 59, 68, 155
Divine love, 39, 59
Divine mercy, 25, 68, 108, 119-121, 141, 152-153, 155, 158-159
Divine sovereignty, 41-43, 54
Dominant culture, 6, 73, 82, 84, 134, 139, 143-144, 149, 155
Dry bones, 63
Dynasty, 15, 18
Early prophets, 7
Ecclesiastical documents, 13
Ecological, 93-94, 97, 109, 125, 152, 157
Ecological education, 97
Ecology, xxiii, 72, 88, 95-97, 138, 156
Economic crises, 94, 113
Economy, 84, 88, 96-97, 113, 129, 134, 156
Edom, 20, 31, 53, 61, 68
Education of children, 106
Effect on the U.S.A., 127
Elijah, 6, 21-26, 71, 73, 90, 115, 155
Elisha, 21-28, 90, 155
Elite class, 29-30
Enemies of holiness, 110
Environment, xxii, 6, 64, 72, 76, 87-91, 94-98, 118, 124, 129-130, 136-137, 139, 150, 151, 156-157
Environmental issues, 90
Environmental policy, 95
Environmental threats, 91
Esau and Jacob, 61-62, 68
Eschatology, 34
Ethical conduct, xiii, 25, 28, 36, 73, 84, 95, 155
Ethics of ecology, 97
Evangelii Gaudium, xiv, xvii, xxii, 34, 37-38, 56, 60, 66, 75, 81, 125, 151, 156
Evangelization, 14, 60, 64, 77, 81-86, 125, 154
Exegetes, xxiii, 150, 159
Exegetical evaluation, x
Exhortation, 6, 14, 32, 34, 37, 56, 60-62, 66, 69-70, 81-85, 92, 99, 101, 105, 108-109, 110-114, 117, 123, 135, 140, 151, 154-155

Subject Index

Exiled, 63, 132
Ezekiel, xiv, 2, 7, 28, 62–64, 67, 73, 131–133, 155
Ezekiel's prophecy, 64, 132
Faith communities, xxiii, 159
Faithfulness, 33, 40, 49, 64, 69, 74, 111, 119
Faith-knowledge, 79
Families, xxii, 29, 61, 99–109, 118, 120–121, 123, 125, 129, 144, 149, 152, 154, 157, 159
Family, xxiii, 51, 61, 64, 68–69, 74, 99–103, 106–109, 113, 118, 123–124, 128, 138, 142, 148–149, 153, 159
Fertility, 23, 32–33, 67, 71–72, 155
Fides ex Auditu, 79
Fides ex Ratio, 80
First Isaiah, 34
Flying scroll, 68
Foreign gods, 17
Foreshadow, xvii, xxii, 4, 8, 25, 28, 34, 37, 40, 56–57, 155
Forgiveness, xxiii, 28, 68, 71, 120, 122, 124
Formation, xiv, 75–76, 85, 106–107
Former prophets, 6, 10
Four chariots, 68
Francis of Assisi, 87
Fraternity, 112–117, 120, 125
Freedom, 6, 62, 65, 73, 100–101, 106–107, 116–117, 155
Function, x, xvii, xxii, 1, 3, 7, 9, 23, 75, 155
Fundamentalism, 84, 122, 149
Gaudate ex Exsultate, 75, 109
Gerhring's, 134
Global church, 83
Global effect, 126, 157
Globalization, 113, 147
Globalization of indifference, 6, 23, 62, 77, 118
Global religious leader, xxii, 87, 154
Global warming, xxiii, 96, 136, 137
Gnosticism, 109
God's healing mercy, 25
God's instrument, 54, 57, 66
God's plan, 41, 49, 52, 92
God's sovereignty, 34, 42, 44, 54, 68, 155

Golden rule, 130
Gomer, 32, 33, 54
Gospel, ix, xiv, xvii, 8, 14, 28, 34, 37, 60, 64–66, 69, 72, 74, 80–81, 83–86, 91, 103, 107, 110, 113, 115, 119, 121, 125, 131, 140, 147, 151, 156
Gospel message, 83
Gospel of creation, 65, 72, 91
Gospel of hope, 64
Gospel of the family, 69, 103, 106, 150
Greek Old Testament, 7
Habakkuk, 7, 28, 39–57, 73
Habemus Papam, 77
Haggai, 7, 28, 66–68, 71, 73, 90
Happiness, 113–114, 129
Hebrew bible, 4, 6-7
Ḥerem, 12
High priest, 27, 68
Historical books, 6–7, 10
Historical context, xiii
Historical events, 19, 35
Holiness, 40, 109–110, 112, 125, 135, 157
Holiness of life, 109, 157
Holy One of Israel, 35, 62
Holy Spirit, 14–15, 82, 105
Homily and liturgy, 85
Hosea, 7, 26, 28, 32–35, 54, 71, 73, 99, 155
Huldah, 21, 27–28, 155
Human life, 89, 91
Human person, 117
Humility, xxi, 18, 77, 80, 87, 110, 125, 140, 143, 152–159
Hymn of St. Francis, 92
Hypocritical worship, 30
Idle songs, 30
Idolatry, 12, 20, 22–23, 31–33, 40, 52, 63, 73, 84, 134, 155, 156
Ignatius of Loyola, 103–104, 115
Images, 20, 133, 141
Immanuel, 35
Immigrant, xv, 26, 76, 123–124, 130
Inclusiveness, 70, 73, 84, 140, 148
Indifference, 6, 23, 44, 62, 65, 77, 84, 89, 101, 112, 117–118, 121, 125, 157
Inequality, 84, 90, 134

173

Subject Index

Injustice, xi, xxi, 6, 18, 25, 30–31, 36, 39–42, 44–45, 50, 55–60, 63, 69, 77, 115
Integral ecology, 88, 95
Integral spirituality of creation, 138, 156
Integrating, 107, 124
Intercession of Mary, 80, 98, 121–122
International, 22, 44, 76, 88, 95–96, 116, 124
Isaiah, 7, 27–28, 34–36, 49, 54, 65–66, 69–71, 73, 79–80, 84, 92, 131, 155
Israel's Prophets, xix, xxii, xxiii, 1, 3, 5–6, 8–9, 12, 18, 73, 75, 78–82, 84, 86, 88–92, 94–100, 109, 115, 121, 125, 129, 135, 137, 140, 143, 145, 154–157
Israel as bride, 33, 59
Jehu, 21, 24, 26
Jeremiah, 2, 7, 27–28, 42, 54, 57–61, 63, 73, 81–82, 92, 115, 121–122, 155
Jeroboam, 4, 17–22, 29, 73
Jerusalem, xiii, 17, 19–20, 29, 34, 36, 62, 66, 73, 122, 131–133, 155
Jesus, 27, 49, 60, 73–74, 76, 79–82, 85–86, 93, 101–102, 111, 115, 118–119, 123, 134, 139, 146, 151
Jezebel, 22–25
Joel, 7, 28, 66, 71–73, 88, 90
John Gehring, 131–135, 152, 158
John Paul II, xxii, 13–14, 69, 76, 77, 80, 85–87, 105, 107, 113–114, 124, 136
Jonah, 7, 28, 55, 66, 72–73, 115
Jorge Mario Bergoglio, xxii, 75, 77
Joshua, 10–11
Josiah, 19, 27, 37, 42
Joy of salvation, 38
Jubilee of mercy, 75, 99, 118
Jubilee year, 120
Judgment, xiii, xxi, 19, 28, 31–32, 35, 37–38, 43, 45, 49, 55, 58–59, 62, 68, 71, 73–74, 78–79, 84, 107, 111, 155
Judgment speech, 51
Justice, xiii, 6, 25, 28, 30–32, 35–37, 39, 43–44, 55, 59–60, 64, 68, 70, 72–74, 84, 88, 98, 101, 109, 113, 129, 148, 155
Justice and peace, 70, 95, 129, 155
Kerygma, xiv, 85–86

King Cyrus, 65
Kingdom of God, 14, 52, 111
Knowledge of God, 30, 35
Lack of knowledge, 35, 59
Lament, 43, 45–46, 55, 71
Language, 3, 30, 38, 45–46, 49–50, 53, 71, 78, 83, 86, 101, 114, 142, 154
Laudato si', xvii, 39, 45, 65, 72, 75, 87, 98, 109, 118, 125, 136–139, 147, 151, 156
Leadership, xxi, 9, 11–12, 18, 33, 36, 72, 75–76, 82, 87, 91–92, 125, 140, 145, 150, 153, 155, 159
Letter, 112, 121, 126, 157
Light of the Master, 110
Locusts, 71
Love, xxi, xxiii, 18, 32–34, 39, 55, 59, 65, 69, 71–72, 74, 79, 83, 85–86, 92, 97–110, 115, 119–125, 128–129, 143–144, 148–149, 152–154, 158–159
Love for children, 105
Love for the poor, 70, 129, 144, 154
Love in marriage, 103
Lumen Fidei, xvii, xxii, 53, 75, 77–80, 91, 97–98, 125, 147, 156
Lumen Gentium, 81
Majesty, 53–55
Malachi, 7, 28, 66, 68–71, 73, 90, 104, 155
Man of God, 4, 18–20, 28, 46
Mantle of Elijah, 25
Markets, 88, 95
Marriage, 32, 101–107, 122, 125, 128, 138, 149, 153, 157, 159
Marriage and family, 101, 128
Marriage metaphor, 32
Martin Luther King Jr., xxii, 103–104, 123
Mary, 76, 80, 86, 98, 112, 114, 121, 122
Meaning, 1, 2, 5
Mercies, xx
Mercy, xvii, xxi, xxiii, 33, 37, 65, 72–74, 83, 118, 122, 124, 156
Mercy and poor, 135
Mercy of God, 36, 119
Messages, xxii, xxiii, 75, 112, 125, 156, 157
Micah, 7, 28, 34–37, 55, 73
Micaiah, 21, 26–28, 155

174

Subject Index

Migrants, 86, 112, 117, 124–125
Military imagery, 55
Minor Prophets, 7, 32, 40, 47, 155
Miriam, 8–9, 27, 155
Miserando atque Eligendo, 121
Misericordia et Misera, 112, 116–119, 126, 157
Misericordiae Vultus, 120
Missionary disciples, xiv, 85
Missionary mandate, 82
Mission of unity, 88
Models, 90, 96, 98, 112–113
Modern-day prophet, 135
Modern economists, 94
Monarchy, 10, 21, 59
Moses, 4, 8–11, 23–26, 28, 60, 69, 73, 82, 91, 108, 119, 155
Motif of power, 38
Mount Sinai, 24
Mystery of God, 45
Mystery of God's love, 119
Mystery of the universe, 91–92
Naaman, 25
Naboth, 24–25
Naboth's vineyard, 24
Nahum, 7, 28, 38–39, 44, 55, 61, 73
Nathan, 15–16, 28, 34, 73, 155
National Press Club, 137
National restoration, 63
Nature, 1
New covenant, 59, 64, 69, 151
New Evangelization, xvii, 78, 86
New heart, 64
New lifestyle, 88
New prophet, 74
New temple, 64, 66–67
New Testament, 3–4, 49, 73, 81, 102, 151, 153, 159
New Testament church, 151
New Year Messages, 23, 75, 112, 116, 125, 157
Nigerian bishops, 121, 122
Nineveh, 38, 61, 72
No longer slaves, 112, 116, 125, 157
Non-Catholics, xix, 106, 128, 131, 152, 158
Nonviolence, 112, 123, 125, 157
Obadiah, 7, 28, 55, 61–62, 68, 73

Old Testament, xiv, 2–4, 7, 28, 43, 73, 80–81, 116, 119
Old testament faith, 79
Onesimus, 116
On the light of faith, 77–78
Oppressing the poor, 36
Papacy, ix, x, xix, xxiii, 15, 18–19, 26, 28, 35, 63, 76, 78, 81, 83, 121, 125, 128, 132, 135, 138, 140, 142–143, 145, 149, 152, 156, 158, 159
Paradigmatic achievement, 126
Pastoral achievements, xxii, 73, 152, 154, 157, 158
Pastoral language, 30, 78, 101
Pastoral ministry, xi, 67, 135, 152, 156–158
Pastoral perspectives, 106
Pastoral work, 83
Pastors, xvii, 4, 85, 103, 116
Pathway to peace, 112–113, 125, 157
Peace dialogue, 18, 28, 155
Pelagianism, 109
People of the land, 66
Pew Research Center, 127, 130–131, 152, 158
Philemon, 116
Place of worship, 19
Plague, 53–54, 56, 71, 109
Planet, xxii, xxiii, 76, 88, 92, 125, 128, 134, 151, 154
Poor and middle class, 109, 129, 152, 158
Pope Francis' achievements, 141
Pope Francis' blueprint, 134
Pope Francis's lament, 62
Pope Francis' life, 75, 154
Pope Francis' ministry, 75
Pope Francis' papacy, 132
Pope Francis' theology, 138
Pope Francis' wants, 140
Pope of Mercy, xix, 77, 154
Pope of New World, 77, 154
Post-exilic, xi, 7, 66, 69, 71, 109
Post-exilic prophets, xi, 7, 66, 71, 109
Poverty, xxiii, 90, 95, 96, 101, 113, 117, 124, 130, 147
Prayer, 19, 41, 43, 45, 47, 50–51, 53, 56, 58, 70–71, 74, 80, 86–87, 98, 105, 108, 111, 122, 124–125, 156

175

Subject Index

Pre-classical prophets, 7, 8, 10, 21, 27, 28, 155
Pre-exilic prophets, 27, 37, 41–42, 49, 57, 109
President Obama, 136
Priesthood, 2, 10, 19, 59, 76, 84, 155
Proclamation, xiv, 75, 84–85, 107, 120, 125, 143, 156
Profits, 96
Prophecy, 1–4, 9–10, 18, 26–27, 30–32, 41–42, 45, 47, 49, 59, 62, 65, 67, 69–70, 73, 114–115
Prophetess, 3, 8, 11, 27, 74, 155
Prophetic behavior, 115
Prophetic books, x, 7, 9, 66, 119, 157
Prophetic dimension, 90–92, 96, 133, 139, 144
Prophetic effect, ix–xi, xvii, xix, xxiii, 2–3, 7, 28, 56, 75, 87, 98, 112, 127–128, 134–136, 138–140, 142, 144–145, 148–153, 157, 159
Prophetic effect in Africa, 144
Prophetic effect in Asia, 142
Prophetic figures, xxii, 11
Prophetic ministry, xiii, xiv, xv, 6, 9, 22, 24–25, 28, 49, 59, 60–61, 68, 73, 101, 115, 127–128, 130, 136, 143
Prophetic pantomime, 132
Prophetic renewal, 14
Prophetic role, 7, 10, 13, 15, 18, 26
Prophetic sentiments, 92
Prophetic style, 147
Proselytization, 114–115
Rapidification, 89, 157
Rebuilding, 66–70
Rebuilding the temple, 67–70
Reflection, 14, 47, 105, 107, 112, 149
Refugees, 124–125, 130
Rejected, 12, 17, 58–59, 73
Rejoice and be glad, 108, 112
Religious leaders, xxii, 87, 154
Remnant, 30–31, 34–37, 132, 155
Remnant of Israel, 34, 37
Remnant of Joseph, 31
Repentance, 68, 71, 73, 78–79, 82, 84, 155
Responsibility, 61, 63, 88, 96–97, 117
Restoration, 35–37, 42, 55, 62–63, 65, 68, 71, 73, 78, 84

Restoration of fortune, 65, 68
Restoration of Jerusalem, 36
Restore fortune, 57
Returned exiles, 66, 67, 71
Returning to God, 33
Righteous, 39, 41, 43, 45, 48–52, 55–57, 119
Righteousness, 28, 30–31, 37, 39, 70, 80, 110
Ritual, 30, 102, 133
Ruler, 12, 36, 39, 52, 54, 121
Sacrament of penance, 120
Sacraments, 80
Sacrifices, 12, 19, 30, 36, 68, 69, 71, 112
Salvation, 14, 28, 30–38, 59, 65, 70, 79, 85, 92, 102, 120
Salvation history, 33, 48
Samaria, 22, 25, 30, 32, 36, 54
Samaritan woman, 101
Samuel, 4, 6, 12–14, 17–18, 28, 155
Saul, 12–13, 16
Science and technology, 93
Scripture passages, 124
Second Isaiah, 34, 65, 70, 120
Seduced, 59
Self-examination, 100
Sensus Fidelium, 146, 149
Shaphan, 27
Shemaiah, 18, 20, 42
Signs, 1, 10, 30, 63, 81, 83, 92, 109, 112, 132, 145, 156
Silent, 44–45, 52
Simple style, 139
Simplicity, 36, 63, 74, 83, 87, 125, 142, 154, 157
Slavery, 9, 116–117
Social doctrine, 86
Social gospel, 60
Social justice, 25, 31, 34, 60, 64, 82–83
Solomon, 16–18, 29
Son of God, 49
Sovereign of all creation, 30, 38, 41, 45, 51–52, 65
Sovereignty of Yahweh, 23
Spiritual combat, 111
Spiritual life, 112

Subject Index

Spirituality, 3, 14, 25, 49, 64, 86, 96–99, 108–109, 125, 138, 147, 149, 156–157
Spirituality of action, 147
Spirituality of marriage, 108
St. Augustine, 115, 118
Steadfastness, 41, 49–50
Stories of faith, 80
Style of politics, 123, 125, 157
Suffering, 9, 27, 33, 39–41, 44, 46, 53, 55–58, 61, 65, 73, 80–81, 121–123, 155
Suffering servant of God, 65
Survey, 54, 68, 127, 130–131, 136–137, 159
Surveyor, 68
Symbolic, 17, 32, 62, 131, 154
Symbolically, 17, 62, 131
Symbols of power, 53
Symbols, 53, 132–133
Synod, 32, 74–75, 114, 144, 146, 149, 151
Synod Fathers, 81, 101, 107
Technological paradigm, 94, 125, 157
Technology, 79, 84, 88, 93–95, 139
Tekoa, 4, 29–30
Temple monarchy, 59
Ten things, 139
The Joy of the Gospel, 8, 34, 66, 81, 140, 151, 156
Theodicy, 39–40, 43, 56–57
Theologians, xviii, xix, xxiii, 41, 107, 144–146, 159
Theology, x, xi, xx, 5, 15, 31, 39–41, 43, 49, 53, 55, 57, 60–69, 72, 76, 80, 82, 121, 125, 137–139, 145, 147–148, 151–153, 155–156, 158–159
Theology of creation, 71, 137, 139, 151
Theology of the angel, 68
Theophanic, 39, 53, 55
The poor, xxi, xxii, 3, 6, 23–26, 29–31, 36–37, 42, 45–46, 50, 56–57, 60, 65, 68–71, 76–77, 81–82, 84, 86–90, 94–98, 107, 111, 115, 120, 125, 128–129, 133, 135, 140–141, 144, 146–158
The rich, 3, 29–30, 57
The Twelve, 7, 40, 47–48, 54–55
Third Isaiah, 34, 66, 69–71
Three days, 72
Three-part theological survey, 159
Throwaway culture, 88–90, 125, 139, 157
Traditional institutions, 59
Trinity, 98, 102
Tripartite, xxiii, 114, 144
Trust in God, 32–35, 49, 56, 71, 79, 111, 122
U.S. Conference of Bishops, 76, 137
U.S. Congress, 129, 136
Unethical worship, 55
Unfaithfulness, 12, 30, 32–33
United Nations, 36, 56, 130, 136
United States of America, x, xi, 75, 127–130, 133–138, 142, 144, 152, 157, 158–159
Universal goodness, 93
Vatican II, 41, 102, 107, 109, 134, 145, 147, 153, 159
Vatican reporter, 77
Vigilance, 106, 111
Vision, xi, 15, 30, 40, 48–50, 53, 55–56, 63, 67
Visions, 30, 67
Visits, xxii, 74–77, 112, 125, 128–131, 152, 154, 156, 158
Watchman, 47
Widow of Zeraphat, 23
Wife, 22, 27, 33, 62, 104–105, 132
Win peace, 112, 117, 125, 157
Woe, 39, 42, 50–52, 56
Woe formula, 50
Woe oracles, 39, 50, 52
Women in the basket, 68
World Day of Peace, 112, 123–124
World Day of the Poor, 121
Worship, 17, 19, 22–23, 25, 27–32, 42, 50, 52, 55, 63, 67–70, 111, 155
Writings, xvii, xxi, xxii, xxiii, 7, 28, 31, 34, 39, 61, 68, 74–75, 77, 81, 87, 102, 125, 137, 140, 152, 154, 156–158
Year of Faith, 78, 81
Year of Mercy, 74–75, 118–119
Zechariah, 7, 28, 55, 66–68, 71, 73–74, 84, 90
Zephaniah, 7, 28, 34, 37–38, 55, 73, 80, 84
Zion, xiii, 34, 36–37, 54–55, 63, 66, 68, 70, 73, 86, 121, 155

Scripture Index

OLD TESTAMENT

Genesis

1–6	91
1–2:42	45n135
1:15	91n85
1:26	91n85
1:27–28	116, 116n224
1:27	99n126
1:28	91, 91n85, 99n126
1:31	91n85
2:2–3	91n85
2:15	91n85, 92, 99n126
2:18	99n126
2:20	99n126
2:24	99n126
3:16	99n126
3:17–17:19	91n85
3:17–19	99n126
4	99n126
4:9–11	91n85, 92
4:9	113
4:17–22	99n126
4:25–26	99n126
5	99n126
6:5–6	91n85
6:6	92
6:13	91n85
9:7	99n126
10	99n126
10:10	52
11:10–32	99n126
11:29–23:20	27
12	8
12:13	82
13:16	79
15:5–6	49
15:5	79
17:1	108
17:2–5	99n126
17:16	99n126
20:7	8
22–27	61
22:1–2	49
22:7	79
23:3	99n126
25:1–4	99n126
25:12–17	99n126
25:19–26	99n126
28:18–22	19
35:11	99n126
36	99n126
48:3–4	99n126

Exodus

Reference	Page
1–15	43
2–3	91
3	8
3:17	82
4:22	99n126
5:3	53
6:10	91
7–12	55
7:1	8

Scripture Index

9:7	53	18:1–8	19
9:15	53	18:15–22	10
11:1–12:28	10	18:15	11
12:26–27	99n126	18:18	11, 16
13:14	99n126	18:20	11
15–18	55	18:21–22	11, 26, 27
15	53	22:4	91n85
15:1–18	8	22:6	91n85
15:14–16	54	33	54
15:20–21	8		
15:20	27	**Joshua**	
16	24	1–24	10
16:23	91n85	1:1–9	11
19–24	24	3:5	11
20:10	91n85	3:8	10
20:12	99n126	3:10–13	10
23:12	91n85	3:13–16	11
32–34	24	6:17–19	12
32	8	6:26	11
33:21	47	11:12	11
34:6–7	55, 119	11:15	11
		11:23	11
Leviticus		14:2	11
19:9–10	91n85	14:5	11
21	133	15:13	11
25:1–4	91n85	17:4	11
25:4–6	91n85	19:49–50	11
25:10	91n85	21:2	11
25:23	91n85	21:8	11
		22:5	11
Numbers		23:7–8	11
12:1–12	27	22:9	11
20:1	27	24	10, 23
22–24	9	24:2–28	11
22:38	9	24:2–13	11
23:3	47		
24:1	47	**Judges**	
		1:1–2:5	11
Deuteronomy		2:1–5	11
5:8–9	19	2:6–16:31	11
6:20–25	99n126	2:10–11	11
10:18–19	99n126	3:6–8	11
10:14	91n85	4–5	11
12:5–7	19	4:4–5:31	27
12:32–13:4	10	4:6–7	11
13:1–5	11	4:9	11
		4:17–22	11

Judges (cont)

5	53
5:4–5	54
5:24–27	11
10:13–14	11
17–21	11
18:30	19

1 Samuel

1–2	27
8–10	4
8:10–18	17
9:1–10:16	12
9:8–10	4
9:9	4
10:17–27	12
11:1–15	12
12:13–15	13
13:13–14	12
15:2–3	13
15:15–19	12
15:22–23	12
15:26	18
16:13	18
25:28–31	27

2 Samuel

3–6	13
7	13, 15
7:1–17	15, 16
7:4–7	15
7:11–16	16
7:12–16	18
11–12	13, 15
24:11	4

1 Kings

1	13, 15, 16
11–14	16n59
11:3	17
11:4–8	17
11:9–13	17
11:29–41	17
11:29–37	17
11:38	18
12	30
12:15	18
12:24	18
13:1–10	19
13:2–3	19
13:4	19
13:11–25	19
14:7–10	20
14:12–18	20
14:25–28	20n64
15	21
15:25	21
16:1–4	21
16:30–33	22
16:30–32	22
16:31	22
16:34	11
17–19	22
17	23
17:8–24	23
17:14–16	25
17:17–24	25
17:24	25
18	23
18:21	23
19	23
19:1–4	23
19:5–8	24
19:11–13	24
19:11	47
19:15–21	24
19:15	24, 54
19:19–21	25
20:35	4
21	22, 24, 99n126
21:3	25
21:14	25
21:20	25
22	26
22:5–28	26
22:14	26
22:22	27
24:19–20	11

2 Kings

2–9	25
2:3	4
2:5	4

Scripture Index

2 Kings *(cont)*

2:7	4
2:8	25
2:13–15	25
2:13–14	25
2:15	4
2:21	25
2:23–25	26
3:16	26
4:1–7	25
4:1	4
4:32–37	25
4:33	26
4:38	4
4:42–44	25
4:43	26
5:1–19	25
5:22	4
6:1	4
6:24–7:20	25
8:13–15	54
9:1–13	26
9:1	4
13:14–21	25
14:23–29	29
22–23	27
22:8	27
22:14–20	27
22:15–20	27
22:24–28	27
23:28–30	42
23:33–36	42
24:12–17	121

1 Chronicles

23:14	4

2 Chronicles

26:6–8	29
34–35	27

Ezra

1:1–11	66
1:2–4	66
2:64–65	66
3:2	4
3:8–13	66
5:16	66
9:2	67

Nehemiah

6:14	27
9:17	55, 119
12:24	4
12:36	4

Job

18–19	43
19:7	44
19:13–14	99n126
19:17	99n126

Psalms

8	45
24:1	91n85
27:10	99n126
31:10–31	99n126
33:6	91n85
78:3–6	99n126
85:1–2	119
103	55
103:8–12	119
104:31	91n85
119:103	111
127:1–2	51
127:1	99n126
127:2	99n126
127:3–5	99n126
128	99n126
128:1–6	99n126
128:3	99n126
128:4–5	99n126
128:5–6	99n126
131:2	99n126
136:6	91n85
137	63
137:1–9	63
145:8	55
146:9	124
148:3–5	91n85
148:5–6	91n85
148:12	99n126

Scripture Index

Proverbs

3:11–12	99n126
3:19	91n85
6:2–22	99n126
13:1	99n126
22:2	91n85
22:15	99n126
23:13–14	99n126
29:17	99n126

Isaiah

1–39	34, 35
1	34
1:2–3	35
1:4	35
1:18–31	35
1:27	35
2	34
2:2–4	35, 54
3	34
4	34
5	34
5:7	35
7	35
7:3	131n15
7:9	35, 49, 79
7:10–17	34
7:14–16	35
7:14	131n15
7:18–20	54
8:1–4	131n15
8:3	27
8:8	131n15
9	34
9:3	34, 82n33
9:6–7	34
10:1–4	34
10:5–34	34
10:5–6	51
10:5	54
11	34
11:1–5	35
12	34
12:6	35, 82n33
12:16	34
13–27	34
13–23	54
14:4–23	51n155
14:8	52
20	131
20:2	131
21:6	47
21:8	47
28–30	34
28:16–17	35
30:8	48
30:15	35
32:1–8	34
33	34
38:17	119
40–55	34, 65
40:1–2	65
40:1	120
40:9	66, 70, 82n33
40:11	65
40:12–22	65
40:28–29	65, 91n85, 92
40:31	82n33
41:14	65
42:1–4	65
43:1	65
43:3	65
45:5	65
49:1–6	65
49:15	99n126
50:4–10	65
50:10	65
52:9	65
52:13–53:12	65
52:15–53	44
53:5–6	65
53:8	65
54:5–8	65
55:10–11	66
56–66	34, 69
56:4–7	70
56:10–12	70
59:1–15	70
59:15–19	70
59:17	70
61	73
61:1–3	69
63:1–13	70
65:16	79
65:17–25	70

Scripture Index

66:1–3	70	29:10	91n85, 121
66:18–23	70	29:21–23	122
		30:9	59
Jeremiah		31:31–34	59
1:4–19	57, 60	31:33	64
1:5	57, 91n85	32:17	91n85
1:6–8	58	32:21	91n85
1:7	82	32:40	59
1:8	91n85, 115	33:15	59
2:2	59		36–38
2:12–13	5, 91n85	36:1–26	42
3:5–6	59	36:5	58
4:1	59	36:19	58
4:2	59	37:20–21	58
4:22	59	38:1–6	58
5:1	5	51:7	52
5:5	5		
5:26–28	60	**Lamentations**	
5:27–28	59	3:17	83n33
6:11	58	3:21–23	83n33
6:13	5	3:26	83n33
6:20–25	59		
7:3–15	59	**Ezekiel**	
8:10	5	1:1–3	63
10:7	54	3:7	64
11:18–23	43	3:16–21	63
12:1–4	43	3:17–18	47
12:5–6	43	3:22–27	62, 63, 132
15:10–21	57	4:1–3	62, 132
15:17	58	4:4–8	63, 132
18:18–23	57	4:9–11	62, 63, 132
18:18–20	58	4:12–15	62, 63, 132
18:21–23	59	4:17–20	62
20:1–2	58	5:1–4	62, 63, 132
20:7–18	43, 57	6:8	64
20:7	59	6:59	64
20:8–9	59	6:61	64
20:14–18	59	7:23	63
22:13–14	42	8	63
22:15–16	52	9–11	63
23:9–32	27	12:1–16	62, 63, 132
26:10–11	58	12:17–20	63, 132
26:20–24	42	16:1–52	63
27–28	91n85, 121	17:19	64
29	91n85, 121, 122	18	63
29:1–23	61, 63, 91n85	21:8–13	62, 63, 132
29:5–6	91n85, 122	22:29	63

Scripture Index

Ezekiel (cont)

23	63
24:15–24	62, 63, 132
33:7–8	47
33:21–22	63, 132
34	63
36:26	64
37	63
37:15–28	62, 63, 132
40–47	67
40–44	64
43:1–9	63
44:7	64
47	72

Hosea

1–3	32
1:6	44
2:1–3	33
2:1	33
2:7	33
2:9	33
2:11–14	33
2:12	33
2:16–24	33
2:21–22	33
3:5	33
4–8	32
4:1–2	5, 33
4:3	33
4:12–15	33
5:1–2	33
5:4	33
6:1	33
6:6	33
7:1–10	33
8:4–6	33
8:6	32
8:11	33
8:14	33
11–14	32
11:1–4	33, 105
11:1	99, 100
11:3–4	99, 100
11:8–11	33
11:8	33
12:7	33
13:1	33
13:2	32
14:2–3	33
14:5–9	33

Joel

1:2–2:17	71
1:9	71
2:13	55, 119
2:13–14	71
2:18–29	72

Amos

1–2	30
1:1	29
2:6–16	30
2:6–7	29
3–6	30
3:15	29
4:1–13	30
4:1	30
5:12	29
5:18–20	78
5:21–27	30
6:4–6	29
7:12	4
7:14–17	29
7:14	4
7:15	30
8:4–8	5, 155
8:5–6	29
8:6	29
9:11–15	30

Obadiah

1–7	61
11–14	61
8–18	61
19–21	61

Jonah

3:4	72
3:5	72
4:2	55, 72, 119

Scripture Index

Micah

1:6–7	36
2:1–2	36
2:6	36
3:1–12	36

Micah (*cont*)

3:8	36
3:12	36
4:1–3	35, 55
4:4–8	36
4:6–7	36
4:14	47
5:6–7	36
6:4	9
6:6–8	36
7:18–20	36, 119

Nahum

1:2	38
1:4	38
1:6	38
2:3–12	38
3:1–10	39

Habakkuk

1–2:5	39, 42, 52, 57
1:1	40
1:2–11	40
1:2–4	40, 43, 44, 45
1:2–3	43
1:2	51
1:4	43
1:5–11	44, 57
1:6	44, 56
1:7–8	44
1:7	44
1:9	44
1:10–11	44
1:12–17	40
1:12–14	44, 45
1:13	45
1:14–16	56
1:14	45
1:15–16	45
1:17	45
2:1–20	40
2:1–5	44
2:1	46, 47
2:2–3	48
2:2–5	47, 48
2:3–4	56
2:4–5	49
2:4	39, 41, 57, 79
2:5	50
2:6–20	39, 52
2:6–19	50, 56, 57
2:6–8	50
2:6	51
2:7–8	51
2:9–11	50, 51
2:11	51
2:12–14	50, 51, 52
2:12	51
2:13	51
2:15	52
2:15–17	50, 52
2:16–17	52
2:18–20	50, 52
2:18–19	52
2:20	52
3:1–19	41, 53
3:2	53
3:3–19	57
3:3–15	40
3:3	53
3:5	53
3:6–8	54
3:8	55
3:9–11	55
3:10–11	54
3:13–15	55
3:13	56
3:15	55
3:16–19	40, 55
3:16	55
3:18–19	56

Zephaniah

1–3	55, 78
1–2	37
1:2–18	37
1:7	52

Zephaniah (cont)

1:18	38
2–3	37
2:3	37
3:1	37
3:9–10	37
3:12–13	37
3:15–17	37
3:17	82n33, 84

Haggai

1:4	67
1:9–11	67
1:12–2:9	67

Zechariah

1:1–6	68
1:7–6:15	67
1:7–17	67
1:18–21	67
2:1–5	68
3:1–10	68
4:1–14	68
5:1–4	68
6:1–8	68
6:9–15	68
7:8–14	68
8:1–3	68
8:14–17	68
8:20–23	68
9:9	82n33
14:9	55

Malachi

1:2–5	68
1:5	68
1:6–2:9	68
2:8	69
2:10	69
2:11	69
2:14–16	104
2:16	69
2:17–3:5	69
3:5	69
4:4–5	69

NEW TESTAMENT

Matthew

1–7:27	108
2:11	99n126
5:3–12	110
5:12	108
5:13–14	151
5:17	13
5:45	91n85
6:3–4	97
6:3	91n85
6:26	91n85
7:24–27	99n126
8:27	91n85
9:9–13	99n126, 121
10:34–37	99n126
11:19	91n85
11:25	91n85, 93
13:31–32	91n85
16:15	14
18:3–4	99n126
18:22	81n33
19:3–9	99n126
19:4	99n126
19:5	99n126
20:1–16	99n126
20:25–26	91n85
21:28–31	99n126
22:1–10	99n126
22:39	99n126
23:8	113
25	121
25:35–36	111
26:67	27
28:19–20	82
28:16–20	151

Mark

1:30–31	99n126
5:22–24	99n126
5:35–43	99n126
7:11–13	99n126
9:17–27	99n126
12:1–9	99n126

Scripture Index

Luke

1:28	81n33
1:41	81n33
1:45	80
1:46–55	74

Luke (cont)

1:47	81n33
1:68–79	74
2:1–38	74
2:19	99n126
2:48–50	99n126
2:51	99n126
4	73
6:20–23	110
7:11–15	99n126
7:36–50	99n126
8:21	99n126
9:59–62	99n126
10:21	81n33
12:6	91n85, 93
12:13	99n126
15:7	81n33
15:8–10	99n126
15:11–32	99n126
16:1–31	99n126
19:1–10	99n126
22:19	81n33

John

1:1–18	91n85, 93
1:14	91n85
1:39	81n33
2:1–10	99n126
3:29	81n33
4:19	81n33
4:35	91n85
8:1–11	99n126, 118
8:56	79
11:1–44	99n126
12:46	78
13:34	99n126
15:11	81n33
15:13	99n126
16:20	81n33
16:22	81n33
18:22	27
20:20	81n33

Acts

1:8	151
2:46	81n33
8:8	81n33
8:39	81n33
13:52	81n33
16:34	81n33
18:3	99n126

Romans

1:17	49
5:5	80
10:10	79
10:17	79
11:33	82
12:1	97
16:5	99n126

1 Corinthians

3:7	81n33
4:12	99n126
9:12	99n126
9:16	81n33
13:2–7	103
15:3	80
15:28	91n85, 93
16:19	99n126

2 Corinthians

5:14	81n33

Galatians

3:11	49
3:28	116
5:6	83

Ephesians

5:21–33	99n126
5:22	104
6:11	111

Scripture Index

Philippians
2	99n126
4:4	82

Colossians
1:16	91n85
1:19–20	91n85, 93
4:15	99n126

1 Thessalonians
4:11	99n126

2 Thessalonians
3:1	14
3:10	99n126

2 Timothy
1:5	81n33

Hebrews
1:1–2	xxi
4:12	111
10:37–39	49
11:7–70	80
11:16	80
12:1	81n33, 109
13:2	124
13:7	81n33
13:8	81n33

1 Peter
2:5	99n126
2:10	86
4:8	108

1 John
4:19	81n33
15:11	81n33
16:20	81n33
16:22	81n33

Revelation
3:20	99n126
6	81n33
11:15	52
15:3	91n85
21:2	99n126
21:4	99n126
21:9	99n126

www.ingramcontent.com/pod-product-compliance
Lightning Source LLC
Chambersburg PA
CBHW060608230426
43670CB00011B/2030